The Clinical Operation of

Imagery Communication Psychotherapy

Other Related Titles from World Scientific

Crime and Behaviour: An Introduction to Criminal and Forensic Psychology
by Majeed Khader
ISBN: 978-981-3279-33-9

The Psychology of Problem Solving: The Background to Successful Mathematics Thinking
by Alfred S Posamentier, Gary Kose, Danielle Sauro Virgadamo and Kathleen Keefe-Cooperman
ISBN: 978-981-120-570-5

Unlocking Consciousness: Lessons from the Convergence of Computing and Cognitive Psychology
by Charles T Ross
ISBN: 978-1-78634-468-7

The Clinical Operation of
Imagery Communication Psychotherapy

Yuan Yuan
Central University of Finance and Economics, China

World Scientific

NEW JERSEY • LONDON • SINGAPORE • BEIJING • SHANGHAI • HONG KONG • TAIPEI • CHENNAI • TOKYO

Published by

World Scientific Publishing Co. Pte. Ltd.
5 Toh Tuck Link, Singapore 596224
USA office: 27 Warren Street, Suite 401-402, Hackensack, NJ 07601
UK office: 57 Shelton Street, Covent Garden, London WC2H 9HE

British Library Cataloguing-in-Publication Data
A catalogue record for this book is available from the British Library.

THE CLINICAL OPERATION OF IMAGERY COMMUNICATION PSYCHOTHERAPY

ISBN 978-981-3278-93-6

For any available supplementary material, please visit
https://www.worldscientific.com/worldscibooks/10.1142/11232#t=suppl

Typeset by Stallion Press
Email: enquiries@stallionpress.com

Foreword: "Shu" and "Tao"

In traditional Chinese culture, people always distinguish different levels of "Shu" and "Tao". "Shu" refers to the level of method, which means people who know about a kind of "Shu" can do things with a method. Compared to the ignorant, a man who is learned and has methods will be very effective. A slim woman who knows martial arts can defeat a strong man who knows nothing about martial arts. However, the Chinese are not content with "Shu"; they want to pursue a higher level — "Tao". "Tao" is the source of the matter, the way of things. People having a sophisticated mastery of "Tao" have gone beyond the fixed and specific "Shu". The state of "Tao" — "Do nothing yet everything will be done" is beyond the reach of those who know only about "Shu".

I know that there are some people who have gone beyond the "Shu" to "Tao" in certain things. Once upon a time, I saw a piece of calligraphy artwork by one of the outstanding Chinese calligraphy artists, Su Dongpo; I found that some of the words were very large, some very small, some very tidy, some very illegible, and the layout was not in accordance with the requirements of calligraphy, but it was so beautiful, which stunned and amazed me with no words to praise.

Such a high state is what we aspire to, but the yearning for this state is not the same as knowing it. We hope for "Tao", but it is hard to reach. The method of drinking tea is called the tea ceremony, the method of arranging flowers is called ikebana, the method of wrestling is called judo and the method of action is called taekwondo, but not every person knows the "Tao" of tea, flower arrangement, wrestling or martial arts. People who do not understand the "Tao", often mistakenly assume that "Tao" and "Shu" are opposites, thinking that "Shu" is the low level of things and "Tao" is the higher level of things. They think that people with "Tao" no longer use any "Shu", so they abandon any techniques to pursue "Tao", with the thought that as long as they do not use any techniques, they can reach the state of "Tao".

Actually, this is a big mistake — if martial art novices try to restrain all the moves of the opponent without using any moves, the result can only be a dead end. "No techniques" is also a technique, not "Tao". As a martial art novice meets the master Pharmacist Huang, he decides not to make a move, admitting that he has no chance of beating Huang, expecting Huang to do nothing out of pride in this situation. This is also a kind of technique. This technique may or may not be useful, but it is not "Tao". People with "Tao" may not use techniques, but they do not refuse to use them. They use them at the right time. "Tao" has nothing to do with the fact that whether "Shu" is used or not.

If we know a little bit of humility, we'd better not consider what "Tao" is before starting to learn anything. What is the point of guessing something lofty? In the beginning, mostly the first 10 years of our life, we should give priority to learn "Shu". Su Dongpo can write like running water, but when he first learned how to write, he also needed to imitate calligraphy masters and learn the basic laws of writing. The precondition of surpassing "Shu" is to understand it first.

However, when we are studying "Shu", we should remind ourselves that there is "Tao", so that we can avoid being obsessed with "Shu", and learning it too rigidly. Some people learn "Shu" rigidly and are limited by it, which blocked their path to reach "Tao". These people can never reach the state of perfection. We should know the existence of "Tao", and also know that we do not reach "Tao". We should learn "Shu" seriously, but know that "Shu" is just "Shu"; only in this way can we have a sense of future and hope.

Imagery Communication Psychotherapy (ICP) includes "Shu" and "Tao" at the same time. When learning ICP, we all start with "Shu", but there is always "Tao" implied in the teaching. Learners may still not know "Tao", but they will be immersed in it. This book can be used as a reference or guide for clinical practice.

ICP is a psychological therapy full of practical value. It is easy to study, so many psychologists can use it. Its potential is huge, and skilled ICP therapists can use it in a highly complex or deeper way to explore the deepest parts of the human personality.

Over the years, ICP has become the most popular method of psychotherapy in China. According to the ICP Psychology Research Center, as of May 2017, more than 30,000 people have received systematic training of ICP. In addition, this psychotherapy has been used to solve a variety of psychological problems and psychological disorders, and served tens of thousands of clients, who have achieved significant results. We are proud to say that this approach is very useful.

However, there are two things I want to remind everyone: First, ICP cannot be learned through self-study. Do not assume that you can copy what you have read in this book; because if you go against the way of ICP, using these technologies may be ineffective or even harmful. Second, do not assume that these methods are rigid. Actually, they can be applied flexibly. If you remember the two points, you will use the book efficiently.

Here, I want to say thanks to Yuan Yuan and all those who have contributed to the development of ICP. I sincerely hope that ICP will continue to benefit people.

Zhu Jianjun

Preface

In my mind, Imagery Communication Psychotherapy (ICP) is like a child who is raised by senior masters, dedicatedly created by Professor Zhu Jianjun, and co-supported by the ICP team.

The child not only grows up in the care of family but also witnesses the growth of each of its members. The feeling of this companionship is intimate and warm.

As a member of the ICP team, I always want to do something for ICP. This desire came from both gratefulness and responsibility. I feel grateful for the things it has taught me, for the way it accompanied me when I wanted to cry or laugh and when I went through periods of my own mental journey. In addition, I feel the responsibility of the parents to help children grow.

The Clinical Operation Guidelines of Imagery Communication Psychotherapy and *The Summary of Imagery Communication Psychotherapy Clinical Techniques* are two signature books in the history of the development of ICP, which are also the periodical summary and historical summary of ICP. These two books mark the completion of the rapid development of ICP and the coming of the transitional period. ICP has formally become a school of psychology. It has formally completed the transformation of both management and academy. It has also formally completed the transition from "Zhu Jianjun's personal ICP" to "ICP academic community".

This book is rearranged and expanded on the basis of the Chinese version of *The Clinical Operation Guidelines of Imagery Communication Psychotherapy*, with the aim to be a more practical

English version. There is no elaboration of what has been published, only a summary of the outlines. This book aims to provide a guideline which is convenient to consult, practice and consolidate for all the readers and ICP therapists. Some important theoretical content and clinical cases are new in this book. For example, Chapter 2 (The core psychological qualities of Imagery Communication Psychotherapy) is added to present the cultural value of ICP more clearly.

We believe that we should maintain vigilance for any living thing to ensure that he/she always develops in the direction of health and beauty, which is also the core value of ICP. Therefore, to adhere to the idea of health and the spirit of self-exploration and self-growth, it is necessary to practice some important content over and over again.

Jung creates the term "the wisdom of unconsciousness", which apparently includes the imagery. Hopefully, the English version of *The Clinical Operation of Imagery Communication Psychotherapy* can accomplish the goal of communicating the wisdom of unconsciousness.

While writing this book, I received the warmest help from my mentor Professor Zhu Jianjun and my close friend Cao Yu. I sincerely thank Professor Xin Ziqiang, the Dean, for his great support to me. I convey my special thanks to Professor Zhao Ran for her encouragement and help. I am so lucky to get the careful guidance from my colleagues Dr. Fu Xinyuan and Dr. Zhang Ning. I really appreciate you!

The cases and consulting segments used in the book are basically from my clinical practices. Here, I would like to pay my sincere tribute and gratitude to these genuine and brave clients. To protect their privacy, all personal information that can be identified in the cases has been anonymized.

I am particularly grateful to my graduate students, Liu Lei, Liu Yang, Yu Xiaoxia and Gong Yu! They were also involved in writing a part of this book. Liu Lei helped with Chapters 6 and 13 and prepared the references. She also translated the preface by Professor Zhu from Chinese into English. Liu Yang helped with Chapters 1, 3 and 11. Yu Xiaoxia was responsible for Chapters 4 and 5. Gong Yu helped with Chapters 8 and 9. I wrote the rest, expanded and revised their writing.

These four beautiful, intelligent girls have been willing to support me and continuously dedicate to spread the wonderful psychology gift from China to the world. We hope that more and more people know it, understand it, apply it, and gain much more health and growth from it.

Special thanks to Dr. Jiang Ge and Ms Terigele! They have proofread and reviewed the manuscript. They completed undergraduate studies in Psychology at the Central University of Finance and Economics. Jiang Ge completed her doctoral studies in Psychology at the University of Notre Dame. She is now an Assistant Professor at the University of Illinois at Urbana-Champaign. Terigele is pursuing a PhD in communication studies at the University of Kansas.

The famous American psychologist, M. Scott Peck, writes in the book *The Road Less Traveled*: “Love is not the feeling, but the actual action and the real effort.”

I love ICP. I know there are many people like me.

Yuan Yuan

Contents

Chapter 1

Introduction and Overview

1. What is imagery?

The psychological experience is the basis of any mental activity. The so-called psychological experience refers to the psychic contents that we have perceived but without any further information processing involved.

Theoretically speaking, psychological experience must be perceived by a person. In practice, however, most of our psychological experience cannot be captured by our consciousness. In our standpoint, the most reasonable explanation is that people are unaware of these "subconscious activities" or "experiences that pose a threat to the self"; just because of their low level of awareness, or due to suppression, these unconscious experiences are unable to enter into our daily awareness.

Information processing transforms mental experience into a psychological symbol, while this process is built on the existence of the symbol. Thus, any information processing is, in fact, a procedure of "symbolization".

Through symbolization, we are aware of the symbols. The symbols are interlinked and form a symbolic system, and thus the subjective world comes into being. The regular psychological contents that cannot be arbitrarily changed as well as the psychological world formed by these psychological contents constitute the background of our psychological activities. We name it the psychological reality. The meaning of "Reality" is that it is true, has its own characteristics and has its own law. Even if facing the same stimulation and producing the same psychological experience, a different psychological reality can take shape. There are three primary symbols used by human beings. The first one is language and logic. The second one is the symbols in conditioned reflex. The last one is psychological imagery.

Psychological imagery is "a mental picture of things that do not exist".

However, if we analyze carefully, we will find that this meaning can be divided into two kinds: one is the outside diagram. For example, a child who has never seen a snake asked me what kind of animal it was. I would imagine the picture of a snake in my own mind before I give him a response. This diagram of the image is more appropriately called "representation". There is another kind of imagined image with symbolic significance. For instance, you dreamed of a snake during your sleep. The significance of the snake was often no more than a representative of the reptiles without feet on the lawn. It might have had other significances. Perhaps it represented an insidious villain in your life, or perhaps it was on behalf of a man's sexual desires because the shape of a snake and the male genitalia are so alike, and so it may have stood for a kind of intuition. The imagery with this kind of symbolic significance is called psychological imagery or imagery in this book and in Imagery Communication Psychotherapy.

Imagery is not equal to visual imagery. It could be categorized into visual imagery, acoustic imagery, gustatory imagery, tactile imagery and olfactory imagery, all of which are based on different ways of sensation and perception. Foremost among these is visual imagery. Therefore, we mainly discuss visual imagery in this book.

In the imagery activities, the role of imagery is equivalent to "Term" in logical thinking. It is the basic symbol of "original psychic mechanism". The most fundamental characteristic of imagery is it is symbolic. In other words, imagery can express meaning. The symbolic features of imagery can be seen much more naturally in some conscious or unconscious activities, such as dreams, literature, arts, myths and fairy tales, psychosis hallucination, and the imagery used by primitive man.

Imagery could express significance, which is not the superficial and direct meaning of the image usually. It could reflect mental activity hiding behind the image. Imagery could convey every mental aspect.

Imagery is a symbol used in unconscious language — a kind of language which expresses unconscious things or activities by the symbolic sign. Imagery is also the essential matter of unconsciousness — which could be conveyed by imagery; individual unconsciousness could be conveyed by individual imagery, and collective unconsciousness could be conveyed by primordial imagery and archetype.

Imagery activity is primordial cognition. Compared with daily logical thinking, imagery activity has the following five characteristics:

(1) Imagery activity uses original logic that follows fundamental primitive principles such as similarity and so on.

Once it finds similarities between the two images, a link will be established between these two images. The image of a snake is similar to male genitalia; thus, in primary cognition a snake can be used as a symbol of the male sex organ. This process is vague and flexible and is not as definite as logical thinking.

(2) Although imagery activity does not accept the control from the will directly, it is indirectly affected by the will.

Consequently, imagery activity achieves the highest efficiency in the absence of obvious efforts. Incidentally, to force one's own will to control the mental activities that cannot be directly controlled is always one of the sources of psychological disorders such as obsessive–compulsive disorder.

(3) Much more emotion is involved in imagery activity.

At the same time, it reflects the state of psychological energy. The reason that imagery links closely with emotion is that imagery is a more primitive cognitive function. In the imagery activities, cognition and emotion are not separated yet. We can start with images to regulate emotion, and it will be much more direct and influential than beginning with thinking activities.

(4) There is some dissident sense in imagery activity.

Maybe we have experienced the kind of feeling more or less: some ideas were not from our own but suddenly came into our minds, as if they were dissident things. This is the so-called dissident feeling. For example, some dreams give us a sense of dissidence sometimes. In fact, this sense of dissidence emerges mostly because the imagery activities indeed do not come into being in the consciousness field for the daily consciousness — it comes from a different part of the brain. In Freud's words, it originates from another "primitive mechanism".

(5) The precision of expression of psychological reality is highly conveyed by imagery activity.

Imagery is much more useful than logical thinking when it reflects the things in one's inner heart and psychological reality. We cannot find an appropriate word to transmit certain kinds of real emotion accurately and have to reluctantly choose a similar word to express the approximate feeling. We can precisely express these complex emotions and any minor differences in degree and nature by making use of imagery.

In anger, for example, a girl saw an image of a burning lion guided by the method of imagery communication. This image can express many specific details of her anger. The intensity of fire is the token of the intensity of her anger. The color of fire symbolizes the degree of suppression. The closer to pure red the fire is, the less repressed is her anger. More purple means more suppression. It represents severe suppression if the color of the fire changes from purple to black. We can also get to know a great deal about the reasons for the occurrence of her emotion and her characteristics through other symbolic meanings of fire and lion, which reflects the superiority of imagery. The famous psychologist Fromm clearly expounded on such superiority of imagery.

2. What is Imagery Communication Psychotherapy?

Imagery Communication Psychotherapy is a type of psychological counseling and psychotherapy which was established in the 1990s by Professor Zhu Jianjun, a famous Chinese psychologist. It is also the second type of psychotherapy that was founded by a Chinese psychologist; it followed Professor Zhong Youbin who created the Cognitive Comprehend Therapy in the 1970s.

Imagery is the most commonly used cognitive symbol in primary mental mechanism. Consequently, the complex is often stored in the deep mind with a psychological imagery approach, and the archetype is almost permanently laid in the deeper psychological level that was called by Jung as the collective unconscious in the way of imagery.

Using image as media, imagery communication technique helps people to communicate on a deeper level through the method of primordial logic. It emphasizes experience and interaction. Clinically, the process is completed by an imagery communication psychotherapist and a client together. When both the psychotherapist and the client are reaching the state of imagery communication, their communication is subliminal. Although they do not put the cards on the table at the cognitive level, the improvement caused by Imagery Communication Psychotherapy (ICP) will happen gradually since the unconsciousness of the client at that time is fully understood. It's just a matter of time.

In other words, the ICP psychotherapist communicates with the client on the subconscious level by using the symbolism of imagery, in order to dissolve the negative emotions, eliminate the complex, explore the deep mind, integrate personality and promote the development of spiritual growth and health.

ICP is a scientific psychological counseling and psychotherapy method, but the whole process is quite like a psychotherapist working with a client to weave a daydream or like co-directing a spiritual story. If the client is a child, the process will become easier, as it resembles an imaginative and engaging game and can be directed.

In this process, the psychological state of the client can be vividly presented. The psychotherapist can guide the client to release and regulate all kinds of negative emotions in the case of self-awareness, correct irrational beliefs and improve character, and then make his personality structure more complete and more harmonious. The psychotherapist is also able to develop targeted treatment for the clients with mental trouble and psychological disorders.

In some cases, psychotherapy can even be done only in the imagination, not on a conscious level, so as to avoid the awkwardness of certain sensitive topics and moral norms; this is usually done when topics such as sex, sexual assault, violence, etc. are considered. It still has a very significant clinical effect.

In Chinese, there is a word called "heart house". In fact, the house imagery does show one's mental state at a certain stage.

In terms of imagery, the house itself symbolizes a person's psychological tone and basic personality state. For example, the material of the house symbolizes basic personality traits.

Bamboo house and wooden house represent nature, simplicity, modesty and peace, but they are not fire-resistant. People who have a bamboo or a wooden house as their dominant personality are afraid and unable to express their anger. They can even be extremely patient and repressed in order to avoid interpersonal conflict.

Grass house highlights insecurities and emotional fragility. People who have a grass house as their dominant personality are pretty sensitive. They are often afraid of many negative emotions, which are a high level of neurosis, especially phobia, depression and anxiety.

Stone house is a symbol of stronger self-defense. But it represents stability, toughness and even stubbornness.

The pavilion image is a symbol of great self-openness, flexibility and lack of a spiritual self. The reason is that there is no mental limit. A large number of clinical cases show that the borderline personality is often represented by the pavilion image.

Here is a transcript of communication regarding the house image with a client.

Psychotherapist: Slow your breath. Relax your body . . . Please imagine you are walking to a building . . .

Client: Well, I see . . . it seems like a house.

Psychotherapist: Look at it. What is it made of?

Client: A crystal house. It is transparent.

Psychotherapist: Are you willing to live in such a transparent house?

Client: It is very beautiful. But I cannot live in it for a long time.

Psychotherapist: Why?

Client: Anything can be seen outside.

Psychotherapist: What does it feel like?

Client: I feel unsafe and uncomfortable.

Psychotherapist: Do you have any ways to make yourself more comfortable?

Client: Well, I would like to install a big curtain . . . Oh, I feel better now.

The client was hysteric. In the imagery communication above, we can clearly see the female client's "heart house": beautiful, smart, transparent and affective fragility. The crystalline texture creates a sense of illusion. On the symbolic level, its positive aspect is that she is clever and has a sense of identity. And its negative aspect is transparency and affective fragility. That means, "People can see through me at any time. I have no place to hide. So, I have to be extremely good in the eyes of others." Besides, transparency is demonstrated. Therefore, a crystal house also represents a kind of enactment. Affective fragility is mainly a reflection of the texture of the wall. If the client wants to change her fragility, she needs to change the material of the wall in her image. The psychotherapist could discuss with her about what materials she is willing to use against foreign aggression such as storms or hail.

People living in the crystal house are usually enactive. They pay special attention to themselves and always want to maintain a good impression in the eyes of others. This client did not want to live in such a house for a long time because she was constantly exposed to others while she exposed herself to the outside world. Thus, there is no secret and privacy. Accordingly, she added curtains in the image.

The psychotherapist can help her realize that the curtain is like a curtain on the stage — opening means start and closing means end. The curtains in the house are never always open or closed. However, she could be ready to "perform".

During the process of psychotherapy, as seen earlier, the psychotherapist did not impose his/her will, but activated and applied the client's own mental resources. In this sense, it was the client who helped herself, and the psychotherapist was more like a facilitator and a companion.

3. The history and development of ICP

Speaking of the history of ICP, we have to start with its creator Prof. Zhu Jianjun.

Prof. Zhu majored in meteorology during his undergraduate studies. His Master's degree was in clinical psychology. He earned his doctoral degree from East China Normal University under the supervision of a famous Chinese psychologist Prof. Zeng Xingchu.

He is a man of extraordinary talent, diligence, persistence, honesty and wisdom. He was destined to make a difference in his life. Prof. Zhu learned the state of the atmosphere, changes and phenomena and moved between the clouds and rain when he was young. Later, he delved into the vastness of the human psyche and was trying to explore a pathway to unconsciousness, and worked professionally in a therapeutic capacity in this deep world. Maybe his life has a deep affinity with the different levels of "wind and cloud".

When he first came into contact with psychodynamics, he was very interested in Freud's psychoanalysis, especially in the interpretation of dreams. Being so obsessed, he was once nicknamed "Zhureud". However, as the research went deeper, he identified more and more with Jung's theory. He argues that dreams are the language of the subconscious mind, which is the symbolic meaning of using imagery to express extremely rich inner activities. Dreams have unique cognitive styles and expressions. Prof. Zhu called the dream "a letter from a primitive man".

Starting in 1990, he absorbed the thought essences of humanism, western psychology, oriental traditional culture, Buddhism and Taoism, and was committed to applying symbolic meanings of imagery to communicate with clients at the subconscious level.

Since ICP's inception in 1990, it has gone through three stages of development.

The first stage, 1990–2000, the establishment stage of ICP: The creator Prof. Zhu tried ICP in the field of psychological counseling and psychotherapy and gradually improved and enriched it in practice. Dr. Sun Xinlan in East China Normal University made a groundbreaking contribution in the research of deconstructing personality imagery. In addition, a few of his colleagues used this method clinically and offered valuable advice.

The second stage, 2000–2008, the rapid development stage of ICP: As Prof. Zhu's monographs *Who Am I — psychological consultation and Imagery Communication Psychotherapy* and *How Many Souls Do You Have* were published, he introduced ICP at the International Conference on Psychotherapy in Kunming, China, where some outstanding experts recommended it, thereby spreading ICP rapidly across the country.

In 2004, the Beijing Imagery Communication Psychotherapy research center was formally established. ICP has obtained the certification of China Labor Department and becomes a special skill of psychological consultation that is recognized by the government. Only after formal training and assessment can the psychological consultant or psychotherapist who has obtained the certificate become an imagery communication psychotherapist.

In 2006, Beijing Qiande Imagery Culture Co., Ltd was formally established. It is committed to spreading the culture of mental health, which is an important platform to promote and develop ICP.

A series of academic findings based on scientific research have been published by Beijing Qiande Imagery Culture Co., such as *Self-Acceptance and Imagery Communication Psychotherapy, Photophemodialysis — Imagery Communication Psychotherapy to Watch Movies, Meet the Ghost in Your Heart, Interpret Dreams by the Imagists, I Draw My Heart, Love Could Be Less Painful — Notes of Imagery Communication Psychotherapy.*

In this period, thousands of psychological workers and amateurs across the country studied ICP. Zhao Yancheng, Yuan Yuan, Cai Chenrui and many others made important contributions to the development of its theory and practice. We cannot name them all. It was the collective contribution of these dozen core members that made Imagery Communication Psychology more mature.

At this point, ICP has become one of the most influential domestic psychological counseling and psychotherapy methods in China.

The third stage, 2008 to present, the transition stage of ICP: During this period, we formally completed the transition, from management to academic transformation, from "Zhu Jianjun's personal ICP" to "team's ICP".

It is worth mentioning that the book *The Psychotherapy from the Orient: Imagery Communication Psychotherapy* (in both Chinese and English) was published by Anhui People's Publishing House at home and abroad in 2008. Its Chinese author is Zhu Jianjun, and the English translator is Yuan Yuan. This book was published in Polish in 2016.

In July 2008, Yuan Yuan gave an oral presentation titled *The Method of Imagery Communication Psychotherapy* at the *29*th *International Conference of Psychology* in Berlin, Germany.

On the basis of more than 20 years of knowledge accumulation and expansion, ICP is preparing to enter into a period of relatively steady development. Currently, it is at this stage. As a method of psychotherapy, 20 is a prime age. There is still a long way to go. We can only promote its healthy, harmonious and sustained development with constant care, assiduous study and continued growth.

4. The implementation conditions of ICP

(1) The arrangement of treatment rooms: Since Imagery Communication Psychology does not have special demands on the environment for treatment, we could use a general psychological counseling room or psychotherapy room to carry out ICP. The basic principles of arrangement include silence, convenience, good ventilation and lighting. With regard to some details such as color of the wall, carpets, placing of the sofa, table lamps, curtains, decoration pictures, clock, tissues, trash bin, green plant and so on, these are generally the same as in other counseling rooms and psychotherapy rooms.

A client could remain seated or partially lie on his back if there is a deck chair. A psychotherapist decides which posture his client will take. The principle is to relax the client's body and mind. In general, lying partially on one's back is more comfortable than sitting. However, it could readily give rise to anxiety if a psychotherapist is not well acquainted with his client, especially when this client is of the opposite sex and particularly conservative in terms of sex. We should guide a client to adjust his body and breathing when we notice that the client is uncomfortable in a posture, such as holding his arms, etc.

It would be better if the light in the psychotherapy room is adjustable. For example, thick curtains that stop the light from entering the room can be taken into consideration for all kinds of clients. Some clients like to have imagery communication in a dark environment while others do not. Some of the clients even feel very uncomfortable in dark surroundings.

There could be some paintings or photographic work hanging on the wall, but it should not be too much. It is worth noting that we should choose an image which is neutral and does not easily cause nervousness and excitement. For instance, images of peaceful grass, a calm sea, or a forest do not look dense. In some cases, a psychotherapist could use these images as the starting point to guide a client to imagine.

(2) Arrangement of time: Generally, a consulting session lasts for 50–60 minutes. For ICP, 60–90 minutes is appropriate. We advise 90 minutes to be reserved every time because the consulting session cannot be planned accurately for ICP, and we may not have to use ICP every time. Sometimes we need to intervene with a brief imagery communication.

(3) Telephone guidance: We do not allow imagery communication psychotherapists to guide a client to experience imagery communication on the phone, except for a few special cases. Telephone-guiding ICP is prohibited.

(4) Autodidact should not apply ICP: Besides the unconscious activity involved, the negative mental energy during deep unconsciousness is the main objective of ICP. Therefore, it is not suitable to self-study ICP, or to apply ICP to oneself or others without systematic training and practice in lights of the risk of being unable to handle it well. We are against learning ICP via reading related books. We are opposed to taking risks with ourselves and others by self-study.

5. The primary goal of ICP

It is not surprising that we can find and solve psychological problems by ICP because it can delve deeper into the unconscious world. The final goal of this psychotherapy is to promote the growth of our clients, lift their level of mental health, enhance their physiological function and social competence, cultivate better personality and help them live a happier life, just as all of the psychotherapies. Specifically, it includes the following:

(1) Make a client obtain what he lacks, such as sense of security, relief, love, attention, understanding, support, self-confidence, self-power.
(2) Eliminate unhealthy behavior and learn healthy behavior.
(3) Cripple or alleviate a psychological complex.
(4) Comprehend the complex or original cognition in unconsciousness, make a client efficient at controlling his unconscious activity and obtain much more autonomy by perception.
(5) Enhance one's self-perception, self-control and self-autonomy, and then demonstrate the psychological or spiritual qualities that the client had.
(6) Build and develop an empathetic relationship. Enhance the ability of empathy through experiencing each other.
(7) Learn or improve the ability to express love, attention, respect, comprehension and support.
(8) Develop positive and healthy values, beliefs and attitude toward life.

(9) Deepen self-exploration and self-acceptance and improve self-development and self-realization.

6. The indications of ICP

6.1. *The indications*

Mental problems, psychological disorders (all kinds of neurosis included), psychosomatic disease, parent–child education, potential development, human resource management.

6.2. *Be careful with the following people*

Pregnant women (avoidance of negative emotions), special groups such as prisoners and drug addicts.

6.2.1. *Not for the following people*

(1) Psychiatric patients;
(2) Patients with severe personality disorder: Schizoid personality disorder, antisocial personality disorder, borderline personality disorder;
(3) Some patients with physical disease (for example, cardiovascular disease, brain disease, cancer);
(4) Mentally handicapped.

7. Why does ICP work?

Imagery communication is not only a psychological theory to meet the needs of cognition, but, more importantly, it is also a psychotherapy with quite practical values used to eliminate psychological disorders.

The reason why ICP is able to get the desired result is roughly due to the following:

(1) The imagery communication psychotherapists provide clients with the psychological elements they lack.
(2) Providing clients an opportunity to express themselves and release their negative emotions with self-awareness.

(3) Leading clients into deep self-exploration.
(4) Using the appropriate thoughts, emotions and behaviors instead of the inappropriate.
(5) Enhancing self-perception and crippling or alleviating a complex.
(6) Giving clients an opportunity to surpass themselves and contact others sincerely.

8. The emphasis of ICP

(1) Getting involved in positive factors to change the vicious circles

Psychologically disordered patients always get bogged down in a vicious cycle. The past traumatic events make them form inappropriate cognitions and behaviors that give rise to negative environmental changes and new traumatic experiences. A positive event or intervention of benign factors may change this cycle. This positive incident might be the wanting for love, concern and support, which a psychotherapist gives to his client. We transmit love, concern and support deep within one's personality through images in imagery communication.

For example, a depressed client is imaging: "I'm walking in the desert without any life all around. I'm walking lonely without any goal. I know what will happen, that is, I will be dead and I am not afraid of it."

An ICP psychotherapist could express his/her support like this: "Walking ahead straight is hopeful. Many explorers have finally found life in such circumstances. Furthermore, it is impossible to have nothing even in the desert. Let's have a look. Perhaps there are small insects and grasses." Or he/she could say: "It looks like you are lonely and helpless. Please imagine that I'm looking for you with water and food."

It is an opportunity to break down the old vicious cycle for a client who has been short of love in the past. He may show slight improvement of his negative emotions and then change his opinion on the world to a lesser or greater extent when he can accept and absorb a little love. The environment would be ameliorated to a certain extent, leading to upset of the vicious cycle and the building of a positive cycle, if these changes could be reflected in his action.

(2) Transform the negative imagery into positive imagery naturally

Negative imagery refers to the images with a negative image and unhealthy symbolic meaning. "Naturally" means the smallest intervention. Negative imagery has different levels of generality.

Usually, everyone has only one highest level and the highest general image. All aspects of this person will be under the influence of it and his entire life will be shrouded in this shadow if it is negative. It is hard to be aware of the consciousness. However, once this image is transformed positively, the whole personality of this person will change dramatically.

It is true that there is a close relationship between the high images and low images. They are not dissected and independent. Weakening the negative images at lower levels can weaken the power of negative images at higher levels. Likewise, those negative images of higher levels will use their strength to resist changes and try to restore the shifted negative images. Thus, to transform negative imagery is a hard job that requires a high degree of creativity.

The mental energy carried by negative images will become more vigorous with the transformation of negative images into positive ones.

Compared with psychoanalysis, ICP can directly solve a psychological complex by dealing immediately with the images which are the embodiment of the psychological complex.

(3) Eliminate or dissolve negative imagery

The transformation of the negative into the positive is an admittedly good solution, but not the sole and the best one. One of the reasons is that, as we have previously stated, the inversion of psychological energy is never complete. A better solution is to eliminate a negative image and dissolve the complex that this image represents. It is not yet free although its form has changed. The psychological energy may become free provided that negative imagery is digested.

In ICP, a mentally healthy person doesn't have to be positive or negative, and he/she just reflects this world as it really is. It is true that the negative imagery is the culprit of psychological disorders, and the positive imagery that cannot reflect the world strictly according to the facts is also not ideal.

The way of eliminating negative imagery is mainly to release psychological energy under the circumstances of perception. Generally speaking, so far as a psychological disorder forms, one's mental energy has been transformed more than once. We usually begin with one's current emotional and mental state, guide the person to detect his/her own feelings and desires, wipe out his/her suppression, and encourage his/her emotions and desires to be expressed and discharged. After this step is completed, the person will be able to realize from what emotions the current mood is transformed. Then his/her psychotherapist can lead the individual to notice the more primitive emotion and to express and release it gradually, until the initial source of the problem is found and solved. And this complex will be fully resolved.

(4) The principle of consultation and treatment is return to the original and reduction of the fixation

Fixation is an important factor for the formation and maintenance of psychological disorders. The principle of ICP for the fixation is to return to the origin.

A client fixes on a certain image, a certain person or a certain kind of behavioral pattern simply to satisfy his own wants spiritually or biologically. His fixed object may be because of some previous satisfaction or a symbol of satisfaction, or it may have a specific implication for him. By way of imagery communication, a psychotherapist can guide him to discover what he needs isn't this image, this person or this pattern, which are only a means of satisfaction. In that case, the mental energy fixed in them can be "reduced" to return to his real needs.

Prof. Zhu Jianjun once analyzed one of his personal experiences:

I traversed a small park not far from home the day before yesterday — Shi Jingshan Sculpture Park. Suddenly an idea emerged: If only I could go there for a walk!

It was free and there was no obstacle preventing me to walk there. But I was too busy to find time. Walking in the Sculpture Park became my wish in last days. I thought of it like a child thinking about toys.

The Sculpture Park was an image in my mind symbolizing leisure and rest. The desiring energy is fixed in this image.

People pursue it as the formation of image. The corresponding energy is released when the image becomes a reality.

How would the results change if I went to another park rather than that Sculpture Park?

Perhaps I would be unsatisfied because I would feel that my wish was not satisfied — I did not go to the Sculpture Park. My energy of leisure was mostly fixed in the image of Sculpture Park and other parks were unable to release it.

This is the fixation.

What I should do is to try to understand in my mind what I want is not necessarily the Sculpture Park, but leisure. My psychological energy will come back to its starting point without changing its direction. This is reduction. Since I needed a rest, other parks would also satisfy me, thereby the psychological energy would be capable of shifting into another goal or image and the fixation be digested.

We can use the "contamination" if it is extremely hard for a client to release the energy and we need to break his fixation with an image. For example, Prof. Zhu may find out the similarities between the Sculpture Park and another park. His psychological energy will be able to transfer from the Sculpture Park to the other one.

(5) Reduce the level of psychological contamination, improve awareness and ability to distinguish

Contamination is one factor that leads to psychological disorder. We can reduce or eliminate psychological disorder by decreasing contamination.

As other therapies of psychodynamics, we also believe that "reality testing" is an effective method to remove psychological disorder. Reality testing can clear up the contamination between images and perceptive realities; thus, the perception of clients gets more accurate and effective. Imagery communication names this process as "distinguishing between imagination and reality."

In addition, we also do everything possible to guide clients to lessen the contamination between the past memory and the present perceptions.

What is much more important is to decrease the contamination of clients' feelings of self and of others, as well as those between the self-images and the perception images for others.

The constant distinction of various images is able to cut down the contamination gradually, make clients have more ability to create new images according to the current reality, reflect reality more accurately and achieve increasingly high psychological health.

It should be stated that we do not wipe out the contamination in actual ICP; on the contrary, we are likely to use it to achieve certain therapeutic purposes. We do not immediately reduce or eliminate any contamination at any time. The practical psychotherapy process is flexible without a fixed procedure. There is no contradiction between the two.

(6) Find and initiate clients' own positive mental resources

ICP emphasizes minimal intervention in the process of counseling and psychotherapy. We believe that everyone has his own mental recovery ability. He also has his own unique positive mental resources, even if his mental state is very poor. The art of psychotherapy is whether one is willing or able to find these mental resources.

An excellent imagery communication psychotherapist cannot impose his will on any client although he always has this opportunity, especially when it comes to imagery communication.

(7) Maintain an empathic attitude

Rogers pointed out that empathy itself has the effect of psychotherapy.

A psychotherapist cannot empathize arbitrarily. The result will be terrible if a psychotherapist has no ability to sympathize but deliberately attempts to do so. Imagery communication has the advantage of making it easier to achieve empathy in imagery communication. This is because other people are prone to misunderstand when we apply current languages to express our emotions. However, when a person makes use of images to express his mood and feeling, it is relatively easy for others to be infected by his emotions, just by imagining on the basis of his description and understanding his emotions, which is beneficial to accomplish empathy.

The ability of empathy relates to the personality cultivation of psychological counselors. It is not true that each one can be sympathized with the imagery communication method. Nevertheless, we can say that imagery communication is good for increasing empathy.

Besides these, other methods are practiced to dispel psychological disorders in imagery communication. For instance, it absorbed some methods of the oriental culture in order to improve the perceptive ability of clients. Better perception promotes their psychological health.

9. The danger of misusing ICP and how to deal with it

9.1. *Making clients superstitious*

Some clients confuse the world of mental image with the objective material world. Few of them even mistakenly believe that the images of ghosts and gods have physical objects. It is dangerous to confuse psychological reality with objective reality.

Coping strategy:

Explain patiently to clients to make them understand that all images are mental symbols of one's inner activity, including individual unconsciousness and collective unconsciousness. It is not objective reality, but psychological reality.

9.2. *Loss of self-control*

Some clients may sink in the strong mental energy. They might be frightened or tempted.

Coping strategy:

(1) An imagery communication psychotherapist should control the rhythm of resolving a complex further, not too fast.
(2) An imagery communication psychotherapist should provide emotional support, company and guidance to his client.
(3) Do not leave clients alone to complete thorough imagery tasks.

9.3. *Be addicted to ICP*

Some clients may be addicted to ICP and ignore the demands of reality. They escape the reality and even lose the interests in affection, study, work or life.

In other words, they regard ICP as a new defense mechanism. This is unhealthy because the ultimate goal of psychological counseling and psychotherapy is to lead people to live a better life in the real world.

Coping strategy:

(1) An imagery communication psychotherapist should remain alert. Stop the progress as soon as possible once they find the potential of addiction.
(2) Make clients realize that he is trying to escape the difficulty by being addicted to images.
(3) Help clients formulate plans and focus their attention and help them in executing the plans to achieve their specific goals in real life.

Chapter 2

The Core Psychological Qualities of Imagery Communication Psychology

Imagery Communication Psychotherapy (ICP) is not only the intervention method of certain mental disorders, but also one universal psychological adjustment method. In the world of imagery, through the presence of an imagery communication psychotherapist, one's "story" changes, even the "life-script" is changed, thus transforming his/her entire mental world. The inner transformation will change the way he/she sees the outside world, consequently changing his/her mindset, emotions and behaviors, in order to improve his/her mental health, relationships and lifestyle.

ICP assesses one's basic psychological quality in the four dimensions of belief, love, knowing and action, which are referred to as "the four moral characters". Any mental disturbance is related with a lack in or more of "the four moral characters" (Zhu Jianjun, 2006).

Why should Imagery Communication Psychology choose the four psychological qualities as basic moral characters? This is because belief, love, knowing and action are the necessary resources for mental growth.

First of all, these four qualities are summed up in our clinical experience. We find that they are very important for mental growth. At the same time, we also find that they are the main core of each stage of personality development.

The "oral stage", as per classic psychoanalytic theory, is the first stage of life. It is the stage ranging from 0–1 years after birth. At this stage, human babies have to rely on the full care and protection of adults to survive. A baby in this period has no ability to live independently. Therefore, the first psychological quality the baby developed was “Belief”.

If a baby at the oral stage obtains good care and protection, it will think that the adults (usually the mother) can be trusted and will believe that it is good and worthy of being cared for, protected, loved and supported. But at this stage, if the mother or other caregivers do not give enough care, protection, love and support, the quality of the baby’s “Belief” will suffer. The baby will not believe that its mother can be trusted and that its behavior is good, and so will not believe that it should deserve to be cared and loved.

The second stage of life is the “anal stage”, according to classic psychoanalytic theory. It refers to the period of 1–3 years after birth. All kinds of practical activities such as talking, walking, etc. have started. A baby must act boldly at this stage and learns to control the physical body and physical world by this practice. Thus, the second psychological quality the baby developed was “Action”.

If a baby at the anal stage receives good support and control from the parents, he/she will bravely explore and succeed. This would motivate and create a mental quality of “Action”. A man with “Action” has the curiosity and understanding of the real world to be able to express and communicate with it, thereby striving to achieve his/her goals.

If parents are too strict with their children, the children will become self-styled, timid, cautious and afraid to explore. They will have no ability to face possible difficulties and failures. This is because, for them, the failure is not just a failure to do something, it also means losing the love of their parents. Likewise, if parents are overprotective of their children, that is, avoiding all dangerous situations, the children will be afraid to act. The psychological quality of “Action” will thus be impaired.

The third stage of life is the “Oedipus stage”, according to classic psychoanalytic theory. It refers to the period of 3–6 years after birth. A child begins to realize relationships and is aware of the complicated relationship between themselves and their parents at this stage. The child needs to learn how to love. Therefore, the third psychological quality the child developed was "Love".

If the parents provide a model of love for their children at the Oedipus stage, they love each other, and both of them love their children, the potential of love will be aroused. The children will enjoy and express love, and then understand love. So, they are able to love themselves and others.

Last of all, the fourth stage of life according to classic psychoanalytic theory, is the "latent period". It refers to the period of 6–12 years after birth. This period requires the development of the "Knowing" quality. Children go to primary school to gain cultural knowledge to expand their horizons. They not only learn about their life but also learn more about the outside world. Crucially, this stage will create a curiosity that transcends the utilitarian mind.

If a child's unpractical curiosity and thirst for knowledge are not destroyed by educators at this stage, he/she can happily study and never be bored by it. The child will "jump out of his/her daily life" to see the world. The child will become a rational and wise person when he/she grows up. Truly, the failure of education could completely destroy this. The failure of education makes children hate learning or regard studying as a utilitarian activity, because it makes learning dull and boring.

It is worth noting that belief, love, knowing and action are relatively independent. They can promote and push each other and evolve in 12 ways. For example, "Knowing" could transform into or contribute to "Love" when we have enough understanding.

For instance, we will love our parents much more when we know that so many injuries stem from ignorance, especially parents' love for their children.

In many cases, parents thought that they gave the best love to their children, but they did not know what the children needed. A parent was constantly giving money to her daughter, but the daughter needed the company of her mother and her father's approval more. A father scolded his son repeatedly even if the son performed well and got good grades. The father used to think obstinately that it would prevent his son from complacency.

Then one day, these parents met an excellent psychotherapist or a psychological consultant. Not only did they learn that love and way of love are two different things, they were also unconditionally accepted by the psychology expert. When the parents start to realize that they should focus on their children's spiritual needs, the "Knowing" of parents will transform into healthy "Love".

In the same way, when their children know that their parents thought they gave the best love to them, they understand that their parents love them so much and the parents' way of love is not healthy. This "Knowing" will turn into understanding their respective mother and father. This understanding can be sublimated into "Love".

The formation of the framework of "the four moral characters" was derived from the clinical practice of ICP. However, it is not limited to ICP. A psychotherapist can promote a client's belief, love, knowing and action by whatever psychotherapy he/she uses.

1. Belief

"Belief" is like the earth. It has a sense of stability, security, carrying or bearing. A person can be much more realistic and independent only if he/she has "Belief". "Belief" creates self-confidence internally and manifests as faith in the world and others externally.

Lack of "Belief" will result in a lack of security. For a man lacking "Belief", it is easy to feel anxiety and inferiority. He/she is always worried about the dangers outside and requires reassurance from others. He/she wants to control everything or know everything.

In particular, for a person who is insecure, he/she will always be worried about the outside world and not trust it if the person gives oneself limited belief. The person will suffer from mental illness if this is serious. However, if the person gives limited belief to someone else, he/she will have a low level of self-esteem and not believe in themselves.

That is to say, someone with a lot of mental resources of "Belief" could believe in oneself, others and his/her future, despite "insufficient evidence" sometimes. While this belief can go wrong sometimes, more often than not, it has positive consequences. Trusting others can lead to positive rewards. Trusting yourself can give you an opportunity to try and succeed.

2. Love

"*Love*" *is like water.* It has a sense of vitality, nourishment and creativity. The power of "Love" develops into "loving oneself" internally and evolves into "loving others" externally.

Lack of "Love" often leads to hardships in establishing good interpersonal relationships. A person lacking "Love" feels lonely and helpless easily. He/she does not understand love even if someone else has it. However, he/she is apt to feel poor, unhappy, depressed and sad.

In particular, love is a feeling that brings happiness and meaning. It is difficult to experience this feeling for a person who is incapable of loving. On the one hand, it is not easy for others to arouse the person's love. On the other hand, it is not easy for the person to love others either. His/her heart is not pleased and the people around him/her are hardly happy. Misunderstanding and difficulties in interpersonal relationships cannot be easily solved due to lack of love.

Furthermore, "Love" begins with loving yourself or loving others when the resources of love are full. Your heart will be nourished. Love can inspire love.

3. Knowing

"*Knowing*" *is like the wind.* It is full of intelligence and has a sense of flexibility and smartness. A person can be much more curious and studious without vanity only if he/she has the "Knowing" attribute. The person will have rational capability and logos wisdom.

Lack of "Knowing" will lead to lack of desire for knowledge and joy of knowing. A man lacking "Knowing" cannot perceive things objectively because of being short of non-utilitarian perspectives.

In particular, for a person who is not full of resources of "Knowing", it does not mean a low IQ. It means a lack of desire to know, lack of joy in the process of knowing, and lack of non-utilitarian perspective. The psychological problem is that the person cannot see things objectively. The person's desire and emotions interfere with the way things are thought and explained. Distorted perceptions can further lead to irrational emotions and inappropriate behavior

Alternately, if the mental resources of "Knowing" are sufficient, wisdom and knowledge will follow. Persistent learning will bring on continuous improvement.

4. Action

"*Action*" *is like fire.* It has a sense of motivation, energy and efficacy. A person can be much more courageous and put his/her ideas into practice only if he/she has "Action". The action itself can be sublimated into wisdom and lead to results.

Lack of "Action" will lead to daydreaming or procrastination. The ability to convert mental activities into actual actions is inadequate. A person lacking "Action" easily feels unfulfilled and not confident. The lack of eternal success will do great damage to his/her self-efficacy. He/she will have less consciousness and ability to cooperate due to being deficient in patience and courage.

In particular, for a person who is lacking "Action", all his/her ideas and plans would be blank checks that cannot be cashed. Without action, there is no possibility of success and achievement. Lack of achievement is bound to harm self-efficacy. This can result in a series of secondary issues.

Operation:

We can see one's specific state of "Belief", "Love", "Knowing" and "Action" in his/her unconsciousness through the method of ICP. In other words, according to the law of primitive cognition and the symbolism of images, the sights and things seen in the door reflect the psychological qualities that one person has in his/her "Belief", "Love", "Knowing" and "Action".

(1) Guide the client to be relaxed and imagine himself/herself in the middle of a room. This room is foursquare without any furniture. There are two doors side by side on every wall.

(2) The two doors on the first wall are labeled separately as "Belief" and "Unbelief". The client is guided to walk to the door of "Unbelief" and open it and look inside in his/her imagination. Then, he/she is guided to open the door of "Belief" and even go in to see what the scene is. He/she can watch while walking in the imagination and tell the guide what was watched in words.
(3) Guide the client to turn right to the other wall on which two doors are labeled separately as "Love" and "No Love". The client is guided to observe and describe, in accordance with the method mentioned in (2). The point of guidance is the door of "Love" and the scene inside.
(4) Guide the client to continue to turn right to the next wall on which two more doors labeled separately as "Knowing" and "No Knowing". He/she is guided to observe and describe the situation, in accordance with the method mentioned in (2). The point of guidance is to experience and perceive the scene of "Knowing".
(5) Guide the client to continue to turn right to the last wall on which are two doors labeled separately as "Action" and "No Action". He/she is guided to observe and describe the setting, in accordance with the method mentioned in (2). The point of guidance is deep observation and feeling the scene of "Action".
(6) In order to intensify these four mental qualities in the subconsciousness, the psychotherapist can emphasize that, "you will be unwavering in your choice of belief, love, knowing and action, and believe that they can bring you wisdom and power".
(7) Guide the client to go back to the seat in the middle of the room. Let them breathe slowly. Then, they can be allowed to open their eyes after hearing the guide count several numbers.

Chapter 3

The Operative Principles

1. The insistent principle of Imagery Communication Psychotherapy

The insistent principle is a part of the values of Imagery Communication Psychotherapy (ICP).

1.1. *Self-perception oriented — the basic principle*

ICP must be applied to improve the self-perception of clients. We are not allowed to solve only the specific problems and ignore self-perception. Weakening or concealing self-perception is strongly disallowed. All other principles must not violate this fundamental principle. Even in cases of psychological crisis intervention, for the short-term purpose of "urgent bandage", we may not be able to take care of inspiring clients' self-perception, nor can we destroy and suppress self-perception.

1.2. *Real love oriented*

ICP regards true and sincere love as the basis of psychotherapy. Deliberately pursuing and expressing love is opposed. We should encourage love to take place naturally and authentically.

1.3. *Trust and responsibility oriented*

ICP sticks to the principle of "seeking the cause in oneself," especially when there is a problem with a relationship. It encourages a person to try to look into oneself and find the reason for himself/herself rather than blame others, whether this person is a psychotherapist, a psychological counselor or a client.

We oppose the use of rationalization, isolation, avoidance and other self-deception to beg the question. We must be brave to hold on and bear the responsibility for our destiny. We must undertake the suffering in our life and what we have horror of. And we must bear the pain of mental problems.

Trust the power of quality such as wisdom and true love. Trust the vitality and growth potential of people.

1.4. *Behavior in reality oriented*

Spiritual values could only be realized when we are exposed to the real reality. ICP encourages clients to act boldly in reality. It is ICP's "reality principle".

1.5. *Life and growing oriented*

ICP insists on life and spiritual growing as its own.

In ICP's view, life is an attitude that persists and does not give up even while suffering. Therefore, whether it is to use ICP for psychological counseling and psychotherapy, or ICP psychotherapists to self-grow, both need to endure discomfort at a certain stage. This uncomfortable feeling is the price of spiritual growth. It is a valuable process.

2. The opposed principle of ICP

The opposed principle is another part of the values of ICP.

2.1. *Oppose the control of others or seek rights in order to control others*

The ethics of ICP is unconditional acceptance and equal respect for clients. It never allows a psychotherapist to deprive the client of free will.

2.2. *Oppose overly "adapting to society"*

ICP believes that the mentally healthy people should adapt to society selectively. Consequently, we encourage clients to adapt to the positives of society. In other words, mentally healthy people should be able to distinguish between right and wrong, not simply and mechanically adapt to everything.

2.3. *Oppose "mental health means happiness"*

Imagery communication does not regard the pleasure of clients as the primary goal of psychotherapy in that the mentally healthy people are not happy sometimes.

People with mental health can still experience all kinds of unhappiness, such as anger, anxiety, sadness, etc., but they are less likely to experience unhappiness. And when they are unhappy, they are doing better than the average person in terms of self-adjustment and healthy coping.

2.4. *Oppose "mental health means equilibrium"*

Peace is just one of the forms of life. Simply pursuing peace is the same as the death of spirit. The mentally healthy people change as the situation changes, by being peaceful or excited.

Chapter 4

The Process of Imagery Communication Psychotherapy

1. The initial stage

1.1. *Developing an effective therapeutic alliance*

In this kind of psychotherapy, particular emphasis is placed on the development of an effective therapeutic alliance. Essentially, the key points of this process are the personality, mental status and empathy ability of an imagery communication psychotherapist as follows:

(1) It is necessary for the psychotherapist to fully focus on the client during the whole treatment.
(2) Deliberate loving care toward the client is not encouraged. It is believed that love arises spontaneously when the psychotherapist endeavors to understand the client and can deeply feel his/her inner world.
(3) The psychotherapist is encouraged to be as genuine as possible. Although recognizing this kind of genuineness may hurt the client, the psychotherapist needs to reflect on whether he/she could accept some issues related to the client and become aggressive or not, and then deal with his/her own complexes.
(4) In situations where an imagery communication psychotherapist lacks necessary and basic trust from the client, he/she can use some techniques to increase the client's level of security and trust.

For example, apply simple imagery communication to solve a slight problem and thus prove its effectiveness, or bring out the sub-personality that is the most unsatisfied with his/her own mental status.

If a client habitually says, "forget it!", the psychotherapist can ask, "Who likes to say that?" Then guide the client to close the eyes and read the following: "What does this man look like? Age? Gender? What is he/she wearing? What is his/her mood at the moment?" The psychotherapist can also ask the client to name the image in order to identify and communicate in future consultations. This is a common technique of personality image deconstruction in Imagery Communication Psychotherapy (ICP). It is somewhat helpful for the client to explore and grow at the personality level.

It not only embodies the flexibility of ICP but also enables the client to be aware of his/her present and specific personality state. Psychotherapy begins in a subtle way.

1.2. *Preliminary assessments*

ICP conducts assessments in the context of psychodynamics, with two aspects as its foundations: a favorable psychotherapist–client relationship and the basic understanding of the client's issue.

Mental assessment of ICP runs through the whole counseling and therapy, and is not rigidly distinguished from therapeutic intervention.

(1) Evaluation of the category of mental problems and disorders

ICP operates on categories of mental problems and disorders as the present clinical category system. The primary approach is to search for characteristic images during the therapy and in the meanwhile to observe and refer to general diagnostic symptoms as well as the client's behavior pattern.

(2) Evaluation of personality

The main method is Deconstructing Personality by Imagery (PID). There are concrete techniques for this, including a graph of relations between sub-personalities, and internal harmony, hostility, isolation and indifference of one's personality, psychological age, psychological gender, and psychological complexity.

The procedure of this method is detailed in the following chapter.

(3) Evaluation of mental health

This aspect mainly focuses on those psychological factors related to mental health, including capacity of mental energy, levels of repression, duration of psychological problems, and quantity and feature of negative images.

(4) Evaluation of the psychotherapist–client relationship

The major reason for this type of evaluation is to assess how the following aspects reflect in images: encounter relation, love and care, genuineness, respect, trust, transference and projection.

Two-person imagery is another way to evaluate the psychotherapist–client relationship. Two-person imagery means that the psychotherapist is always with the client, and participates in the client's imagery experience during the imagery communication process; furthermore, the psychotherapist should tell the client images and responses he/she has seen in this process.

All initial images in ICP can be used to carry out two-person imagery by adding one sentence into the instruction: "Imagine that I am with you whenever you see anything".

In this situation, what the client describes about the psychotherapist in his/her imagination represents the figure of the psychotherapist in his/her mind.

(5) Keeping an eye on symbolic imagery in psychological transformation

Symbolic imagery can usually indicate the direction that the client's mental status is transforming to.

The major foundations of this evaluation aspect are individual development and clinical experience of the psychotherapist.

To avoid or at least reduce unhealthy motives of the client, and in case the novice psychotherapists rigidly use these symbolic images to mislead the client, we recommend all ICP therapists to not tell clients about these images used for psychological evaluation or make them public through publishing or teaching.

1.3. *Setting therapeutic goals and establishing plans*

ICP is an in-depth psychotherapy that enables crippling or alleviating complex that elicits symptoms, and thus its essential goals are to remodel one's personality.

This therapy usually does not provide a precise, fixed or inflexible therapeutic plan but will persist in therapeutic goal orientation and make an adaptable adjustment in each therapeutic stage.

1.4. *Reaching a consensus with the client*

It is necessary to reach consensuses on therapeutic goals, plans, schedule, expense and exceptions with the client.

In this stage, the imagery communication therapist has responsibility to inform the client that with the progress of treatment, he/she will experience a period of mental distress which is necessary for personal growth. No matter what happens, the psychotherapist will accompany him/her, support him/her and guide him/her on the spiritual plane.

2. The corrective stage

The major tasks of the corrective stage are alleviating negative images, improving the mental status of the client, and weakening or eliminating his/her psychological problems or disorders.

2.1. *Exploratory phase*

At the beginning of the corrective stage, a client is usually tentative about psychotherapy and is not determined to change himself/herself.

An imagery communication psychotherapist should keep a sharp eye on the client's means of psychological control. Meanwhile, the psychotherapist is required to keenly reflect on themselves, break through resistance, promptly identify problems and deal with negative images.

2.2. *Hesitation and first-decision phase*

When the psychological treatment begins to work, there will be some hesitation and worry in the client's subconsciousness. At this point, the psychotherapist needs to get on with his/her problem as well as wait patiently till the client makes a decision.

In this way, a significant change can be observed easily when the client has determined to devote himself/herself to psychotherapy.

2.3. *The advanced phase of issues*

This is an apparently accelerated phase where many negative images and internal problems reflected can be alleviated, and thus the client will perceive more substantial progress and have a sense of fulfillment and obtain pleasure.

However, when new problems arise, such as psychological conflicts, complexes, and deeper and more general negative images, the client will feel fatigued and reluctant, and once again become hesitant.

At that point, if the psychotherapist cannot find any mistake about the therapeutic direction after a prudent evaluation, he/she should be bold in insisting his/her judgment and should try to understand and deal with the client's negative transferences, blame and hesitations.

2.4. *Hesitation and secondary-decision phase*

This phase will come as long as the client and the psychotherapist get through the previous phase. Here, the client will find it more difficult to make a choice as he/she must improve his/her personality to resolve the problem ultimately.

The imagery communication psychotherapist cannot force or induce the client to make a decision but should be more patient and confident to stay with him/her to get through this tough period.

2.5. *Personality reorganization and deeper problem-solving phase*

Once the client has made a secondary decision, he/she may make some kind of a breakthrough. The client has been qualified for self-exploration and self-coping. In other words, he/she has become psychologically healthy and even more perceptive than average.

At this juncture, there is no need to make too many interventions. Moderate guidance and assistance will be beneficial.

2.6. *Hesitation and tertiary-decision phase*

Clients at this phase may be hesitant whether or not to go beyond themselves. The psychotherapist will have little impact on their choices at that time. However, the psychotherapist can give some support and ensure that proper help will be provided when the client needs it.

2.7. *Emergence of the most general imagery*

The most general imagery, closely related to Jung's Archetype, will emerge when the client decides to surmount himself/herself. At this very moment, the only concern for the psychotherapist and client is to fully feel and perceive it.

It is extremely important to note that most of the clients will not get to the seventh phase and only a few of them can even arrive at the fifth one.

3. The terminating stage

The termination of ICP depends primarily upon the client.

No matter which phase of the corrective stage the psychological counseling and psychotherapy will end with, the psychotherapist needs to make objective evaluations for self as well as with regard to the therapeutic effect, and deal with the separation from the client in a proper manner so that the genuine nature of the psychotherapist can be felt.

As a whole, the technique of ending is divided into two categories. One is the ending technique of not realizing the goal. Another is the ending technique of realizing the goal.

3.1. *The ending technique of not realizing the goal: Steady retreat*

When using the "confrontation" in ICP, one of the principles is in for a penny and in for a pound. What it means is that for a difficult complex, if we do not have the full grasp, we cannot apply ICP to reach the core. This is called "in for a penny". But if we have begun to engage in ICP, some frightening images emerge, such as vipers, monsters, ghosts, devil, etc., and we should be brave enough to face them.

In the process, even though the clients are afraid, we should encourage them to insist as much as possible until the terrible images are drained of negative energy and become less frightening. We could encourage and support the clients, even order them when necessary, and let them stand by and never give up until they reach that goal. This is called "in for a pound".

What shall we do if a client is unable to stand up to it? ICP suggests that the client will do his/her level best to keep going. If they cannot hold on indeed, we can use the "steady retreat" approach, leading him/her in his/her imagination as leisurely as possible away from that terrible image.

For instance, the imagery communication psychotherapist guides the client to confront the image of a ghost and slowly steps back in his/her imagination, until he/she leaves the place where the ghost is, to a sunny spot.

Before "steady retreat", the psychotherapist must tell the client, "you have been holding on for a long time today. You have successfully completed today's task. Now you can transfer it in imagery." That way, the client does not feel like a failure.

After "steady retreat", the psychotherapist must tell the client, "later on, when we have done more and better preparation, we will look at this image together. Next time, we will face it more successfully." In this way, a temporary withdrawal will not become a permanent fear and lead to retreat.

3.2. *The ending technique of realizing the goal: Storage*

The storage technique was designed by Cao Yu, the wife of Zhu Jianjun. This technique can be used extensively at the end for achieving the therapeutic goals in ICP.

(1) Design background

During the psychotherapists and psychological consultants' mental development, periodic "repetition" occurs frequently. We found that some of the major traumatic complexes that have been dealt with before bounced back to the origin after a period of time. This often confused us regarding the usefulness of previous work.

As a matter of fact, a traumatic event or experience that has a profound effect on us always infiltrates into all aspects of our subconscious. It has existed as a subconscious negative script and belief and as a negative behavioral response habit. Or it has already existed as a part of our self. Therefore, it is not enough to simply dissolve a single complex in slices. The problems and habits associated with this complex still exist. They are like "potential", intangibly pushing us back to the original system.

(2) Working principle

Aiming to solve this difficult problem, Cao Yu designed the technique of storage according to the human psychological rules. "The new arrival, the old ones are still alive." By covering the timeline in time, the "old files" are replaced by modified "new files" to become a mental version of the upgrade.

As a result, at the level of primary cognition, the two beliefs of old and new have a subconscious connection in our deep inner core. Our subconscious is beginning to know that the "old files" have become obsolete documents of the past, and our belief base will be these updated "new files" from now on.

The storage technique aims to compensate for the lack of rebound in the dealt complex. Especially, the major complex cannot be cured in one shot, we need to constantly add and solidify the current resources with time, and prompt the rebound to auto-update by establishing the connection between the past and the present. After extensive clinical practice, this technique has proven to be effective in preventing the complex rebound.

(3) Basic operation

When a certain complex is relatively completely cured and improvements are seen, the psychotherapist immediately takes the client back to the beginning of the scene of negative image or life script and, with the current awareness, guides the client to see the old and the new in the same field of vision, and to use the new vision for updating, naming and storage. At the end of this imagery communication, according to the client's feeling, he/she is led to put the new file stored in his/her body somewhere in order to connect, extract and apply the new resources when needed later.

It is a remarkable fact that the clinical experience shows that the heart region or the instinctive region is better, and it is easy to bounce back in the brain region. In spite of this, for the respect of the clients, the imagery communication psychotherapists need not be eager to guide them, but only enhance their self-awareness in line with the specific situation in practice.

For example, when a client stores the processed version of the mental script in his/her brain region, the psychotherapist can encourage and lead him/her saying, "You did a very important little step today! We will continue to focus on it."

There are three purposes of this sentence. The first is to indicate full approval of the client. The second is to remind the client that this processed complex may somehow spring back in the future. The third is to enhance his/her awareness and to encourage him/her: even if there is a rebound one day, there is no need to worry, because the "new seed" has been planted today.

(4) Sample application

To facilitate the readers' and users' understanding, here is an example of a developer's work.

The client saw a personality image in his imagination, that was a ragged man, hunched over and sorrowful, bearing the pressure of all the family members. The psychotherapist led the client to stare at this image. This figure soon turned into a dirty and tattered trash can.

Through the method of Imagery Communication Psychotherapy, the client transported the trash can to the garbage power station and cleaned and maintained it. In his images, electricity was channeled into all parts of his body and became a mental resource. At this moment, the client was guided to look at the trash can in his imagination. It had been completely new and finally become a healthy and happy sanitation worker.

At this time, the psychotherapist used the storage technique. The client was led to look at the past photo of the sanitation worker and acknowledged the existence of the past. Then the new image of the sanitation worker covered the original. The client named it and stored it.

After this passage of imagery communication was over, the psychotherapist informed the client: although this sub-personality became the sanitation worker, he may think of his past at some point in the future. That is ok. By then, you can extract the new file and let yourself know that you are different now from you used to be.

About two years later, the psychotherapist received feedback from the client. In the face of the high-intensity pressure, the client felt that he returned to the original state for two or three times. But immediately, the old image could automatically evoke the new image of sanitation worker. Whenever that happened, he felt like he had a new coping model. He did not even have to take the initiative to extract that new file. He identified the healthier stress response model.

(5) Range of application

The storage technique is applied to mental troubles, various types of neurosis and mild borderline personality disorders.

Additionally, it can be applied to people with psychological trauma, self-growing psychological consultants and psychotherapists.

(6) Announcements

Note that if a client chooses to put the "new file" in his/her head region in the "storage", this indicates that he/she is still rational or in rationalization. We recommend that an imagery communication psychotherapist guide the client to take the initiative to extract the "new file" in the following psychotherapy session, and then reexperience the positive resources of the new coping model and consolidate it. Generally, the "new file" will be stored in the heart or chest region after an active extraction and experience.

In the application, we found that if the consultative relationship is safe enough, the clients can fully experience the new positive images, and most of them will be automatically stored in the chest region (representing the emotional region).

In rare cases, there are barriers or tight bands in the storage region to indicate that the client still has resistance and is not used to this new positive coping model.

Under such circumstances, the psychotherapist can guide the client to carefully observe the location of storage and to let it be covered and hooped. The first step is to break through the impedance. The next step is to give the correct guidance to the client so as to experience self-awareness. The final step is to complete the storage work.

If a negative image does not transform into the new one completely, this indicates that the client still has a strong resistance, or that the psychotherapist's operation is inappropriate. Please do not use the storage method.

Caution: Please do not use the storage method on beginners of ICP.

Chapter 5

The Techniques and Procedures of Imagery Communication Psychotherapy

1. Micro techniques of Imagery Communication Psychotherapy

Micro technique refers to the smallest technical unit for a certain stage of the psychological counseling and psychotherapy process.

1.1. *Substitution and modification*

The simplest intervention technique of Imagery Communication Psychotherapy (ICP) is substitution. It refers to the way in which the client, under the guidance of the psychotherapist, imagines a positive image and substitutes it for the previous negative one.

With an unacceptable attitude, this technique cannot really resolve the client's mental problems. For this reason, substitution is not recommended as a general rule. But there is one exception. When conducting mental crisis intervention or meeting a client with rather intense negative sentiments, the psychotherapist can use it to temporarily alleviate the client's suffering. And after that, further treatment must be provided in this case.

For instance, a girl who attempted suicide was in a very depressed mood. In the event of crisis intervention, a bleak cemetery and a perfect coffin appeared in her imagination. No matter how hard the psychotherapist tried, she wanted to lie in her coffin and sleep forever. This image showed that she really wanted to die. In the case, in order to save her life, the psychotherapist could guide her: Please imagine that there is a bright house next to this cemetery. It is very warm and peaceful. You try to walk into the house. . .

This is an example of substitution in ICP.

When using the technique of modification, the psychotherapist works on the client's previous negative imagery — usually a more superficial and less general one. Experienced psychotherapists can use it to address deeper and more general negative ones.

Modification can be used as one of the conventional methods in primary intervention of ICP. When the modified imagery reappears, the psychotherapist can persevere with the modification or use some deeper and more effective methods such as confrontation and acceptance, as will be evident in the following.

For example, in a client's imagination, his house was covered with dust. The dust image symbolizes depression. The thickness and coverage of dust indicate the degree of depression. The psychotherapist could guide him to sweep the dust in his preferred way, such as with a rag wipe, a feather duster or a vacuum cleaner. This is the modification in ICP.

To be sure, we encourage the latter be used when comparing modification, confrontation and acceptance.

1.2. *Confrontation*

Confrontation is not so much a micro technique at the method level, rather it is a basic counseling and psychotherapy attitude. In the context of ICP, it refers to the frightening and uncomfortable image that occurs in the process of imagery communication; with the guidance and support of the psychotherapist, the client is encouraged to look at the image without evading, attacking or doing anything about it, just waiting for it to change spontaneously.

Confrontation is a kind of proactive effortless action, being particularly applicable for dealing with terrifying images. It is one of the most effective ways to resolve negative imagery and cope with fear.

And what it does is, the client is encouraged to stare at terrifying imagery in imagination and to make no other behavioral responses when it appears. At the same time, the psychotherapist leads him/her to relieve tension by muscle relaxation. Once the client shows signs of escape or self-deception, the psychotherapist should stick to the procedure.

There are three principles of confrontation: no escape, no assault and no coping in the face of images.

The most typical terrifying imagery is ghost imagery. In this way, we will briefly interpret the ghost imagery and how to confront it.

The ghost imagery is the symbol of all kinds of negative emotion, mood and mental disorders in people's inner hearts. People who do not understand the ghost imagery tend to go into the wrong places: it is either an objective existence or a mistaken belief that ghosts do not exist, or that ghosts are rare. In fact, there is no ghost in the objective world. Ghosts do not belong to the realm of matter. However, so many people see ghosts in their dreams, illusion, imagination, feeling and other inner activities.

The reason is that a ghost is a kind of a cultural symbol, which exists in the spiritual world of human beings. In other words, it is not uncommon for people to see ghost images in the spiritual world. If a person mistakes the ghost of psychological reality for the existence of objective reality, then that means something is wrong with his/her spiritual world. The problem is psychotic.

If we could understand ghosts and bravely confront them in our imagination — no escape, no assault, and no coping, just look at them — we would have the opportunity to see that they are also a life force, just a strange energy of life. Like us, ghosts are filled with longing — to love and be loved, respected and understood. They become these terrible images only because of their misfortune and trauma.

In this case, we accompany and support them to "look at him/her" when a terrible ghost image occurs in the clients' imagination. This is a painful and hard process. However, as long as the confrontation is persistent, the clients will have a chance to see the ghosts' true colors and have an opportunity to convert the negative mental energy carried by the ghost imagery into the corresponding positive mental energy.

It turns out that the ghost with fangs and sharp claws is just burning anger, the grim reaper in black robes is only human fear of the instinct of death, and the ghost of the white lady with weak breath is just deep depression.

Because of understanding, we will be merciful.

1.3. *Acceptance*

The attitude of acceptance should be the quality of all psychotherapists, especially unconditional acceptance.

As far as ICP is concerned, acceptance means accepting uncritically, but it is not equal to identification or connivance. Acceptance still has the ability to identify right from wrong. It is just not critical in attitude.

This technique can better apply to the disgusting and menial imagery. Like confrontation, acceptance is also one of the most effective ways to resolve negative imagery.

Basic methods of acceptance include: no aggression, no hurt and no humiliation. In other words, it means that we do not do anything that signifies no acceptance. When the client continues to do this for a long time, he/she can be recommended to communicate with these negative images in imagination.

The familiar disgusting and menial imageries are of mollusks, maggots, cockroaches, rats, toads, homeless animals, decomposed bodies, stupid people, downtrodden people, ugly people, dirty people, cowardly people, incompetent people and so on.

When faced with such images, the client is prone to habitual reactions or has an impulse to refuse them, such as to spit at them, to be far away, to bury, to burn, to throw them away or to kill them.

These psychological actions represent the inner conflict of the client. The conflict arises from the lack acceptance of a certain part of self. It can only be repressed. Using these methods does by no means eliminate those negative images, thereby losing the opportunity to transform mental energy.

As a result, the ICP psychotherapist should sincerely accompany the client to experience these negative images, and guide him/her to actively communicate with them, to help them, and even to embrace them in the imagination.

Here, in particular, it serves to be reminded of the fact that hugging is not a technique of counseling and psychotherapy, whether a counselor hugs a client or a client embraces an image in his/her imagination. The reason is that what really matters is genuine sincerity. Otherwise, the hug becomes a physical gesture and lacks the genuine human concern. This is not true acceptance or healing acceptance.

Here is a true example:

Many years ago, a male client imagined that there was a group of ragged people walking slowly in a deep valley. There were blooded and wounded warriors. There were skinny beggars. Some were dirty homeless people. They all smelled bad. His expression was painful. He felt a sense of disgust and nausea.

His consultant was a pretty woman who just began to learn Imagery Communication Psychotherapy. She told her client that she was standing on the top of the hill in that valley, she was wearing a long white dress, and she was looking down at the crowd with her arms wide open. She guided him to look up at her in his imagination, to experience her acceptance, and even to feel her embracing.

At first, he felt a little better. But soon he felt a greater sense of inferiority and incompetence. He even had a vague anger at his consultant.

Obviously, this is not true acceptance. In a sense, the high profile of the consultant deepened the client's sense of inferiority and incompetence. In the presence of this elegant and noble female image, he himself was a sharp contrast. He himself felt dwarfed. This is one of the sources of his anger even though we all know that there was an element of transference.

In this case, the real acceptance would be when the consultant accompanies the client to fully feel the pain of that group or empathize with him, and encourages him to express his deep feelings and wishes with self-awareness. Then, she should guide him to find a way to help those people in his imagination. During the whole process, a good consultant does not allow any unacceptable psychological behavior, such as avoidance, shock, contempt, exclusion, elimination, etc.

1.4. *Support and directive of images*

Without unified forms and procedures, this technique is used based on the analysis and judgment of the psychotherapist.

In the situation that there are some images lacking love and caring, the imagery communication therapist can provide some support in terms of imagery. It must be noted, however, that this technique cannot be used too frequently; it must be used accurately and moderately so as to reduce the dependency of the client.

The purpose of directive is to help the client to make an accurate and more beneficial choice, and to take the correct measures to deal with the current situation. After all, the client is influenced by the complex of the past and does not understand the symbolism of imagery. Some of the client's choices are not healthy and correct in an imaginary situation and may be wrong and dangerous or harmful. At this point, we need to direct the client to know what is healthy and how to respond correctly.

Some clients cannot help avoiding or attacking ugly or dirty images, such as toads, lizards and stray animals, when they see them in their imagination. At this point, we have to do some imagery directive work. We must inform the clients that avoidance and attack are not good solutions, but only lead to more inhibition and feelings of disgust. We could encourage toads, lizards and stray animal images to bathe in clean water and bask in the sun in the process of imagery communication. The images of water and sunshine have the effect of decontamination and symbolic significance of healthy and effective nourishment.

1.5. *Insight and catharsis*

The effect of insight is highly valued in ICP. Insight is perception with the purpose to facilitate the client's exploration of the truth of his/her inner mind.

The contents of insight include: (1) helping the client recognize the underlying emotions and feelings related to those images; (2) helping the client sense the transformation process of inward emotions reflected by interrelations between images; (3) leading the client to find out the cause and process of the complexes.

The technique of insight should follow the principle that the more specific and accurate the insight is, the better.

There is a supporting technique for insight, that is, "Tape Rewinding". When a negative image presents itself in a client's imagination, an imagery communication psychotherapist can guide him to "replay" the imagination. It means going back to a certain point in the past and experiencing how the negative image took shape.

For example, a tree cut off by the waist is in a client's dream or imagination. We could use this technique for guidance, "if you are watching a video now, please imagine yourself playing it back and returning the tape to the moment the tree was chopped. See what happened at that moment? What was cutting the tree like that?"

Catharsis is always valued in psychodynamic psychotherapy. It can release pent-up mental energy and thus become a key factor in the effect. However, the effects of catharsis are also affected by other factors.

First of all, catharsis with insight has great influence. In ICP's view, releasing without self-awareness has no real therapeutic effect. There are side effects sometimes. For instance, some of the clients mistakenly assume that a negative emotion should be cathartic, even to the extent that no suppression is seen as a manifestation of mental health, regardless of the bottom line of moral and mental health. It will destroy their real relationships and lead to an outpouring of impulse.

For this reason, we insist that counselors and psychotherapists guide clients to release their negative emotions with self-detection and self-awareness. At least, this is what ICP asks imagery communication psychotherapists to do.

In addition, the therapeutic effect of releasing the source emotion will be better.

As we know, emotion can be transformed. The sequence of transformations usually occurs unconsciously in many cases. If a client released a transformed sentiment, even transformed many times, but not the source emotion, so the more he/she converted, the less negative energy he/she released, and less the therapeutic effect would be.

As a result, imagery communication psychotherapists must try to guide clients to catharsis of their negative emotions with their insight and self-detection.

In the in-depth phase of ICP, insight and catharsis with self-awareness will be the main techniques, no matter for self-growth or clinical treatment. It will even be the only technique when psychotherapy steps into a quite deep level.

1.6. *Calibration technique*

The calibration technique means that a psychotherapist names the emotions and mood that a client cannot clearly describe or tell. The role of this technique is to help clients understand their emotions and mood, and enable them to compare emotions and mood at different times or moments, thereby increasing their ability to manage emotions.

Moreover, the clients can construct a more stable self-construction by understanding the changing laws of their emotions and mood. Our clinical practice shows that as long as imagery communication psychotherapists consciously use the calibration technique, the clients will generally make significant progress in a few months and have a positive impact on self-construction.

Its operation is simple. When the client shows some emotion or mood, the psychotherapist tells him/her the name of the emotion or mood. For example, "I see you are upset now." "You look a little angry." "It seems to me that you are confused at the moment."

This technique can be seen as a kind of education. It educates the clients to classify emotions and mood, and promote their personal maturity naturally.

1.7. *Other micro techniques*

The core micro technologies in ICP have been mentioned so far. Other techniques are sometimes required to cooperate with each other during the actual clinical operation. The following is a brief overview of other micro techniques. There are no priorities.

1.7.1. *Alternation*

Method: Leading the client to alternatively perceive two objects in different fields.

Purpose: Reducing contamination, increasing the feeling of reality and avoiding indulgence.

1.7.2. *"The word in the heart"*

Method: Searching for the word in the client's heart, and letting him/her repeat it a couple of times with increasing volume till the point the client can speak it out.

Purpose: Releasing the client's emotion with self-awareness and improving confidence.

The point is to let the client experience his/her emotion in a relaxed way, waiting for that word to emerge naturally in the mind. It must be very simple and full of emotions. It is not the one needed here if it is long or reasonable.

1.7.3. *Shooting questions*

Method: Shooting questions at a client step by step and not relaxing till he/she identifies his/her own problem. After that, the psychotherapist can provide some moderate guidance.

Purpose: Enhancing self-awareness.

1.7.4. *Deep thinking and quiet reading*

Method: Stressing, remaining silent for a short while, and speaking or pointing out the pertinent word.

Purpose: Strengthening insight and epiphany.

This is difficult for some clients. The psychotherapist could guide the client to imagine a vast prairie, sea or cloudless sky with relaxed breathing and other conditions to reduce the thoughts. Next, lead the client to speak to himself/herself in the simplest language. Guide the client to speak the first step of the question if it is so complicated.

The client needs to experience this question quietly and focus on his/her feeling. When the inner answer emerges, he/she compares it to the self's feeling and matches them. He/she could ask himself/herself: "Is that right?" and then wait for the inner feeling. Repeat the previous process if not. Otherwise, continue to the next step.

It is worth reminding that at any time, if the mind is found to be in a mess, please stop thinking, relax and imagine the sea or sky to eliminate too many thoughts.

1.7.5. *Conscious behavior correction*

Method: Leading the client to understand his/her own problem, to summarize and analyze the improper behaviors, and to map out the improvement plan that enables him/her to reflect on and deal with his/her situation.

Purpose: Enhancing self-awareness, promoting execution and control.

1.7.6. *Image show*

Method: Letting the client perform what he/she has seen in the images.

Purpose: Expressing and releasing.

This method applies to group training. Other members of the group can play the roles of the client's images. During the performance, the psychotherapist can stop and ask the characters to understand and express their true feelings.

1.7.7. *Stories and slogans*

Method: Sharing the imagery stories of the client and summarizing them into short sentences in the form of a slogan.

Purpose: Enhancing self-awareness and accelerating insight.

1.7.8. *Self-illuminating language*

Method: Creating a set of descriptions that the clients can frequently read for themselves.

Purpose: Enhancing self-awareness to replace subconscious negative beliefs with more healthy and positive beliefs.

The contents of these languages are positive hints. It must be ensured that the language pattern is the one primitive cognition is used to. Its features are simple, smooth and moving, with no academic terms and obscure words. The whole writing process should be in the primitive cognition state.

1.7.9. *Distinguishing emotions of different classification*

Method: Making the client distinguish through analysis and perception "my emotions" and "others' emotions", "the past emotions" and "the current emotions".

Purpose: Increasing self-awareness of emotion and reducing contamination.

For instance, the client can imagine a scene of conflict with another person. Next, imagine a cloud of turbid gas permeated between the two men. Imagine there are two glass beakers near them and the gas can be separated and inhaled into the two glass beakers. Their emotions return into the separate beakers. After a while, the gases become liquid and gradually deposit into several layers. Immediately, the client experiences emotions of each layer in the beaker and the other's specific emotions of each layer.

1.7.10. *Consciousness cleaning*

Method: Spontaneously speaking out the thought contents in consciousness, and at the same time decreasing any further symbolization activity as possible. The client stays awake consciously in the process.

Purpose: Making the client's consciousness clearer, promoting awakening and awareness, and dealing with complexes.

1.7.11. *Ritualization*

Method: Awakening the authentic part by some objects similar to it, with complicated and changeable approaches for this process.

Purpose: Actualizing potentials and increasing perceptibility.

1.7.12. *Expressing desires and waiting*

This is one of the deep-seated techniques.

Method: Expressing the innermost expectation by a symbolic way. Nothing to do after the expression except to tell oneself: "I am willing to wait for this wish to come true whatever the way it is."

Purpose: Deepening self-awareness, expressing the innermost expectation, and declaring one's willingness to wait for its realization and to accept the possible fact that it may not be realized.

1.7.13. *Finding out "seeds"*

Method: Tracing the client's emotions and behaviors to find his/her "seeds of love", "seeds of courage", "seeds of power", "seeds of trust", etc.

Purpose: Searching and utilizing the client's own positive psychological resources, enhancing his/her self-acceptance and self-identity.

1.7.14. *Actively choosing and promising*

Method: Proposing the client to choose self-confidence, love, self-awareness and life; requiring him/her to make a commitment when accepting these choices.

Purpose: Improving the life quality.

1.7.15. *Asking questions*

Method: The common guideline is: "this feeling is expressed in a sentence. What is it?" "This feeling likely seems to say...." The latter is more accessible.

Purpose: Enhancing self-awareness to express further emotion.

1.7.16. *Knowing common archetype and imagery*

Method: Leading the client to know the archetype and imagery in his/her dreams or imaginations.

Purpose: Deepen self-exploration and promote self-knowledge.

1.7.17. *Analyzing imagery in movies, literatures and dreams*

Method: Encouraging the client to consciously analyze imagery in movies, literatures and dreams.

Purpose: Improving the sensibility.

1.7.18. *Stratified empathy*

Method: For different levels of emotional feelings of the client, a psychotherapist shares them and expresses empathy.

Purpose: Enhancing self-awareness to understand the emotional hierarchy of the moment. The client has a chance to experience sincere empathy from the psychotherapist. At the same time, the psychotherapist gives the client a demonstration of emotional expression.

For example, the psychotherapist tells a client: "your attack makes me sad. Your feeling of hurt inside makes me love dearly."

1.7.19. *Detailed inquiry*

Method: Specifically inquire the details of images. It combines the techniques of inquiry with materialization.

Purpose: Clarifying issues and deepening communications.

For instance, a client sees a fish in the imagination and tells his/her psychotherapist. The psychotherapist asks him: "What does this fish look like? What color? How big? How old is it if it is like a person? What are the characteristics?"

1.7.20. *Response inquiry without self-awareness*

Method: In the face of questioning without self-awareness, the psychotherapist should remind the client to focus on his/her emotions, motivations and needs rather than simply returning to the question.

Purpose: Reducing the problem, improving clients' ability to see themselves and to perceive.

1.7.21. *Immediate counter-examples*

Method: This is in essence a confrontation. The psychotherapist clearly points out the apparent contradictions or inconsistencies in a client. The key is "immediate". Once found, identify quickly. If it is not "immediate", the impact will be lost.

Purpose: Increasing awareness and improving detection.

1.7.22. *Break unawareness*

Method: When the client tries to cater to the psychotherapist, whatever the client says, the psychotherapist should reply with a "no". Even if the client is talking about what the psychotherapist has just said, the psychotherapist is looking for reasons to say no. That would put the client into an "unfit" predicament. After that, the psychotherapist reminds the client to detect the unawareness.

Purpose: Breaking the state of unawareness.

1.7.23. *Drawing diary*

Method: This method applies to group training. ICP trainers ask students not to take notes in the usual way when they listen to a class. No words are allowed in the notes. Students can only record what they have heard or understood in the form of comics and short drawings, or leave marks to help them remember.

Purpose: Promoting primitive cognitive abilities, learning to use imagery to express, and reducing reliance on logical thinking.

2. Procedures of basic techniques in ICP

The practice of ICP is so flexible and changeable that it may not exactly follow the prescribed steps. However, there are some indispensable procedures, such as therapeutic interactivities among images, and awakening the client at the end of the psychotherapy session to bring him/her back to the awake state from the imagination state.

2.1. *Introducing ICP*

The contents in this procedure conclude the adjustment of posture and breathing, some brief directions and physical relaxation. The order of body relaxation is from head to toe. The head symbolizes reason, and its full relaxation helps to enter the subconscious state and deep experience.

The common types of resistance when introducing ICP:

(1) The client cannot relax or refuses to keep his/her eyes closed.
(2) The client cannot see any image. This is the most general type of resistance in the introduction stage.
(3) The client has seen some images, but cannot clearly observe them because of the dim light or due to the frequent change in imagination.
(4) Other types of resistance such as falling asleep, jumping or vacillating between different topics, pretending to be clumsy, attacking the psychotherapist, etc.

Some methods to eliminate resistance in the introduction stage:

(1) Eliminating scruples and worries of the client.
(2) Instructing the client to be physically relaxed and to concentrate on the physical sensation.
(3) Utilizing some specific images to guide the client, for example, transforming colors into images.
(4) Continuous guidance with patience.
(5) Making a detour.
(6) Interpretation.
(7) Regulating the pace of guidance and maintaining a firm, slow and modest tone.
(8) Increasing the novelty of the imagery.
(9) Bringing in some common skills such as tape rewinding, slow-motion, photographing and focusing.
(10) Sharing the present imagery and feelings of the psychotherapist.
(11) Switching the medium of imagery perception.
(12) Switching the object of imagery perception.

Note: It is not the method but how the psychotherapist can understand the client that is important for eliminating resistance.

2.2. *Entering imagination*

The psychotherapist can set an initial imagery or use other methods to start up the imagination in this procedure.

Common initial images:

- The house imagery: Basic personality traits, and the general mental and emotional state.
- The pit imagery: The present psychological problem faced.
- The box with something scary: The objects that one fears subconsciously
- Flower and insect: One's attitude toward gender and sex, one's attitude towards the opposite sex and intersexual relationship.
- The cave imagery: Subconsciousness and regression (one of the self-defense mechanisms). It should be noted that novices must prudently use this imagery, because it is easy to touch and trigger a deeper complex and psychological trauma.
- The mirror imagery: The self-image in subconsciousness. We advise caution about novices using this imagery.

Other methods for introducing ICP:

The introduction can also start with the following contents:

- Dream;
- Somatic sensation;
- Specific word;
- Present emotion;
- Body posture;
- A metaphor;
- Memory of one scene;
- A piece of work;
- An imagination;
- A crucial realistic object;
- The five internal organs or other body system;

- Introducing the missed imagery by rewinding;
- Utilizing the specification method;
- Interpreting ICP.

Note: When leading the client to imagine, it is necessary to tell him/her: "it is just an imagination. You can believe that I am always with you, no matter what happens". When having stepped into the phases "entering imagination" and "therapeutic interactivities among images", the psychotherapist can repeat the above instruction which will provide spiritual company and psychological support if some extremely negative images occur to the client or there are some images the client is unwilling or fears to face.

2.3. *Analyzing and understanding images*

The significance of understanding images is much greater than analysis.

Imagery is a symbol with mental energy. ICP relies on the communication between two hearts to achieve the purpose of psychological treatment and spiritual growth. Therefore, ICP therapists should be very careful and show sincere commitment. They should also be mindful of the general atmosphere and emotional feelings conveyed by the images described by the clients, and inner feelings that these images bring to themselves.

The significance of experience and understanding is extremely important. But as an ICP psychotherapist, one still needs "theoretical arms" and masters analytical methods and related knowledge of symbolic meaning. The symbolism of imagery has some regularity. Mastering the regularity can achieve or increase understanding of imagery.

Let's take an example of the most basic initial imagery of house.

House imagery can symbolize the human body as well as the human mind. In the context of psychological counseling and therapy, it is more symbolic of the inner world. The Chinese word for it is "heart house". According to our clinical experiences, the specific features of house imagery symbolize different psychic characteristics.

The degree of dilapidation in the house often symbolizes the self-abasement and depression of a client's mentality. Generally speaking, the more dilapidated the house image is, the worse the client's mentality is. The better the interior and exterior of the house image are, the better and healthier the client's mentality is.

The color of a house always symbolizes one's tone of personality and emotion. Warm colors represent an outgoing attitude and enthusiasm. Cold colors represent an introvert or a darker mood. Every color is a relatively independent image with other rich significances. Concrete scenes need to be combined in order to be analyzed and experienced. Here, there is no discussion.

The size of a house often symbolizes one's mental capacity. Relatively speaking, a bigger house is better. However, a too big and broad house is not necessarily good and healthy. It may involve psychological boundaries and whether there is a mental self.

The material of a house is often associated with one's feeling of security and basic personality trait. Overly strong and thin materials symbolize insecurity, such as stone and straw. Its difference is that the former will use excessive protection to compensate for the lack of security, while the latter has no such compensation.

A house built of natural materials, such as bamboo and wood, symbolizes simplicity, peaceful and un-vainglorious characters. This material is susceptible to fire in real life, so its symbolic meaning can be interpreted as a fear of intense interpersonal conflict and anger. In other words, bamboo or wood-oriented people are good at suppressing anger in order to avoid interpersonal conflict.

With regard to the symbolic meaning of materials and their coping styles, ICP has summarized many detailed clinical experiences. This book is limited in length, and we advise some of the readers and beginners to not mechanically memorize. There is no list.

The number of floors and the number of rooms symbolize "the number of psychological layers" and "the number of psychological states", which is related to the complexity of personality. In general, the more the number of floors the image has, the more complicated the character is. A high-rise building is related to the degree of rationality. The higher a building image is, the more rational the person is. A simple structure of the house image indicates one's purity and simplicity.

The size and state of the door and windows symbolize spiritual openness. A very small and/or closed door and windows mean less openness. Big and easy to open door and windows mean more openness. In order to improve the effect, in the process of imagery communication, we always encourage them to open doors and windows as long as clients are willing. It is much healthier to initiatively open the door and windows than to keep them closed, even if some clients are unwilling or afraid to open them.

A dirty house often symbolizes one's negative mindset and depression or fear. Dust image symbolizes depression.

The mess in a house often symbolizes one's anxiety and irritability.

Bad light or even darkness in a house symbolizes that the client knows little about himself/herself. Self-knowledge is an important basis of mental health. Thus, a dark or dim house indicates one's unhealthy mentality. A brighter house means a relatively healthy state of mind. Of course, if the client experiences ICP for the first time, and his mind is filled with fear, his house image will be dim or dark.

In any case, we encourage clients to make the house brighter in their imagination in any way they like. It can improve their mental health and promote psychotherapy.

The concrete interior decoration and the characters, animals, plants and human creations in a house image are all symbolic. The general principle of analysis is to contact "context", which is to combine the overall house image. To explain an image in isolation is unscientific and inaccurate.

There are a few points that need to be noted in the analysis and while experiencing images. These are explained in the following.

(1) The ultimate and overly perfect imagery does not necessarily mean good mental health. If a client's house image is pretty neat, it is often the manifestation of obsessive–compulsive disorder or obsessive–compulsive personality. If a client's house image is extremely beautiful or luxurious, it is often performance due to hysteria or hysterical personality.

(2) The symbolism in this book is only a matter of probability, not of necessity.

The symbolic meaning is flexible, not rigid, mechanical and invariable. The same symbolism can be expressed by various forms of imagery. The same image has multiple meanings. In addition, the combination of several images and the whole image will constitute a new symbolic significance.

It is forbidden to mechanically apply symbolism. In ICP's opinion, this is savage analysis!

(3) The same image has many variations. Each variant represents an overall, in general, but not identical, state of mind.

Take water for example. There are some basic symbolic meanings of water imagery: vitality, nourishment, femininity, sexuality, fertility, creativity, love, care and so on. There is a correlation among these basic symbolic meanings.

Imagery communication psychotherapists should analyze an overall water image according to its specific variants and status appearing every time with the purpose of interpreting accurately. The sea, the stream, the river and the spring must be interpreted as sea, stream, river and spring. The water imagery has many variants, such as ice, snow, rain, cloud, fog, blood, milk, wine, tear, poison, etc. They are inseparable from the basic meaning of vitality and emotional nourishment, but each has its own focus.

For instance, "ice" image emphasizes emotional freezing and condensation. "Milk" image emphasizes maternal love, nurturing and caring. "Wine" symbolizes intoxicating emotions. "Poison" symbolizes indulging and harmful emotions.

(4) An imagery communication psychotherapist does not interpret the symbolic meanings of images to the client in the process of ICP.

This is quite different from classical psychoanalysis. Classical psychoanalysis emphasizes concretization of unconscious contents. ICP works directly at the level of unconsciousness. The deep communication and psychotherapy in the way of "unconsciousness to unconsciousness" are realized through the symbolic meaning of imagery. Therefore, it is not necessary for clients to know the symbolic meanings of imagery on the rational level.

On the contrary, if a psychotherapist leads a client into imagination, especially into the therapeutic interactive stage, explaining the symbolic meanings of his images will take him onto the rational level, out of or breaking the deep communication at the subconscious level, interfering with the whole process of psychotherapy.

(5) An imagery communication psychotherapist could consciously reinforce the singularity of imagination in order to increase the degree of freedom that a client imagines.

Some clients are too rational or nervous after entering into imagination, and the images described are limited to everyday logical thinking. For example, when a client experiences house imagery, what he/she sees in the imagination are usually things "there should be in the house" in daily life, such as desks, chairs, tea table and so on. Although these things have a symbolic significance and analysis value, because they are limited, they can show his/her little inner activities and shallow depth. In this case, the psychotherapist could consciously guide the client:

> In your imagined house, you can see a singular world. Something strange will appear in it. You may see things that are not common in your daily life, even in real life. As long as you relax, you can see. That is ok. I will be with you. Say what you see.

2.4. *Therapeutic interactivities among images*

In this stage, the psychotherapist can have some in-depth interactions with the client by using symbolic meanings of the images.

On the basis of images described by the client, the psychotherapist can understand his/her state of mind, feel his/her mood and know his/her ego defense mechanism and complexes, and then take corresponding countermeasures. During this process, the psychotherapist can apply any psychological counseling techniques according to the need, such as inquiry, listening, confrontation, materialization, etc.

But the psychotherapist must express by transforming them into the form of images.

Notes:

(i) Unlike classical psychoanalysis, the imagery communication psychotherapist usually will not interpret symbolic meanings of the images. Instead, they will directly deal with the information at a subconscious level.
(ii) At the end of imagery communication, the psychotherapist needs to bring the client back to the real objective world. This is vital for the therapy, as it will have a direct influence on the client's sense of reality.

Here is an example for demonstration:

Client: I am standing outside a stone arch. After entering it, I see a garden similar to Suzhou Garden. There is a stone tiger in it. This gray tiger is like a young tiger. There is a door behind the tiger. There is another door behind the door. I walk inside and see a high stone tower. This tower is also gray. . .

Psychotherapist: Stare at that stone tiger. If he had the human age, how old would he be?

Client: Twelve or thirteen years old.

Psychotherapist: Ok. You keep watching him and do nothing. Just look at him.

Client: . . . There seems to be water under his feet. Well, it is spring.

Psychotherapist: There is a spring under his feet. That is great! Would you like to put some spring water on him?

Client: Yes, I do . . . His head comes alive. His eyes can turn. How strange! I am not afraid of it at all.

Psychotherapist: Your feeling?

Client (eyelashes wet): Love dearly. I feel a lot of pain.

Psychotherapist: So you want?

Client: I want to feed him water. . . I hold water for him with my two hands. . . His body seems to have temperature. He can move. . . I want to touch him. (At this moment, his tears rolled down) He comes alive! He comes alive!

This client suffered from depression and had also attempted suicide. In the process of imagery communication, he and I created a new psychic story on the basis of his original mental images. It was not so much that the stone tiger survived, but that this client came alive.

In the process, the psychotherapist was more of a patient and wise person, guiding and accompanying the client in his deep personality to explore new ways of responding, forming a new voluntary decision.

Many clinical experiences show that the psychotherapist can continue to operate ICP even if he/she cannot analyze the symbolic meaning of the image for a while. As long as the psychotherapist is attentive, according to the feeling of the image and the scene, sometimes even intuition, one could provide guidance on the healthy direction.

When the psychotherapist's mental health is better than that of the client, as well as has no serious complexes about the psychological problem facing him/her, his/her guidance and suggestion would be more healthy and effective for his/her client. Therefore, we attach great importance to the self-growth of ICP consultants and psychotherapists.

During the whole process of imagery communication, consultants and psychotherapists have no escape. Our mental state, including our acceptance and subtle emotional changes, is also exposed to our clients, although at that moment, they may have closed their eyes. The reason is very simple. Both the psychotherapist and client express themselves by using imagery symbols and deeply communicate with each other by symbolic meanings. The two sides can feel each other. The communication can be directly applied to the client's deep personality and primitive spiritual organization. This is the core of ICP.

2.5. *Brief summary*

After finishing the imagery communication, the psychotherapist can ask some simple questions about the client's feeling or briefly answer his/her questions.

However, the psychotherapist does not analyze the process in detail on the whole. Under normal conditions, this time the psychotherapy can be over after a brief summary.

Note: Detailed analysis in general should be avoided in the case that rational discussion weakens the positive impact on the client's personality in depth.

2.6. *Homework assignment*

Some imagery homework that is required to be done at home can be given to the client to enhance the efficacy if necessary. As an internal psychic behavior, imagery requires repeated practice sometimes.

For example, a client was so depressed when she came to ask for help. Her house image was full of dust. As we know, the dust image is the symbol of depression. In the process of imagery communication, her psychotherapist led her to clean the house in her imagination. Her house became bright and clean when this psychotherapy ended. But the dust may appear in her house image in the next psychotherapy session. This shows that either her depression had improved, but bounced back, or had not been cleaned thoroughly last time.

In response to this situation, the psychotherapist could give her psychological homework: clean the dust. She was asked to go home and clean the dust in her imagination. And this exercise would be done for 20 minutes every day.

This homework allows her to continue until her house image becomes bright and clean naturally when she imagines the house again. If her house image had become clean in her homework, she would not imagine a dirty house to clean it.

However, homework related to the following case cannot be used. The first case involves intense negative emotions such as grief and fear. The second one refers to some dangerous situations like ghost imagery. In addition, the homework related to the situation that goes beyond the client's imagination and tolerance should be avoided, for instance, making the client who has just received ICP finish the whole imagery communication process alone.

The above is the basic and standard procedures of ICP.

In clinical practice, it is not necessary every time to apply ICP, and these standard procedures are not taken into consideration completely in each ICP session. Once ICP is carried out, the psychotherapist must lead the client back to a clear state of consciousness at the end of imagery communication and back to the objective reality world to secure his sense of reality.

3. Procedures for deconstructing personality by imagery

3.1. *What is personality imagery?*

Each person has different sides of personality that can be expressed in various images. Resolving the personality by symbolic meanings of imagery will result in concrete images of distinctive characters. Each image is called "personality imagery", and every side of the personality resolved is a "sub-personality".

3.2. *Where does personality imagery come from?*

Professor Zhu Jianjun, the founder of ICP, pointed out five sources of personality imagery in his book titled *How Many Souls Do You Have*. This book was published by the Chinese City Publishing House in 2003.

3.2.1. *Inherent sub-personality*

This refers to the personality character that an individual was born with. Most of one's personality characters are inherent.

3.2.2. *Internalized sub-personality*

The process that a child internalizes his/her parents' personality has been elaborated from the perspective of developmental psychology. When expounding the mechanism of the formation of super-ego, the classic psychoanalysis has also stated that children can internalize their parents' personality for some motives.

Besides parents, some other persons can also be internalized, for instance, the idol at one's adolescence, some important relatives or friends.

3.2.3. *Temporal sub-personality*

Our characters differentiate across the periods of our growth. Some of our sub-personalities, imprinted with signs in one's early years or even in one's infancy, can indicate some kind of fixed mental energy. For this reason, the temporal sub-personality usually has great significance for psychological evaluation. The imagery communication psychotherapist can know through a certain temporal sub-personality of the client what happened to him/her, how he/she experienced it, which kind of trauma had left, and what the client really wanted at that age or period.

3.2.4. *Content sub-personality*

This is the most common personality imagery. It comes from the acquired psychological experience. Although putting emphasis on learned experience, we also acknowledge the genetic effect. At the moment when we make a judgment or form the attitude toward implicit and explicit causes that elicit our affections, or when we have become used to respond to some kind of affection in a certain way, these vivid psychological activities will accumulate and form a vivid personality imagery.

3.2.5. *Role-taking sub-personality*

This side of personality indicates the social role a person has internalized. It is necessary to acknowledge every social role in order to adapt to our society and gain recognition from the society and others. The perceived image of a social role and its character will be internalized when we have established an identity.

3.3. *Symbolic meanings of personality imagery*

First, it should be noted that personality imagery is neither really good nor really bad.

For example, there are many animal images which serve as mysterious and intuitive, including snake, bat, tortoise, cat, spider and yellow weasel. It is hard to say which is good or bad as the character depends on its psychological development — when it develops adversely, there will be something sinister about the person; on the contrary, the person can make good use of mystery and intuition, be qualified with great insight, and become an excellent artist or psychologist.

We may often think something as "bad" because of our unacceptance. The negative feeling and experience toward it thus leads to the fact that we reject it, fear it and dislike it.

Second, with symbolic meanings of personality, the personality imagery has value for psychological analysis, and then has far-reaching influence on the individual's self-acceptance and mental development.

Finally, theoretically, symbolic meanings of personality imagery can be elaborated from the following five aspects:

3.3.1. *Humans*

Human imagery, usually originating from primitive images or the combination of some archetypes, is the commonest from of personality imagery.

For instance, "mother", as a human imagery that people always see, is varied: either benevolent or stringent, old or young, mentally healthy or morbid, having good or bad relationship with her children.

Whatever the specific mother images look like, all of these images have a root and primitive archetype, that is, Great Mother, which is the typical archetype of mother in the collective unconscious of humanity. As originating from the earth, it may sometimes arise in different forms of the earth and ground.

In a word, personality images belonging to the type of "mother" may not be called as "mother" (the name given to the image by the client), they can, however, highlight the function of breeding, nourishing, bearing, healing and rearing, and have salient characters like kindness, love and tolerance. Admittedly, there is also another character of "mother" — phagocytosis, similar to the process by which the earth derives nutrition from fallen leaves and skeletons. To be more precise, Great Mother Archetype unconditionally waits for and accepts the return of all life, but she does not actively kill any life. It is her unconditional acceptance that drives life.

3.3.2. *Animals*

The animal imagery usually "represents the innate traits of one's diathesis and nervous system, or can be called 'temperament' according to Soviet psychologists. As temperament is the foundation of disposition, we can have a rough idea of the person's disposition by analyzing what kinds of animals can be found in his/her subpersonalities." (Zhu, 2003, p. 97) As a whole, animals can stand for dispositions.

The categories of animal imagery are related to but not in conformity with animals in reality, mainly based on their respective characters and anthropomorphic symbolic meanings.

The animal imagery can be divided into four categories including "Earth", "Water", "Fire" and "Wind". In this way, elephant and bear fall into "Earth", fish is a representative of "Water", lion and tiger belong to "Fire", and birds are part of "Wind". They have particular features, respectively, land is thick, authentic, steady, fecund, bearing, tolerant, accepting, mild and real; water is nutritious, caring and affective; fire is masculine, passionate, candid and dangerous; and wind is free, motive, flexible and instable.

When understanding the symbolic meaning of an animal image, we should not only take the general meaning of its category into account but also recognize the subtle difference in dispositions between images.

3.3.3. *Plants, minerals and implements*

Although plants, minerals and implements are not easy to be personified, they also have symbolic meanings in the personality imagery. They lie at an in-depth position of personality imagery, deeper than other categories such as human, animal and ghost. It is, therefore, not easy to see these images for many people during the first time to deconstruct personality by imagery. Actually, they exist in the personality context of each person, and belong to the area of archetypes.

For plants, taking trees as example, Jung suggested that trees are sometimes the token of life because the earth can stand for subconsciousness. The observation and perception of the concrete state of the tree imagery can help us understand one's present life state. It is certain that one can have different feelings when faced with a tall pine with luxuriant foliage compared with a slender swaying willow.

As for minerals, they can be regarded as the Self in Jung's psychological theory. They can stand for the self in deep subconsciousness and are the self's status. For instance, crude oil stands for the mental energy in subconsciousness; various jades or gemstones are emblems of the extent of integration, accomplishment and purification that the real self has reached, and thus can be thought as the sign that the person has achieved a great level of psychological health.

Another expression of implement is object. Weapon can stand for sex or masculinity, and can also represent aggression, hostility and anger sometimes. The contents of telephone and television usually reflect one's subconsciousness. A mobile phone symbolizes the connection of relationship and emotional communication.

3.3.4. *Death, devil and ghosts*

The ghost imagery symbolizes intensive negative emotions. All kinds of ghost images come from three typical archetypes — the Death Archetype, the Devil Archetype and the Witchcraft Archetype.

The Death Archetype may disguise as the Death, or other images such as Yama, Ghost or the Black and White emissaries.

Although the Devil Archetype does not symbolize death itself, it may frequently combine with the Death Archetype and transform to a devil. The devil imagery may be ugly looking, might wear a black cloak or be originally a black shadow, be rather powerful, and sometimes have a pair of ox horns on the head. It can also be neatly dressed, but can make people feel uncomfortable and dislike it.

Whether the client has seen a depressed female ghost, vampire, ferocious ghost, sex maniac, coward ghost or hanged ghost, nobody is a real devil in reality. These images are just representatives of humans' death instinct.

Note: Do not initiatively seek for ghost images. The Witchcraft Archetype can incarnate as a variety of wizards. Witchcraft stands for one's innate intuition. When an evil witchcraft appears in the client's imagination or dreams, it is of great significance for the psychotherapist to warn himself/herself not to chase the mystery but to focus on the real life. Whether we live happily or not does not depend on whether we have the psi ability. Even if someone has that kind of ability, there is nothing serious, or it is no big deal.

3.3.5. *Deities, Bodhisattva and Buddha*

As personality images, deities, Bodhisattva and Buddha have some desirable characters such as benevolence, wisdom, self-confidence and philanthropism. They will, however, present great temptation and make some people consider themselves as Buddha after they see Buddha in their dreams or images.

While it could be a kind of luck, it could also be dangerous. The key lies in our attitude toward these images. If we just see it, admit it and do not make use of it, we will remain psychologically healthy. Otherwise, it will be very dangerous to have superstitious belief in it and rely on it.

3.4. *Functions of Deconstructing Personality by Imagery (PID)*

(1) It can help to intuitively enhance self-awareness. The personalized concrete imagery can help us positively perceive ourselves, constantly resolve psychological problems, remove mental disorders and improve the overall personality.
(2) As a measurement of personality, it can help a psychotherapist to rapidly understand the client's behavioral pattern and the whole personality as well as to facilitate evaluation and treatment.
(3) PID takes primitive cognition as its tool. With this as a container, multiple psychotherapies can be brought in and work together.
(4) There appear to be many difficulties on resolving most of the psychological conflicts. That is because different sides of the

personality fixed with various affections, trauma, needs and targets have gotten entangled. They cannot be split and get appropriate cure. By splitting these "packed problems", PID can help discern each side one by one and provide specific treatment in order for every sub-personality to return to its original appearance, that is, the one before the distortion resulting from trauma, retrieve the anterior life energy tortured into negative energy by trauma, and thus make some progress.

(5) Transformation of the client's mood state, change in the mental health level, psychological problems or disorders arising in a particular period and fluctuation of emotions can lead to a change in the client's personality images. For this reason, PID can be used to propel psychotherapy and verify its efficacy.

3.5. *Fundamental operation of PID*

The operation procedures of PID are in line with the general way of ICP.

First, it is necessary to briefly introduce analysis on some personality images to stimulate the client's interest. The imagery communication psychotherapist can make modest explanations on the client's worries and queries to dispel his/her concerns.

Note: It is not necessary to tell the client that plants, minerals, deities or ghosts may appear in personality images before PID, because these deeper images will always arise spontaneously. In clinical practice, there is a pattern that after some human sub-personalities of the client have arisen, some animal images or other images like ghosts, deities or Bodhisattva will appear naturally, and plants, or even minerals can be occasionally seen in the personality images.

Second, guide the client to relax. Here, the psychotherapist needs to create a quiet surrounding with moderate light and no intensive dazzling light. The client is required to sit or semi-lie in a comfortable posture, and be instructed to relax.

Third, continue the guidance and make the sub-personalities naturally arise in the client's imagination. The house imagery or grass imagery can be brought for guidance in this step. After the appearance of several or more than ten human images, almost every client will suddenly say "why does animal imagery arise?" The psychotherapist can answer "yes, it is normal to see animal imagery. What kind of animal is that?"

Then, observe carefully. When a sub-personality fully presents itself, the expression, tone and body posture of the client will have some significant change and become consistent with the character of that sub-personality. With careful observation, the imagery communication psychotherapist can quickly and profoundly catch the alternating state of the client's sub-personalities.

At last, record features of the human sub-personalities presented. Generally speaking, there are usually dozens of sub-personalities of each person. It takes a long time to deconstruct personality by imagery completely. It often takes 2–4 hours. Some people take longer.

There are two approaches to this.

The first is to extend psychotherapy once for 2–3 hours. Its advantage is its consistency. Its disadvantage is that both the psychotherapist and client will feel tired.

The second is to break down the deconstruction work several times. Although not coherent enough, its advantage is that the psychotherapist has an opportunity to detect and help those sub-personalities who have contradictions or conflicts in time. If the client's mental symptoms are eliminated, there is no need to continue to deconstruct other personalities by imagery.

3.6. *Recording features of sub-personality*

We may guide a client by combining an initial image with other images. For example, a house or grass image can be a beginning. The instructions need a little regulation. If we begin with a grass image, the instructions may be as follows:

Everybody's character has many different sides. Now you may sit comfortably, close your eyes and relax, you will find these different yourselves. Firstly, you can imagine you are coming to a grass land. Can you see a grass land? Please see it carefully. What color is the grass? Is it dense?

Ok, you can call your sub-personalities now and tell them: I hope I meet you. And you just wait here quietly. Do not consciously think about them, relax your consciousness, and wait for their images to come naturally to your mind. When you see the images, tell me please. Do not pass judgment on them. They are the parts of your personality, neither good nor bad.

Next, just wait and wait. Every sub-personality shall naturally appear in the client's mind, one by one.

To completely and meticulously comprehend each human sub-personality, the psychotherapist needs to record its features such as name, gender, age, appearance, likes, dislikes, character and some extra notes (other useful information, such as relationships between sub-personalities).

It is interesting to note that when a sub-personality expresses itself fully, the client's facial expression, tone and body posture will change obviously and quickly so as to be consistent with the temperament of this sub-personality. His/her facial expression will look rather tranquil and the client will tend to speak in a mild tone in case of referring to a peaceful young girl sub-personality. If this client is a male, his voice will still be male but very gentle. His body posture will also show restraint. His/her voice will become loud and clear, he/she will be full of exaggerations and the body posture would be open, when the sub-personality a client is telling about is easily get into a violent temper.

It is very easy for a psychologist with rich clinical experience to make out alternating sub-personalities based on subtle changes in the client's facial expression, tone and body posture. The facial expression, tone and body posture may vary when a different sub-personality appears on the scene; this is not all, real distinctions may prevail in the handwriting, style of drawing, choice of words, style of dress and so on.

A careful note of these special features of the different aspects can be taken after these sub-personalities were imagined by a client. It seems that star followers establish files for their stars. We should get used to noting these aspects down:

Name: We tell a client that every sub-personality needs a name with the aim of distinguishing it from others and exchanging this information with him/her alone. A client is asked to "throw himself/herself into the sub-personality" and imagine himself/herself as just the sub-personality. I ask him/her: "what's your name? Tell me, please." Then, I let him/her wait for the emergence of a name and for him/her to speak it out.

It is worthy to note that the name that appeared in the client's mind always cannot stand for this sub-personality if a client is not "throwing himself/herself into the sub-personality", because this name is often received by the other dominant sub-personality or other sub-personalities. For this reason, only when a client is "throwing himself/herself into the sub-personality" and identifies it, the name will be the name indeed. This is what we want to keep the minutes of every session.

It is not necessary for animal and ghost sub-personalities to have a name. A dog is a dog. A tiger is a tiger. Sometimes, a dog may be called "baby" and a cat maybe named "Tom" by a client.

Gender: A sub-personality has gender. So, we need to take notes.

Age: A client can reckon the age of the image or ask about it immediately. Sometimes, the psychotherapist can guide the client to intuit the age of an image, whether it is a person, an animal, a plant or something else.

For that kind of traumatic sub-personality, the age the client reports is often the age at which he/she has experienced such a trauma in real life, especially when it comes to traumatic children sub-personalities.

Exterior appearance and dress and personal adornment: It is of importance, particularly, to record the pattern of clothes and their color. The color of clothes is critical information. We need to inquire about the color when a sub-personality is an animal. Its color does not invariably tally with the actual situation in nature. For instance, a client imagines a red cat. That is ok. You write it down.

Character: This is the most important. There is no harm in encouraging a client to talk more. Please take notes without fail and remain unchanged. A psychotherapist must use the words and phrases that the client said to their full potential.

For example, a client uses the word "temperate", and we cannot record "gentle". It is entirely possible that the infinitely small difference in choice of words will lead to a wrong understanding.

Liking: We note down this respect for the mere purpose of more deeply understanding the character of this sub-personality.

Disliking: Its aim is to get a better grasp of the sub-personality. Generally speaking, dislike is the main factor that leads to non-acceptance or dissonance between sub-personalities.

Others: In the end, we must record other useful data.

We would keep abreast of a sub-personality after we make a note of every sub-personality. When animal sub-personalities appear in a client's mind and we estimate there will be nothing new, we can wind up the work at this time.

Ending method: Before ending, we might point out "we will end it in five minutes." You can ask if there will be others (other sub-personalities). The urging can arouse those hidden sub-personalities. We could even tell those sub-personalities who do not emerge, "only five minutes, if you are not going to appear, no chance." Then, they would be in a hurry to "come on stage".

There are many sub-personalities to a person. One integrated decomposition of personality imagery needs more time comparatively. It will last about 2–4 hours. Some need much more time. Hence, we may extend the psychotherapy time to 2–3 hours when we need to decompose personality imagery. The process of decomposition will be organized and coherent. It still has disadvantages. Both the psychotherapist and the client feel tired now and then. We can seek some sub-personalities at one time and then suspend it. We will go into others later.

The matrix diagram can be used to record it.

The following is an analyzing fragment record of deconstruction of personality by imagery from a female client:

Name	Age	Gender	Appearance	Likes	Dislikes	Character	Remarks
Stupid	24/25	Male	Not tall, blue clothes, smiles at me	Look at girls (pretty, long hair, tall)	Be restrained	Joyful, sluggish	Lover of Little pig
Little pig	20	Female	Short, big head, black skirt	Dream, dream to grow up	Be bullied	Not sociable, not amiable	Lover of Stupid
Daddy	40	Male	Blue worn-out clothes, slovenly	Drink	Play	Dejected	Not knowing others
Annoying mum	40	Female	Fatigue, crestfallen, purplish red jacket	Nothing	Insipid life	Happy in a moment, sigh in a moment	Not knowing others
Confident grandfather		Male	White hair, serious, sky blue worn-out Zhongshan clothes, but clean	Nature	Be restrained	Very strong and unconcerned, unsatisfied about his life, many bad men around him	Be sit alone, not return anybody
Sad grand-mother		Female	Thin, always crying, tattered and dirty	Children come to see her	Be bullied	Incapable	Her son is bullying her
Bastard (son)	40	Male	Lean, blue clothes	His wife	His parent (grandfather and grandmother)	Very evil, never say "no" to his wife's superiority	

The disgusting (wife)	40/50	Female	Very ugly, in terrible disorder, dirty clothes	Hit sb. Swear at sb.	Others object her, live the same life every day, yearn for a rich life	Fierce and brutal, lunatic	Knew Little pig but bad relationship, Little pig feared her, she feared grandfather
Victory	27/28	Male	Tall, handsome, green police uniform	Let other people fear him	Trivial matters	Very conceited (hides grandmother being bullied)	Child of grandmother, good relationship, friends with Bastard
Haughty	30	Male	Tall and big, brown clothes	Play piano, Love himself	Work	Cold, selfish, eccentric	Not knowing others
Li Li (teacher)	40	Female	Fat, white, often smile, red clothes	Her students are excellent	Vexing household duties, such as cooking	Cheerful, careless	
Trying hard	24/25	Male	Rather fat, white clothes	Money	No money	Eccentric, study hard, not be with others, thinking others are not as good as him	Stupid's friend now looks down upon Stupid for his prosaic life
Casual	23	Female	Short, curly hair, blue jeans, green sweater	Casual life	Be controlled	Confident, likes contacting others, sociable	Knew Little pig, no time to be with him, busy in casual living

3.7. *Making imagery communication by sub-personality*

In clinical operation, the imagery communication psychotherapist will neither lead nor allow the client to attack or annihilate any negative personality imagery. This is an extremely important rule of ICP.

The methods of conducting psychological counseling and psychotherapy by using sub-personalities include:

(1) Substitution of sub-personality

It must be noted that every sub-personality should have the opportunity to show up.

Under some special circumstances, replacing one sub-personality with another is called sub-personality substitution.

A major reason for some mental difficulties is when the sub-personality a client used essentially on a certain condition was not fit for this condition. However, there is an appropriate one in his/her sub-personalities, and the method of sub-personality substitution can be employed.

The fundamental operation is so simple and clear. Call the name of this sub-personality, let him/her "appear on the scene", realize the feeling of this sub-personality and imagine his/her looks. Immediately you will "become" this sub-personality.

For example, someone did not behave well at work and was criticized by her boss as "not serious, childish and not suited to the occasion". We find that her sub-personality used in her job was a teenage girl. It is obvious that she is not befitting her occupational circumstances. A white-collar imagination was just her another sub-personality. If we make her transfer the white-collar image consciously when she works, her problem can be solved.

(2) Making sub-personalities know each other

The purpose of this method is to enhance self-perception. Each of us has an unknown profile to our personality. Exploring these unknown "selves" is of great significance to our future development.

Making unknown sub-personalities know each other is a kind of psychotherapy. This way works especially for those whose isolation degree was high.

The greatest effect of sub-personality knowing reciprocally is to enhance self-knowledge and have an understanding for those parts of the self not acquainted with each other.

After mutual understanding, these sub-personalities will show relations of liking or disliking one another.

When it is the former, the mutual understanding and liking of these sub-personalities could bring about some striking and good results right away. For instance, two newly known sub-personalities can draw on each other's merits and raise the level together, learn each other's good points for common progress.

When it is the latter, the relation needs to be made further peaceful and changed from disliking to liking. The practical therapy experience told us the latter was much more than the former. Even the reason why some sub-personalities had never met was their bad relations. They were so unwilling to associate with the other side that they became strangers. It is hard to mediate admittedly. But once it succeeds, a client will show very obvious improvement.

(3) Relationship mediation of sub-personality

This method can be used when sub-personalities dislike each other or when there is hostility, contempt and conflict among them.

The animosity between two sub-personalities in a same person may reach a high degree of amazing. It is possible that one sub-personality flew into a towering passion and hated the other sub-personality intensely and would be content with nothing less than the other's destruction whenever he/she saw his/her "sworn enemy".

In imagery communication, one sub-personality wanted to kill another sub-personality with maltreatment, a situation that is often encountered. Cutting, shooting, poisoning, trapping and so on, the only purpose was to kill another sub-personality. They could not get on well with each other because the symbols of both sides had conflicts and the client could not work out this solution. Thus, each stuck to his/her own version and refused to give in to the other.

A common state of affairs is that one sub-personality has conservative and unreasonable sexual ideas while the other sub-personality has unconventional and unrestrained sexual attitude. In reality, people could not have no sex and connive at it. The best state is maintaining a balance. But when one sub-personality goes to an erroneous tendency excessively, the other will overdo too much right and go to the other extreme; finally, the conflict between them will become increasingly sharp.

Disliking is not just because of hatred and hostility. Another reason is that a certain sub-personality looked down upon the other. A conceited sub-personality must have good points, such as power, beauty, smartness or luck, while the other must be weak, ugly, silly or out of luck, and thus inferior. The conceited always expected the other side had better not exist. In fact, both sides actually coexist. When the self-abased side became more and more inferior, because of a kind of compensation function, a more and more conceited sub-personality would appear in this person's mind. As a result, a conceited sub-personality would become much more conceited and a formerly inferior sub-personality may be made even more inferior. At last, the disparities on both sides would get much greater and want good relations all the more.

Although one sub-personality wanted to get rid of the other, as we know, it is completely out of question. Any image with mental energy cannot absolutely vanish from our mind wantonly. Any effort at killing the other side merely leads to depression and sets off much stronger internal mental conflicts and contradictions.

When one sub-personality was depressed grievously by the other, a client perhaps would not admit that depressed "bad", "weak", "ugly", "silly", or "out of luck" sub-personality image had been a part of himself/herself. He/she would rather speak of this image as belonging to other people and project it on his relatives, friends, colleagues, teachers or a bitter enemy. This way of making a thing was bound to transform internal mental conflict into other's interpersonal exclusion. It is hardly impossible for us to desire resolving our own internal mental conflicts in interpersonal relations.

Probably you projected your own disgusting sub-personality image on to one of the staffs. You could fire the staff someday, but soon afterward you would still project this image on to another person if your internal sub-personality could not be changed. Thereupon, you found that there was a disagreeable person again at your side. These disgusting people appeared one by one and you spared none forever. Never will there be a day of peace.

The true effective method is by admitting that these sub-personalities are a prerequisite to mediation of their relations. Mental conflicts will be settled when the relationship of these sub-personalities takes a turn for the better. There is no doubt that mediation is necessary to analyze and resolve the concrete sub-personality character and understand the nature of the contradictions.

(4) Mutually complementary sub-personalities

Our psychotherapy experience indicated that everyone possesses latent capacity of self-actualization. One example of it is: if a certain sub-personality lacks a certain essential psychological factor for mental health, in the same person's heart of hearts, another sub-personality is sure to have this psychological factor.

For instance, a student who was undergoing imagery communication training behaved with braveness, firmness and power in real life. She had high prestige among her relatives and friends. A tiger was her important sub-personality that played a leading role. But she was always weary about her body and mind or fell into a conflict snare owing her poor flexibility and pliability and toughness.

After a session of imagery communication training, a "white rabbit" sub-personality was seen in her. This sub-personality had a gentle disposition, but was small and weak. However, in fact, this sub-personality contained a very important thing for her perfectible personality. It was a great capacity. If she is able to accept her "white rabbit", she will go a step further to accept herself and the part of her personality that seems small and weak. This way, she will be more liable to accept other's weakness, understand and accept other people. It will be of great benefit to her interpersonal associations.

Consequently, a "tiger" and a "white rabbit" were a couple of mutual supplementing sub-personalities. A tiger made a rabbit complete in the aspect of pioneering spirit. A rabbit remedied the defect of a tiger in exquisiteness and gentleness.

Certainly, exactly as an indication of this example, sometimes it happens frequently that the sub-personalities that can mutually complement originally are hostile or scornful in a client. Now and then, this couple of sub-personalities did not know or understand each other formerly. We should lead them to pay attention to one another and then complement reciprocally. Also at times, when we finish mediation and understanding, a mutual complement will happen spontaneously in the client's mind. We need not do anything special.

Generally, a method of sub-personality supplement is to make sub-personalities "body touch" each other, such as by shaking hands, walking arm in arm, embracing and so on. They can exchange mutually lacking psychological factors.

(5) Sub-personality-orientated psychotherapy

The common operation of this method is to orientate a psychological problem or disorders by sub-personality and to resolve it.

ICP does not always need to deconstruct personality by imagery, nor does it always have the time to do it. Actually, ICP of the usual way is just to use a certain personality to position psychological problems or psychological disorders and solve it.

Specific methods include cases when a client appears to have strong negative emotion, or shows some very characteristic patterns of behavior, then we ask him: "Now look at the emotions out of the 'people'. Who does the sub-personality looks like? What is the name?"...

Of course, its premise is that the client already knows what the sub-personality is. If a client has been subjected imagery communication but never heard of sub-personality, our guiding phrase is: "You need to relax to imagine, if there is now another strong emotional person than you, this person should look like? What is the name?"...

By this approach, we can find the sub-personalities who have something to do with psychological problems or psychological disorders and spend no time on other sub-personalities who have nothing to do with psychological problems or psychological disorders. Thus, we do not need much time in those healthy sub-personalities. There will be more savings.

Apart from finding the relationships between sub-personalities, the greatest merit is the therapy of "positioning psychological treatment". A client's sub-personalities in his mind often have opposite characters. If we do not use ICP but other forms of psychotherapy, we will not know which sub-personality heard what we call a sentence. For the same statement, one sub-personality may process it as good and another as harmful. This will offset the effect of intervention greatly.

For example, a client has an extremely inferior sub-personality who needs to be encouraged and commended. On the basis of the compensation mechanism, a special arrogant sub-personality is produced. This arrogant sub-personality is not encouraged since it will become more dominant. If there is no imagery communication, should we encourage the client? It is very likely that you will encourage the arrogant sub-personality and the inferior sub-personality does not benefit. The inferior character cannot gain the much-needed support if there is no encouragement.

We can turn this situation to be a metaphor: an autocratic country seems to have a lot of poor people in urgent need of assistance, but if the funds were sent there, the country's tyrants will receive the money, and the poor will not have benefited. The tyrants might even use the money to buy arms and become more vicious and oppressive toward the poor.

However, during the course of imagery communication, the sub-personality can be oriented and we can deliberately tell a certain sub-personality a word or a sentence. We can call the inferior sub-personality provocatively and then encourage him. If an arrogant sub-personality also wants to hear such words, we should shout his name and tell him, "You do not need to hear this, you need to learn humility."

In other words, we can provide some kind of psychological intervention to a specialized sub-personality, wherein results are particularly notable.

(6) Poker analysis of sub-personality

This method is applicable while presenting the pattern of interpersonal communication and assisting the mental regulation of it.

First, it needs a set of paper bags on "personality files". The side of each paper bag contains the basic information of a certain sub-personality. The information can be shown in tables. The basic information includes a code, name, gender, what the sub-personality likes and doesn't like, its character, its relationship with others and other information. On the other side of the paper bag, the name is written.

Afterward, some cardboard cards are put into each paper bag, with the names and codes written corresponding to the sub-personalities.

When analyzing a social situation, we observe the conditions, frequency and regularity of each sub-personality's "appearance", like when playing poker.

When we analyze the response which reflects the sub-personality, a sub-personality card is removed from the bag onto the table. Necessary attention is given to the other side with opposite sub-personality cards placed in the left or right position. Look at the first personal response. Retrieve the cards on the other side — opposite personality cards in the left or right position. By analogy, we can figure out which sub-personalities were present in that interpersonal communication and how they communicated with each other.

If several sub-personalities appear at the same time, we put the sub-personality playing the main role at the top and put the rest below it in sequence.

According to the arrangement of these cards, we can clearly see one's interpersonal communication state: which is the most common sub-personality, which sub-personality appeared under what circumstances, which sub-personality has good relationships with others, why a certain sub-personality is the most vulnerable, what the inner conflict is, how several sub-personalities in a situation meet or interfere with each other...

Therefore, we can make necessary adjustments for a client to improve his/her coping style.

Deconstruction of personality by imagery is the only method of communication. It focuses on promoting the client's self-awareness, resolving inner conflict and making relationships more harmonious.

In short, in actual psychotherapy, PID and various other methods can be shared with each other. According to specific contexts, we should pick a variety of methods to achieve the best therapeutic effect.

Notes:

- Techniques are inferior to the personality of the imagery communication therapist.
- Do not use unnecessary techniques.
- Imagery communication does not reject the counseling methods and techniques of any other school.
- Imagery communication can combine with methods and techniques of other schools.

4. The technique of transforming mental energy

The transforming of mental energy aims to take forward the self-correction of behavior.

ICP can help us explore the depth of our heart and understand our perception of ourselves, others and the world in the depth of our personality, and it can also transform our primitive cognition into a healthier and more harmonious state. The shift of primitive cognition can lead to a change in mental energy, which can spontaneously affect our behavior and behavioral habits.

Nevertheless, some behaviors and behavioral habits are very stubborn because they have lasted for a long time. Even if we are already aware of a certain behavior or habit at the primitive cognitive level, we are not necessarily able to break through it and change it quickly. At this point, we need more proactive psychological operation to facilitate its transformation to happen more quickly.

The technique of transforming mental energy is a way to drive unhealthy behavior to change faster. Its principle is that the psychotherapist combines the techniques of ICP and behavioral interventions to guide the client to be aware of his/her own ill behavior or bad habit in terms of psychological factors, using his/her will power to try to bring about a change, and reinforce this change by recording the client's behavior.

ICP is a good method for finding unconscious motives. It is adept in discovering internal causes and intervening at the root. The change of cognition and motivation will inevitably affect the transformation of mental energy and thus seep into behaviors and habits. However, it is not easy to rely on it to change the long-term unhealthy behaviors and habits. We need to use our will and endeavor to change them much more directly.

It is more straightforward to use behavioral therapy to correct behavior. However, in the process of correction, we will find that the clients are not aware of their complexes. In the absence of awareness, although behavior can change over time, the subconscious doesn't change. It is difficult to maintain stability and persistence of curative effect. The technique of transforming mental energy unites the superiority of two psychotherapies and avoids their respective deficiency.

This technique is suitable for anyone. It is best adapted to the long-term ill behaviors and addictive behaviors, such as smoking, drinking, interpersonal withdrawal, irritability, etc.

The general steps are detailed in the following.

(1) Identify the behavior you want to correct

The most basic problem is that the corrective action is not very clear. A client usually vaguely describes the behavior he/she wants to correct. For example, "I want to stop being so grumpy." This statement is very vague. What is "grumpy"? Without a clear and operational definition, there is no way to observe and record the results, and there is no way to know if he/she is not cranky after our counseling and psychotherapy. Thus, the corrective action must have an operable definition, and it must be defined as an observable and recordable actual behavior.

For instance, for that client who said, "I want to stop being so grumpy", the psychotherapist should first guide him through a detailed list of what it means to be "grumpy". For the client, maybe the following behaviors are a sign of grumpiness: in work, when others disagree with him, he will shout; at home, when his wife is arguing with him, he will impatiently slam the door and go; when things go wrong, he will casually throw the tools away ... So, he should be sure. First, he should be sure of what behavior he wants to correct. Second, the client needs to be sure if he wants to rectify all these behaviors, or change one of them, such as only the one regarding throwing the tools away.

(2) Identify corrective goals

The corrective goal must be specific and operable. Just saying "I want to be better" does not work. The above example is still used here. If the client wants to change the behavior that he casually throws the tools away when things go wrong, its aim can be that "in the past, as long as things did not go well, I would exert myself to throw out the tools at hand and damage it. I hope in the future I will only throw out my tools 10% of the time. At other times, I will put my tools in place and just stamp my feet and use other methods to vent my unpleasant feelings."

(3) Perform ICP to find out the psychological reasons for this behavior

We can find out the psychological causes of this behavior through various ways of ICP. One of the most commonly used methods is that when the client appears to have the target behavior, the psychotherapist will lead him to experience the following: "please imagine, you who are doing this, if this person looks different from at the moment of you, what does this person look like"?

Or, if the client accepted the deconstructing personality by imagery in the past psychotherapy sessions, he can be asked directly "which sub-personality is doing this"? Next, the psychotherapist can introduce ICP from this sub-personality to explore why he/she has such a behavior. Follow the work principle and method of ICP, seek its cause and effect in the images, resolve the related trauma and complex, transform its mental energy, and solve the client's psychological problem in the images.

To be sure, we can also start with other images without the help of the sub-personality to find out the deeper causes and solutions.

Regardless of any image, the focus of the work is to adjust and transform the mental energy to solve the psychological problems behind the target behavior, so that the target behavior is no longer needed by the client.

(4) Accompany ICP, change behavior in real life

An in-depth ICP can reduce or even eliminate the driving forces behind an ill behavior, and successfully transform its mental energy. In reality, however, most long-term habitual behaviors cannot be lost through just once ICP session.

In this case, the psychotherapist can instruct the client to learn a brief "review" in real life. The specific approach is to withdraw from the current social activity for a while when the client is tempted to repeat the ill behavior. During this time, the client can briefly redo the imagery communication in the previous step. That is, perceiving which sub-personality has this ill behavior, why he/she did it, and communicating with this sub-personality in the image, reexperiencing the underlying causes and solving the problem.

After actively experiencing a brief review on this, the client will again perceive the meaning of the custom action in the primitive cognitive level, and so will no longer need to continue this target behavior at the primitive cognitive level. So, he can replace that ill behavior with a healthier one.

In fact, it is not easy to change your habitual behavior when you are actually doing it. We often find that even though we know the ins and outs of the problem and solve it well by ICP, the inertia of old behavior still exists, and it can even be very big sometimes. At this time, we need to make some conscious effort to replace the old with the new behavior.

When triggered by certain situations, we tend to have an impulse to continue our ill behavior. Whenever we encounter this situation, we can consciously "review" the imagery communication. In the meantime, in action, we try our level best to substitute the healthy behaviors for the unhealthy ones.

In our clinical practice, we summarized a rule: at the beginning, "review" will take a long time, and this will gradually decrease. After a couple of times, the client usually finishes such "review" of imagery communication in just two or three minutes. Then, the behavior will change.

(5) Recording behavior change

We can make a record after every behavior change.

The record is a piece of cake. For example, on successful completion, check or draw a circle on the calendar. When there is failure, that is the ill habitual behavior prevails, draw a cross on the calendar.

Usually, it takes at least three weeks to correct an ill habit. The appropriate time is six months to a year. During this time, the client should try to keep track of changes in behavior. If done well, the client can give himself/herself a small reward for reinforcement. But this reward should not be of too much value. Otherwise, it will steal the show and the effect will be counterproductive.

We may have many behaviors or habits that we want to change. But when using the technique of transforming the mental energy, we can only choose one behavior to correct at a time. After half a year, the corrective action of this behavior has an obvious effect, and then we can choose another ill behavior to correct. Sometimes we find that several different behaviors are the reflection of the same complex. This will make it possible for us to expect to rectify these behaviors simultaneously. However, clinical experience tells us that the most effective way is to do it one by one.

Although this method is not difficult, there are not many people who can do it. The hardest thing is not so much the complexity but the persistence.

Here is a little story:

The emperor found a hermit. It was said that this hermit was actually immortal. The emperor asked him about the art of immortality. The immortal said a very simple method that was to eat some herbal medicine which was not rare.

The emperor and his ministers enjoyed themselves for a while. However, after a long time, they were tired of eating and suspicious. Slowly, they stopped eating the herbal medicine.

Only one of the ministers still kept at it. His mind was particularly simple. He ate the herbal medicine every day and did not think much about it. In the end, only this minister lived more than 100 years.

The technique may also be similar to the simple, inexpensive and not uncommon herb.

Chapter 6

The Ideas and Methods of Imagery Communication Psychotherapy

1. Treatment of neurosis by ICP

1.1. *Depression*

(1) Ideas for the treatment of Depression by ICP

First, depression is a sustained sense of hopelessness and helplessness. Its negative imagery tends to self-deprecate or exaggerate difficulties.

Second, the clients not only have a kind of unrealistic expectation to life, but also do not get the desired spiritual interests due to depression, which leads to potential resentment toward themselves.

Third, depression which stems from loneliness is more self-centered and self-enclosed.

(2) Characters of Depression Imagery

(i) Negative imagery of drought: Dessert, wildness, dry branches, skeleton, dust, desolate dilapidated house, ruins, a soreheaded old man, a white lady ghost and so on.

(ii) Negative imagery of washy: Dark low clouds, drizzle flutters, a run of wet weather, turbid water and the muddy swamp.

(3) The treatment methods of Depression by ICP

The overall treatment: Confrontation, acceptance and understanding.

Through the treatment of trauma which leads to depression, the psychotherapist can change the negative faith in the deep subconscious from the trauma, and then make the negative imagery transform by itself.

In order to make the client willing to give up unreasonable expectations, the psychotherapist can find out the emotional feelings behind the unreasonable expectations, and then satisfy the reasonable part in a constructive way.

In order to make the client willing to give up the desire to benefit because of the illness, the psychotherapist can figure out the psychological benefits and realistic benefits brought by depression, and then guide the client to understand the price he/she is paying while getting the benefits.

In order to make the client be willing to rely on self-growth rather than excessive exterior searching and dependence, the psychotherapist can repair his/her narcissistic trauma, and then rebuild and improve the client's self-esteem, self-confidence and self-efficacy.

Guide the client to find out the seed of "wish" of his/her own life and to nourish it. Guide the client to transform the new positive faith into real action and make a step-by-step psychological preparation and transform it to reality.

The following are some common methods:

A. For the desolate imagery, bring water in the imagination.
B. For the dust imagery, clean the house and wipe away the dust in the imagination.
C. For the isolated and closed imagery, the treatment method is to open up, first in the imagination, then in reality.
D. For the depressed ghost imagery, the psychotherapist can face and ease the client's fear, care about and improve the condition of the house where the ghost lives, and guide the ghost to change his/her own psychological states.
E. For the beggar imagery, the psychotherapist can accept and take care of the client, encourage and help him/her build his/her self-confidence and self-esteem, eliminate the self-destructive mentality, and help the beggar imagery find a new lifestyle and life attitude.

F. When in a serious depressive episode, remind the client to focus on breathing, which can help improve the vitality.

1.2. *Obsessive–compulsive disorder (OCD)*

(1) Ideas of the treatment for OCD by ICP

First, the problem with OCD is the fear and resistance to some psychological experience; thus, the psychotherapist can help the client face and accept the fear.

Second, OCD patients tend to be timid and lack the sense of security; thus, the psychotherapist can help rebuild their security gently and carefully.

Third, OCD patients and people with compulsive personality are strongly addicted to reason, which makes them lack sensibilities; thus, the psychotherapist can guide them to focus on their own feelings, especially their emotional feelings.

Fourth, OCD patients and people with compulsive personality have obvious internal psychological conflicts, which often shows the opposite and conflicting personality profile; thus, the psychotherapist can focus on eliminating internal conflicts and try to contribute to reconciliation and integration.

(2) Characters of OCD Imagery

- First, there are many dirty images, such as garbage, corpse, decay, swamp, blood, dirty things, foul things and so on.
- Second, there are many opposite images, such as sluts and nuns, gods and ghosts, the giant and timid cowardly children or the little mouse, the bravely tall and the cowardly short, man in black and man in white and so on.
- Third, the imagery environment is full of danger, such as virus, death and so on.
- Fourth, there are many images concerned with the armor, such as the man in armor, animals with shells and so on.
- Fifth, when imagining an image like a house, it is always closed and restricts entry.

(3) The treatment methods for OCD by ICP

The most important thing is that the psychotherapist can accept, understand and accompany the weak parts of the impotence and powerlessness from the inside of the client to eliminate his/her fear to fear itself. Then make the client be willing to give up the response patterns of competing with oneself and finally improve his/her real courage.

The following are some specific methods:

- First, for the dirty imagery, guide the client to learn how to distinguish between imagination and reality in order to enhance his/her ability of reality check.
- Second, for the opposite imagery, the first thing is to adjust them, to try to weaken their inhibition. The psychotherapist neither agrees nor criticizes in the face of compensatory and self-deceptive "positive" imagery. The psychotherapist can encourage the client to face reality and accept negative images gently. One thing should be known, that the accepted negative images sometimes can change spontaneously in the imagination, while sometimes help is needed to motivate the change.
- Third, for the environment full of dangerous imagery, many subtle ways of "facing" can be used to guide the client to face all the dangers and scary things.
- Fourth, for the imagery concerned with the armor, accept it gently. Guide the client to experience and face the fear of insecurity behind the armor and other negative feelings, such as powerlessness, weakness, incompetency and anger, and to release those negative feelings with self-awareness, so that the fixed negative mental energy can make a positive transformation. For those animals with shells, the psychotherapist can look for and activate the internal psychological resources of the client, and then settle them in a safe environment or provide a security guarantee.
- Fifth, for the seriously resistant imagery like a house which prohibits entry, the psychotherapist can guide the client to notice the physical sensation and express it first, and then go back to

the imagery to perceive it after the physical discomfort has been pacified.

- Sixth, guide the client to find the internal weak, powerless and panicking sub-personalities that were ignored and focus on them, and treat them. Next, find and activate the inner resources of the client, which can give sustained support to those sub-personalities, nourish them, and promote their self-growth.
- Seventh, after the treatment to a certain depth, the psychotherapist can guide the client to connect with the archetype of the Great Mother and Wise old man at a proper time. Through the deeper and more powerful psychological resources from collective unconscious, the psychotherapist can help the client repair and rebuild his/her personality in much deeper unconsciousness.

1.3. *Phobia*

(1) The principle of the treatment of phobia by ICP

Above all, eliminate fear and disgust of the phobia patients in their imagination. And then, guide them to through the systematic desensitization training in reality.

(2) Ideas of the treatment of phobia by ICP

- First, the things or the situations of which the phobia patients are afraid may be the symbols of some other things that they are really afraid of.
- Second, the situations of which the phobia patients are afraid may be a situation where something happened, and being afraid is a way to protect themselves from encountering this event.
- Third, the things of which the phobia patients are afraid may be something that the other side of their mind pursues.

(3) Characters of phobia imagery

- First, imagery reflects the things that the client really fears in the unconscious directly in the form of a symbol.
- Second, when engaging in Deconstructing Personality by Imagery (PID), some sub-personalities concerned with the symptoms of

terror will show up. A common scenario is that in a couple of sub-personalities, one of them is on behalf of the longing for a desire, the other represents the oppression and rejection of this desire.

(4) The treatment methods of phobia by ICP

- First, the key points of treatment: Eliminate fear and disgust of the client by those negative images, and then perform systematic desensitization training in reality.
- Second, the commonly used strategy to treat phobia is confrontation. Guide the client to relax during confrontation. It is important to note that imagery communication should not end before the terror goes down.
- Third, the psychotherapist can mobilize the more powerful and braver sub-personality of the client to face the terrible negative imagery.
- Fourth, find the source of horror and original trauma point, and then heal at the source. This can alter the traumatic "sources of infection" behind the symptoms, which means making repairs at a more fundamental level to prevent the horror symptoms from remodeling or relapsing.
- Fifth, the psychotherapist should always keep an eye on the security of the counseling relationship.
- Sixth, once the sense of security is truly established, the psychotherapist can guide the client to discover and confront those hidden timid sub-personalities, allow them to exist, and find an internal support system that they are willing to accept, so that they can achieve healing and growth step by step.

Instructions:

A. The treatment methods of the neurosis mentioned above are principled and informative, rather than the treatment procedures that must be complied with.

B. The ideas and methods of treatment mentioned above are also appropriate for psychological counseling and treatment of similar neurosis or for normal people with characteristics of neurosis.

2. Treatment of psychosomatic diseases by ICP

2.1. *Understanding of psychosomatic diseases by ICP*

Some psychological problems can transform into psychosomatic diseases.

(1) The reason why psychosomatic diseases occur is because of the long-term accumulation of pent-up negative emotions.
(2) The long-term and destructive response to emotion and desire cause psychosomatic diseases.
(3) When people use their body as a symptom, psychological problems will cause psychosomatic diseases in the form of symbols.
(4) Early psychological trauma of an individual, especially before two years of age, can create an unconscious expression in the form of psychosomatic diseases.

2.2. *Ideas of the treatment of psychosomatic diseases by ICP*

In the first place, we should find out the primary complex and early psychic trauma that caused the psychosomatic diseases. Second, unblock and positively transform the long-term pent-up negative energy by accompanying, understanding and expressing consciously. Then guide the client to replace the old destructive response pattern with a new response pattern with attention and constructive expression, so that the source of psychosomatic diseases can be eliminated.

Specific treatment methods: The most important is to provide fundamental solutions to the problems and combine the temporary and fundamental solutions together.

2.3. *The treatment methods of psychosomatic diseases by ICP*

(1) Medical treatment is the most basic treatment. The client should first go to the hospital for symptomatic treatment to prevent the somatic symptoms from getting worse.
(2) For the psychogenic physical illness caused by inappropriate response patterns, the psychotherapist can guide the client to transform the psychological source and harmful response

patterns that cause psychosomatic diseases through imagery, make the fixed negative mental energy transform into the mental energy that are good for health.

(3) For the psychosomatic diseases that use the body as a symbol, the psychotherapist can use imagery communication to deal with the psychological problem, and enable the client to grasp the psychological content that "body disease" is trying to convey. The psychotherapist can help the client improve the ability of inner listening and constructive expression so that the client no longer needs to subconsciously express himself/herself in this "sick" way.

3. Treatment of interpersonal relationship problems by ICP

3.1. *Understanding of interpersonal relationship problems by ICP*

Interpersonal relationship problems are the externalization and projection of individual internal mental conflicts and psychological problems.

3.2. *The principle of the treatment of interpersonal relationship problems by ICP*

The psychotherapist asks the client to "seek the cause in oneself".

3.3. *The treatment methods of interpersonal relationship problems by ICP*

The most suitable technology to solve the problems of interpersonal relationship is PID.

3.4. *The treatment of marriage problems by ICP*

(1) *Treatment principles*: People with marriage problems should start from self-recognition and end with real action of constructive communication.

(2) *Treatment methods*: If a couple comes for counseling, the psychotherapist can use PID to let both sides pay attention

to heterosexual sub-personalities with conflicts in their own hearts as well as ambisexual relationship between these sub-personalities. Next, through the coordination of the therapist, they can communicate with each other in a constructive way, so that both sides in the conflict can reach a settlement with understanding. The couple will build and apply the new constructive and flexible pattern of coping with and resolving conflict in a real relationship interaction.

(3) *The imagery technology of assessing the status of marriage relationship*: "head, chest, abdomen" — guide the client to imagine in order that there is a small person in his/her head, chest and abdomen, and say a sentence to each of the spouse or lovers, in the meantime, focus on his/her current emotional feelings.

3.5. *The treatment of family relationship problems by ICP*

(1) The treatment principle is the same as above.
(2) For very young and very old family members, the psychotherapist encourages the adults in a family to adjust themselves. Through their positive transformation, the adults can disturb the original "problem relationship network", so that the positive transformation of the related overall relationship system will be eventually facilitated.
(3) For the family with too many members and complicated relationships, the psychotherapist can use the imagery sand-play technique to adjust systematically or combine imagery communication with other therapies such as systemic constellations, Satir psychotherapy and psychodrama.

3.6. *The treatment of idolatry problems by ICP*

(1) Understanding of interpersonal idolatry problems by ICP

First of all, we should make a distinction between idolatry and admiration. The focus of the mental energy of the former is on the idol, but the latter is on the good quality. Thus, idolatry is harmful, and admiration is beneficial, which is a kind of model identification in essence.

(2) The treatment step of unhealthy idolatry by ICP

It is hard to treat idolatry, and the later it is, the harder it becomes. Hence, we need quite detailed steps for the treatment.

- First, the premise of psychotherapy is that the necessary counseling setup is needed to break the absolute control of the worshipped to worshipper.
- Second, start from the acceptance gently, dissolve the resistance and build the consultation relationship with initial trust.
- Third, after building the security in consultation relationship, the psychotherapist could use ICP to find out which qualities of the idol are worshipped by the client, and then separate the worshipped personality traits within the idol from the idol himself/herself gently and carefully, and restore the idealized object to idealization itself.
- Fourth, personalize all the qualities that are fixed on the idol in sequence, which means that the sub-personalities represent different qualities that are transformed from the inside of the client. The externally projected mental energy is taken back, and these beneficial qualities can be transformed as the inside model, which is to be the psychological resources. If the consultation relationship in this stage is good enough, the psychotherapist can decontaminate between the inside model sub-personality and outside idol. Pay attention to not make idolatry be autolatric in this stage.
- Fifth, explore the unconscious reason of idolatry, which is always related to the topics such as ideal, idealization and narcissism. The key point of the treatment in this stage is to repair narcissistic trauma gently, allow the existence of the ideal and give a suitable place for it.
- Sixth, discuss the understanding across the consultation with the client deeply, make him/her realize the reason and the cause of the idolatry and the real need of self-actualization from inside,

and make a real operational plan with the client to prepare for going back to real life.

- Seventh, give subsequent psychological assistant after going back to real life.

4. Treatment of other psychological problems and psychological disorders by ICP

4.1. *Alleviation of complex by ICP*

A person whose psychological state is in the normal range also has complex, psychological conflict, suppression and indulgence.

The client needs to haul his/her attention back to his/her own inner world to some extent to find out and alleviate the complex deep in the unconscious. It is not a good time to alleviate the complex when all the attention is focused on external life. The method to solve this problem is to let the client find a loose time to reduce and even eliminate the influence on his/her work state.

In the early stages of alleviating the complex, the potential psychological problems caused by the complex begin to go through the suppression of resistance and emerge from water. Over a period of time, the client may subjectively feel that his/her psychological state is worse than before, which is a normal phenomenon. The psychotherapist should let the client know the truth from the beginning of therapy. The psychotherapist must respect the choice of the client if he/she does not want to use ICP to alleviate his/her complex.

ICP is an effective method to alleviate a complex. The psychotherapist can help the client learn how to use imagery communication for mental self-help, which means that the psychotherapist can not only give a fish to a person, but also show him/her how to fish. If the client has been through some miserable psychological disorders or psychological diseases, he/she is usually willing to accept the use of imagery communication to alleviate his/her complex.

4.2. *Development of potential by ICP*

- First, after alleviating a complex by ICP, psychological conflict of the client is reduced and mental energy for development and creation is increased; thus, the potential of the client has an opportunity for a large degree of development.

- Second, after finding out and eliminating the psychological factors which suppress the client's potential by ICP, the potential of the client will be fully developed because of relieving the mental resistance.
- Third, for the clients who work on literary creation and painting art, the psychotherapist can help them improve the ability of imagination, thinking and self-artistic creativity and expression. Initial images of these people show up in a variety of forms with strong mental energy, which can be so infectious when transforming them into art work.
- Fourth, for the potential development of different areas of life and work, the psychotherapist can use PID to help the client analyze and experience the deployment of sub-personalities and find the sub-personalities that are suitable for a certain life or work.
- Fifth, imagery communication enables the imagination and thinking system. Memory can be improved effectively by knowing and applying this system. For example, the information capacity of picture memory is larger than logical memory.

4.3. *Treatment of obesity by ICP*

Most of the time obesity is psychogenic. Some people cannot accept themselves as being skittish and cannot resist the temptation of sex. So, they become fat so that there is no sexual attraction and no chance of promiscuity. Some people worship an idol who is fat, so they become fat because of identification.

Obesity caused by different psychological reasons has different imageries with their own characters. For example, the reason why some people become fat is due to dissatisfaction of emotional feelings, where eating is the compensation for self-gratification. So there always are images like that of a glutton, vampire, hungry ghost and fat diners with big bellies.

Ideas of treatment: In view of the treatment of psychogenic obesity, the psychotherapist can solve the problem by finding out the unconscious reason why obesity is desired by the client.

- First, analyze and experience these images. The psychotherapist can guide these images to sufficiently express the feeling of dissatisfaction of emotion in the client's imagination, which always is sad or empty. Then transform these feelings to solve the problem of eating too much.
- Second, for the client who is getting fat because of laziness or being spoiled, the psychotherapist can guide the images like the fat person to stand up and go outside in the imagination. Encourage them to do sports outside and experience some hardships. When the client can do these in imagination, the psychotherapist had better encourage him/her to do something like this in reality. This method is very effective. Not only the body of the client can be changed significantly, but also the character can be transformed to be more self-confident and active.
- Third, for the client who has many negative images concerned with sex rather than obesity, the psychotherapist should pay more attention to his/her sex psychology and use ICP to adjust his/her unhealthy sexual attitude and opinion.

4.4. *Treatment of anorexia by ICP*

Ideas of treatment: Explore the unconscious content that "anorexia" wants to express, especially the symbolic meaning of the food to anorexia nervosa, and find out the reason for the resistance to food in the unconscious and repair it suitably.

- First, the psychotherapist needs to find out the specific symbolic significance of anorexia to the patients. It is important to note that the symbolic significance of anorexia to anorexia nervosa can be totally different. For example, for one person, anorexia might mean that the love the person gets is not what he/she wants, but for another person, anorexia might mean that the person subconsciously rejects the values imposed by the nurturers.
- Second, suit the remedy to the case according to different symbolic meanings of anorexia. For example, if anorexia means rejection of mother's love, the psychotherapist can use PID to find out the subpersonality who senses the lack of mother's love, guide him/her

to express his/her feelings and needs sufficiently, communicate with the sub-personality of the mother to get her love and nourishment.

- Third, in view of the anorexia with the sub-personality of the fat person in the subconsciousness, the treatment principle is to improve the self-acceptance of patients, encourage them to admit that the sub-personality of the fat person is also a part of their personalities. And let them know that the sub-personality of the fat person is a symbolic imagery, which represents their negative evaluations, such as foolishness, incompetency and disfavor. At the same time, guide them to distinguish between imagination and reality.
- Fourth, if the negative imagery of anorexia is often associated with sex, the psychotherapist should pay close attention to their sexual psychology, for example, the disgust to sex, and regulate their attitude to sex or the sexual trauma associated with it by ICP.

4.5. *Treatment of sexual deviations by ICP*

Ideas of treatment: Find out the unconscious reason that causes sexual deviations, repair the related psychological trauma at the original beginning point of the complex, and guide the client to find new and constructive psychology and behavior coping style to treat his/her sexual desire.

For example, people with prospective anxiety show negative imagery in terms of sex, and this causes sexual dysfunction, the most common of which is impotence or premature ejaculation, so positive implications are needed.

Specific treatment methods: Use symbolic sexual activity to represent direct actual imagination. The most commonly used images are knocking a big round log into a gate, breaking a dam with a big hammer and a butterfly sucking on a flower bud.

Another example is when the sexually deviated client always has narcissistic trauma and frustration concerned with self-identification in deep unconsciousness. It often happens that sexual deviance is the outward response or compensation mechanism of that trauma. Find out the primary trauma and repair it, and the unconscious driving force of sexual deviation can be eliminated.

4.6. *Treatment of hysteric psychological disorders by ICP*

Hysteric psychological disorders include hysteria, psychological problems which are similar to hysteria but do not reach the diagnostic criteria and hysterical personality.

(1) Imagery characters

There are always some images which are highly histrionic in subpersonality or animal images, such as an actor, exceedingly beautiful young lady, sexy girl, lovely child, poor child, man held up by an evil spirit, monkey, orangutan and so on. House imagery is always specifically magnificent.

(2) Imagery understanding

These clients are usually willing to accept the images mentioned above, but they do not want to accept the opposite images, such as a toad, devil, ugly man, impuissant servant, broken house and so on.

(3) Treatment principles

Find out the benefit behind the disguise with the attitude of acceptance. Go through the performance, connect with the deeper, real emotional feelings and desire, and make conscious expressions directly.

(4) Treatment methods

Make the treatment relationship steady with the attitude of consistent acceptance and tolerance. Promote clients' auto-criticism by improving their self-awareness constantly and deeply understand the psychological needs which are suppressed behind the performance. The psychotherapist needs to empathize their true feelings behind the disguise subtly and gently, guide them to face their true inner desires and emotions, break the indulgence, search for the real psychological problems, and deal with them.

(5) Technical level

By waiting for the right time, which means the psychotherapist can use images like opening the mill, slate or iron plate to break the insulation in place of the diaphragm, guide the client to pay close attention to his/her abdomen and face the real mind. All these have to be done under the premise of the acceptance of the client.

It is worth remembering that the psychotherapist can easily have the countertransference to the client's performance, which can cause a situation like rough debunk or false acceptance. Therefore, the psychotherapist should remain highly self-alert and self-aware at this time.

4.7. *Treatment of addictive behavior by ICP*

The addictive behavior here means the behavior under the state of being indulgent, including drug abuse, alcohol abuse, internet addiction, gambling, sexual permissiveness, bulimia and so on.

Imagery characters: Generally speaking, these behaviors are related to "eating the inedible, dirty, tainted or something with thick mucus". Repetitive patterns in imagery often appear.

Common imagery: Bloodsucker, a ghost or an animal which eats rotten things or corpses, people who eat shit, maggots or mud. Image patterns like "enter nowhere" are commonly seen. A rotating round object can often be seen when people are in a state of indulgence.

Treatment principles: To begin with, guide the clients to stop eating dirty, tainted and inedible things. Next, find out the reasons and desires behind the addictive behaviors and perform the relevant treatment by imagery communication. Finally, conduct behavioral training of addiction withdrawal in reality.

Treatment steps include the following:

(1) Keep the attitude of acceptance for the present situation of addiction of the clients. Then, distinguish "people with problems" from "problems". And set an example for the clients: I accept a person with symptoms of addiction.

Note: Acceptance is an attitude, not identity. It does not mean agreement without giving serious thought. We accept all people with psychological problems, but it does not mean that we think their problems are good or agree with their pathological behavior.

(2) After establishing a good consulting relationship, an ICP therapist can help the client with imagery exploration: The reason why the scavenger feels hungry, what they lack, what is the benefit of being a scavenger, why he/she can only eat decayed food, what prevent him/her from eating more healthy and delicious food.
(3) At this stage, the psychotherapist should focus on the client's disappointed attitude or despair and his/her addictive behaviors, and then fix them. Only in this way can we change the client's belief that "my addictive behaviors cannot be changed", and lay the foundation of real change of psychology and behavior.
(4) In the process of imagery communication, the psychotherapist should help the scavenger put up with hunger and find healthy food. When the client understands what he/she really wants and does not eat decayed food anymore, the client's taste will be restored in his/her subconsciousness; at this time, the psychotherapist should encourage the client to proactively search for healthy food and choose it in his/her imagination.
(5) Use methods like the technique of self-conscious behavior modification and imagery desensitization techniques of ICP to guide the clients to conduct behavioral training of addiction withdrawal in reality, and direct them on how to deal with mental anxiety and realistic pressure when facing the addiction according to their own characteristics.
(6) When the behavioral training is confronted with the bottleneck, ICP therapists can use the opportunity to further discover and solve the mental reasons which cause the clients' behavioral change. Relive their security threats and mental anxiety caused by behavioral change timely, and use language to supervise, support and encourage the level of imagery communication.

(7) Help the client to find out the internal and external resources that can support his/her behavior modification. It is better to help the client to establish a psychological support system in reality. For example, the important family members of the addicts can be invited to participate in the process of mental growth and behavior modification.

Note: The psychotherapist should not use ICP one-sidedly to treat internet addiction of teenagers before receiving formal ICP training! Otherwise, youth addicts will be more depressed and passive, which is bad for their healthy growth.

4.8. *ICP used in the enterprise*

(1) ICP used in the business interpersonal relationship regulation

Management principles: Because of objectivity and complexity, the particularity of the enterprise should be paid more attention, except for the general principle of interpersonal relationship regulation. An enterprise is a group that is structured to achieve a common realistic goal, so the principle of actuality and operability needs much attention. Each part of the enterprise has its specific function; in the meantime, each component must form a harmonious organic whole. Thus, the following principles should be remembered from every part — the functional principle, the matching principle and the organizational principle.

There is a high degree of flexibility and applicability of enterprise psychological adjustment, and it is difficult to make it clear in a uniform way or with steps. For this reason, we will not go into that.

At the same time, business consulting of imagery communication requires a high level of personal literacy for lecturers or trainers. In order to ensure the interests of corporate consumers, untrained lecturers or EAP consultants are not allowed to use ICP to diagnose, train and conduct group psychotherapy for an enterprise.

(2) Work pressure problem

To achieve the effect of reducing pressure, the following are some simple and safe imagery communication techniques. They can be used for group counseling in an enterprise.

- First, the simplest technique is "Place for spiritual cultivation". Guide clients to imagine a situation that can make him/her feel relaxed, and make this situation as the place for spiritual cultivation. When feeling stressed or tired, imagine this place consciously and experience the feeling of relaxation to relieve stress.
- Second, "My nepenthes". Find out some items or activities which can make clients feel relaxed and set them as their own nepenthes. This technique aims to guide clients to find out their personalized decompression methods.
- Third, "The cat's life". Guide clients to imagine and identify the cat image. From a symbolic point of view, a cat is naturally a confident animal that is often languid and relaxed.
- Fourth, "The falling mud shell". This imaginary training is suitable for the start of the weekend. The mud shell symbolizes accumulation and fixation of stress or negative emotions.
- Fifth, "Drawer". The key point is to remind the clients to dispose the things in the drawer at the right time. A drawer is a relatively closed container that can sometimes symbolize repression.
- Sixth, "The homing bees". As an insect image, the bee symbolizes industry, devotion and sweetness. The main focus of this image exercise is to relieve clients' anxiety and irritability.

Note: ICP therapists can combine the techniques above with relevant techniques of other psychotherapies to improve the treatment effect.

(3) Career choice and talent evaluation

Management methods: Analysis of animal images. This technique relies on PID.

Chapter 7

The Strategies of Imagery Communication Psychotherapy

Based on the evaluation of the client, after determining the general goal of psychological counseling or psychotherapy, the psychotherapist needs to have an overall strategy. The strategy of psychological counseling or psychotherapy is similar to a framed script that is a summary of the whole process. It has a prediction and a brief description for the psychological counseling or psychotherapy that will occur.

Here is a simple example. A client was treated for acrophobia. The psychotherapist thinks his acrophobia stems from his relationship with his parents after a preliminary understanding of his conditions. So, the psychotherapist and the client discuss whether or not he is willing to go further to see if his acrophobia is just a matter of his family relations. The client offers to do so and has the time to accept more psychoanalysis.

In this case, the psychotherapist assesses two strategies. One is to use systematic desensitization to alleviate his acrophobia. The client will have greater confidence after the symptoms are relieved. Then, the psychotherapist analyzes and eliminates the complex behind the symptoms, so that his acrophobia will no longer relapse or turn into other symptoms.

Another strategy is to start with the complex, regardless of acrophobia. When the psychotherapist gets a good result after psychological analysis and the client understands the source of the fear of heights, the underlying motivation for acrophobia will be weakened, and behavior correction will become very easy.

Now let's compare these two strategies.

If the first strategy is carried out, and the first stage successfully reduces his symptoms, it will boost his confidence in psychotherapy and make the psychological analysis easy. However, the client may not be willing to continue the psychological analysis once his symptoms disappear. His problem won't be solved at all. Maybe after a year or two, his acrophobia will reoccur or turn into other symptoms. By that time, the client's confidence will be impaired. He would even think that psychotherapy could not solve his problems. Or alternatively, if the first phase cannot successfully reduce his acrophobia symptoms, then subsequent psychotherapy would be difficult to implement.

If the second strategy is executed, removing the internal obstacles can make it easier to eliminate his acrophobia. But if the psychotherapist is always talking about something other than the acrophobia, the client is likely to become increasingly impatient. Once the client gives up, the psychotherapist can hardly go on.

What kind of strategy should we use? The psychotherapist needs to make his own judgment on the basis of the specific analysis of the client.

In a sense, the strategy of psychotherapy is similar to that of politics and military.

It is important to note that the strategy is different from a plan.

On the one hand, a plan is more fixed. We need to know more about internal and external conditions when planning. For each step, there should be definite requirements in the plan. Although the plan can be changed, it generally remains the same or is not characterized by major changes. *A strategy is a rough story script of psychological counseling and psychotherapy, and a synopsis of what to do in case the general conditions are known.*

On the other hand, planning is an everyday logical thinking activity. *Strategy is the narrative thinking activity.*

In all psychological counseling and psychotherapy, a strategy is used intentionally or unintentionally. However, ICP mainly uses primitive cognition and narrative thinking much more than everyday logical thinking, thus focusing more on the strategy and its uses.

For ICP, the value and function of the strategy is to provide a direction and goal to the primitive cognition of the subconscious mind. When a plot summary about "the psychotherapy to be such a development this time" occurs in the mind, in the process of psychotherapy, the subconscious will give what happened a corresponding meaning and understanding of what to do next, and there is also a base of imagination.

1. Different types of strategies

There are various types of strategies. Psychological consultants and psychotherapists can choose the right one.

1.1. *"First add" or "first vent"*

"First add" is a type of strategy. Generally speaking, the psychological consultation choosing this type of strategy should first use the support method to improve the client's self-confidence, self-esteem and some ability to meet some psychological needs. The purpose of this is not only to give the client these mental benefits but, more importantly, to give the client the resources, power and confidence to accept the subsequent psychological intervention. "First add" is for later psychological intervention to be conditional implementation.

"First vent" is another type of strategy. The psychological consultation choosing this type of strategy should first guide the client to vent his/her long list of negative emotions. Thereafter, other psychological interventions, such as behavioral guidance, will be implemented.

1.2. *"Test" or "lock-in"*

The basic story script of "test" type strategy is that the psychotherapist asks the client about the various difficulties in the previous stage, or tests him/her with strict demands, in order to strengthen the client's motivation and desire for help. After this, the psychotherapist will take a more moderate approach to communicate with the client.

The basic story script of "lock-in" type strategy is to let the client trust and accept the psychotherapist and the psychology through a lot of encouragement, support and help. After that, the psychotherapist will make some difficult requests of the client. From a certain point of view, this process is similar to courting. The pursuer first presents flowers for the pursued, and invites the pursued to a dinner and a movie at the beginning of the pursuit. When the pursued accept the pursuer, especially after marriage, the pursuer will ask the spouse to do housework and take care of their children.

1.3. *"First cut the branches" or "first cut the roots"*

In psychotherapy, "first cut the branches" strategy means that the psychotherapist first solves some specific mental troubles and problems, and does not rush to explore the root causes of the most fundamental complex. The nice thing about this is that the psychotherapist will encounter a smaller resistance and it is easy to get results. Sometimes, after some specific mental troubles and problems are solved, resolving the more profound problems won't be hampered by those trivial problems. It will be easier to solve the underlying problem.

Nonetheless, there is a risk in "first cut the branches" strategy. When the root of the deep complex is not touched, it is possible that a problem has just been resolved and a new one arises. The deep psychological problem can change its form and be expressed in a new way. As a result, the solution to the surface problem will be endless. We are constantly obsessed with these shallow issues, and there is no way to free our hands to touch the deep ones.

In psychotherapy, "first cut the roots" strategy means that the psychotherapist does not dwell on specific issues, not solve those shallow and trivial mental troubles, but single-mindedly and directly steers towards deeper and deeper psychological problems in order to find the underlying fundamental complex, to explore the roots of problems and the place where it stuck, and then go directly to resolve the root cause.

Once the underlying complex is solved, the psychotherapist will then guide the client back to the various specific mental problems and find it easy.

Similarly, there is also a risk in "first cut the roots" strategy. We can choose not to dwell on specific issues, not solve those shallow and trivial mental troubles, but these unsolved problems may interfere later. Our vision may be so confused by these specific mental problems that we cannot find the deepest complex and its root at once. In that case, we can neither find the root nor resolve the specific problems. This will make subsequent psychotherapy more difficult.

The strategies given above are the more common ones. There are many types of strategies in practice. We are not going to list them all.

2. Choosing different strategies

CChoosing and determining the psychotherapy strategy depends on multiple conditions.

2.1. *The base of various mental qualities of the client is the important condition for choosing the strategy*

For instance, for those clients who are more capable of detection and introspection, "first cut the roots" may be more appropriate. The reason is that with the help of psychotherapists, we can find the main clues to the mental problems of the forest. However, for those clients who are less capable of detection and introspection, "first cut the branches" may be more appropriate because they are more likely to maintain behavior changes. It will contribute to the following psychotherapy sessions.

Besides, the factors affecting the psychotherapy strategy include confidence, decision taken, willpower, resolution and love of the client. For example, if the client has enough confidence in the psychotherapist and psychotherapy, the psychotherapist can choose the more difficult but effective strategy. Choosing such a strategy means that the client may feel "worse" at some stages because of the mental problems suppressed for so long. When faced with this difficulty, the client can persevere and tide over it as long as he/she has the confidence. But if the client's confidence is insufficient, the strategy of psychotherapy must be conservative. Slowing down the pace of psychotherapy can prevent the client from giving up because of doubt.

2.2. *The psychological development phase of the client is another important condition for choosing the strategy*

The stage at which the client's personality becomes fixed is very influential for us.

When a child is very young, we give milk to the child. When the child grows up, we provide dinner. The same is true at a psychological level. We should give the person more unconditional positive attention if his/her psychological level becomes fixed before the age of one. However, if the fixation occurred in the later stages of psychological development, we would need to ask him/her for a certain request to enhance his/her sense of reality, instead of blindly giving unconditional positive attention. In the early days of mental energy fixation, its negative printing can have a relatively large impact. Thus, the psychological intervention should be more about how to deal with this printing.

In ICP, we can judge at which stage the client's fixation occurs by observing his/her images. For example, the existence of the vampire sub-personality may be due to the trauma and fixation of the client during his/her incubation period. This kind of primitive image occurs very frequently and often suggests that the fixation occurred before the age of one. The simplest way to judge the age during which the fixation occurs is through the existence of a sub-personality of this age. Furthermore, this sub-personality is usually in a bad shape, such as a dead baby or a weak and fearful kid.

2.3. *Assess the mental conditions and resources of the client*

The age, physical condition, physical illness and pregnancy of the client can affect the selection of the strategy.

For instance, in the face of clients with physical infirmity or physical illness, we need to avoid the action of emotional shock when choosing the psychological treatment strategy to prevent hard-to-bear actions for their bodies. If the psychological intervention is too strong and the mental conflict is too violent, it will not be conducive to the treatment of somatic diseases. For older clients, we should choose a more conservative and safe strategy, rather than pursuing a too deep and overly intense clinical practice. When we give psychotherapy or psychological counseling to a pregnant client, it is important to take into account the effects on the fetus and make sure to avoid the experience of strong mental conflicts and negative emotions during therapy.

Moreover, the knowledge background of a client has an impact on the strategy. As an example, in the face of a client with abundant natural scientific knowledge, ICP seems to be more unexpected, thus avoiding the transformation of the result of ICP into intellectualized knowledge. To be sure, it is also necessary to see whether the client has faith in psychotherapy. If the client's confidence is so weak, the unexpected strategy will undermine his/her sense of security.

In addition, the religious belief of a client also influences the choice of strategy. As a rule, at the beginning of psychotherapy, it is best for a psychotherapist to adopt a practice similar to the client's religious belief. In that case, the client can easily adapt.

2.4. *Different psychological problems have different choices of strategy*

Common psychological problems, personality problems, hospice care and self-growth of psychotherapists, etc. have different goals. All of these affect the strategy we adopt.

Here is an instance. Compulsive clients are often used to protecting themselves by the type of approaches such as intellectualizing. They are terrified deep inside. This is always shown in the image as a hard shell. For them, the more radical approach is to break the hard shell or to steer them away from it. This will lead them to a state of self-disorder. As long as they are brave enough to face the state, they will build a new self. A more stable strategy is to lead them to convert the rigid shell into "a suit of armor that can be put on and off". The psychotherapist allows them to have more control over their psychological defenses and then slowly solves their more profound problems. It is slow, but it is safer.

For the impulsive clients, it is advised not to let them give up the hard shells quickly or slowly in their imagination, but to guide them to learn more about self-awareness and to avoid automatic reactions when stimulated.

As another example consider the following case. For depression or other problems of depression, the selection of strategy should be taken together. If our supportive and nurturing actions are too much, the clients may not recover from their illness. It is bad for psychotherapy. Furthermore, in the case that the clients' belief system has not changed, even if we provide psychological support, their level of consciousness doesn't feel that this is useful to them. However, if we do not offer mental support at the start, but use more confrontation, they will feel frustrated. Therefore, we must consider multiple factors comprehensively to choose a strategy suitable for a client.

2.5. *The goal of psychotherapy is different and the strategy must be different*

The strategy is to serve the goal of psychotherapy. Hence, the goal of psychotherapy is different and the strategy must be disparate.

For a client personally, if the objective of psychotherapy is to resolve a specific mental trouble but not to pay attention to the underlying complex, "first cut the branches" will be the most appropriate strategy. After solving the specific mental trouble, if the client still has no interest to continue to explore, psychotherapy can be finished. However, if the client has developed an interest in exploring the deep psychology or source of the issue, we can go on.

For those clients who crave spiritual growth, it is necessary to choose the strategy of "first cut the roots".

2.6. *Assess the extrinsic resources of the client*

If the family does not agree with a client to receive psychotherapy, the psychotherapist needs to deal with some specific mental problems for family members to see clinical efficacy, which might garner their support for subsequent psychotherapy sessions. Moreover, the psychotherapist has to mobilize and utilize the extrinsic resources of a client, so as to obtain more social support, which in itself has psychological therapeutic significance.

2.7. *The personal characteristics of the psychotherapist, the distinguishing features of psychotherapy and the mode of consultative relationship should not be ignored*

(1) The personal characteristics of the psychotherapist determines what kind of strategy he/she is better at using, what kind of mental resources he/she has and what kind of strategy is right for him/her.

This is a metaphor for animal hunting. The leopards run fast but have bad stamina, so they fit the strategies of the raid. The wolves do not run as fast as leopards, but they have far more stamina than leopards, so they are suitable for long-distance pursuit strategies.

If the psychotherapist is good at showing resourcefulness during an emergency, maybe he/she is fit to wait for a chance to break through. Whereupon, it is necessary for him/her to set a condition for waiting in strategy, then wait. If the psychotherapist is very patient, but not adept at playing to the score tactically, he/she is more suited to a step-by-step strategy.

(2) The skills of the psychotherapist in terms of the kinds of psychotherapy and counseling techniques also influence the strategy selection.

If the psychotherapist is good at analyzing the personality topology, it is appropriate to have a bird's eye view of the overall situation and further break it down into segments. Actually, if the psychotherapist is not efficient at the analysis of the personality topology, he/she can start with some concrete images, resolve some of the most important complexes, and then consider the overall situation. It is easier to find the main clue by understanding the local and then examine the whole personality of the client.

(3) The mode of consultative relationship is distinct and the choice of strategy is diverse.

In the consultative relationship, if the psychotherapist is like the client's good mother, in strategy, he/she can first replenish mental resources for the client, and then deal with difficult psychological problems. If the relationship between the two parties is rational in the initial stages of psychotherapy, the psychotherapist can understand the client at the rational level and gradually deepen the perceptual level.

That is, the psychotherapy strategy is a brief narrative script and a summary describing the communication among the images and the process of their changing. With such a script, ICP process is more orderly and effective.

Chapter 8

Deal with Special Problems

1. Deal with strong resistance

1.1. *The principle*

Reassure a client and increase trust in psychotherapy and the psychotherapist.

1.2. *The basic steps*

(1) Accept and face the various resistances of a client, whether conscious or unconscious.
(2) Understand the resistance and grasp its psychological benefits.
(3) Use resistance as a point cut or guidance to discover the negative emotions behind it, such as fear, anger and so on.
(4) Find out the reason about resistance and then resolve it.

1.3. *The processing method*

(1) Before the start of psychological counseling or psychotherapy, the imagery communication psychotherapist should give the client a brief explanation of ICP and its benefits to ease the insecurity of the unknown.

(2) Persistence and insistence

When the client has a strong resistance, the psychotherapist should be patient and confident. What often happens clinically is, when the psychotherapist is close to the core of mental problems, the client will bypass it or confuse the psychotherapist and use various methods to make him/her leave the key point due to resistance. During this point, the psychotherapist needs to make a judgment on whether the timing is suitable for the client to address the issue and whether the client has the necessary mental preparation and psychological resources.

The so-called insistence means that the psychotherapist must bear in mind very clearly which issue of the client needs to be solved at that time and tell quickly and sharply which discourses and behaviors show avoidance and which is in contact with the real issues. The psychotherapist must adhere to the direction of the concerns of both sides and pull it back to the core again and again.

According to our experiences, this is the best way to distinguish whether a psychotherapist has adequate work force at that moment.

(3) Auxiliary imagination

For example, the client can be guided to imagine "being kidnapped". In his/her imagination, the client is blindfolded and sitting in a car that is traveling in various different directions. Then, he/she is saved and taken from the car. The blindfold is removed. The client opens his/her eyes and looks around...

(4) Roundabout

The psychotherapist leads the client to imagine other images. After his/her resistance becomes weak, the psychotherapist brings the client back to that initial image.

(5) No matter what manners the psychotherapist chooses to guide, the client's imagination is always "a piece of white paper", this kind of "white" itself is an image, the psychotherapist could directly analyze and experience it as an image.

For instance:

The psychotherapist can give the client guidance: What do you think the white looks like before you?

The client: White cloth.

The psychotherapist: What is in the white cloth?

The client: I do not know. (I cannot see it clearly.)

The psychotherapist: That is ok. Please relax. It is just an imagination game. You can unmask it in any magical way and take a look at what is inside.

Another example:

The psychotherapist can give the client guidance: What do you think the white looks like before you?

The client: White fog.

The psychotherapist: How are you feeling in the fog?

The client: Nervous. I am a little afraid.

The psychotherapist: How old are you in fear now? What does he or she look like? What is he or she wearing? What is his or her body posture at this moment? What scares him or her?

(6) When a perceived medium cannot continue due to resistance, the psychotherapist can lead the client to switch the perceived medium or the perceived object for maintaining uninterrupted awareness and confrontation.

For instance, the psychotherapist can ask for his/her physical sensation when a client has difficulty in imagining or describing his/her inner feelings, and then direct the client from the physical sensation to the inner feelings.

At this moment, which part of your body is the most uncomfortable?

What is this uncomfortable feeling?

Metaphorically, what is that feeling like?

What is the mood of this physical discomfort?

No matter what, we need to remember that the imagery is just a medium or carrier in ICP. Its load of psychological energy, mental reality and its symbolic meanings are the key points of the work.

2. Deal with transference

Transference is a "contamination".

The principle is to distinguish and exfoliate it with awareness and experience.

We can apply a variety of specific imagery communication techniques to help clients to distinguish between what they think of as a psychotherapist and what a psychotherapist looks like.

One of the techniques is that the client closes his/her eyes and asks himself/herself: "who does this psychotherapist's image remind me of?" when he/she has a particular emotion or feeling for the psychotherapist. When the client finds the remembered person, he/she carefully experiences the emotion or feeling that the person brings and releases it. After completing the release with self-detection, the client opens his/her eyes and looks at the psychotherapist in front of him/her. The client carefully discriminates: "Is there any difference between the psychotherapist I see now and the one I just saw? What's the difference?" This difference is the distinction between contamination and non-contamination.

We can also ask clients to be aware of their transference.

What do you feel most about me?

What is this feeling?

In your past life, especially as a little child, who else gave you this feeling?

Here and now, we sincerely invite this person to appear in your mind (imagination). Look at him or her... what is he or she saying or doing?

Here and now, how old is that child watching him or her?...

Chapter 9

The Symbolic Meanings of Imagery

1. Principles of interpretation of the symbolic meaning

(1) *To avoid being rigid and ossified*

The symbolic meanings of imagery are not fixed and changeless. The same image in different circumstances could have different symbolic meanings. Therefore, we cannot simply match the "image" and "meaning" or just put them in the right place.

(2) *To avoid being mechanical*

The categories of imagery and their symbolic meanings listed in this book are limited, that is, they serve as only a guide and reference. This book cannot be regarded and used as a dictionary.

(3) *To avoid being single*

Imagery communication psychotherapists should combine an image with the "context" and a client's personal situation and details to comprehensively interpret the symbolic meaning of the image.

(4) *To remember the therapeutic goal*

When we deeply communicate with our clients through the symbolism of imagery, we must set the therapeutic goal to promote the client's spiritual growth. We cannot impose our will on our clients, nor can we "label" them.

(5) *To understand the relationship between "universality" and "individuality"*

The explanation we are going to make here is based on the commonality of the symbolic meanings of imagery. In clinical practice, when we apply some symbolic meaning to a particular client, we must "tailor" it.

2. Methods of interpretation of the symbolic meanings

(1) Imagery communication psychotherapists need to constantly upgrade themselves on a theoretical level by learning psychodynamics theory and improving their knowledge, especially Jung's analytical psychology.
(2) Imagery communication psychotherapists need to continue with their personal growth and even regular supervision, to enhance their psychological quality and deep insight into various complexes, so that their insight and perceptivity could become clearer, their complexes could be less contaminated, and their love could become purer and nourishing.
(3) Imagery communication psychotherapists need to constantly sum up their experiences with their peers and enrich their understanding of the symbolic meanings of imagery, so as to avoid subjective speculation and closed doors.
(4) It is necessary for imagery communication psychotherapists to respect intuition. In the understanding of all the basic meanings of the primary image and the common imagery, psychotherapists could interpret symbolic meanings of images in a comprehensive way according to the intuition and feelings at that time as well as the whole imagery communication process.
(5) During imagery communication, the psychotherapist should constantly check with the client to verify his/her own judgment and constantly improve the ability to empathize.
(6) Imagery communication psychotherapists need to have the courage to face the truth and admit their ignorance and mistakes.
(7) When the imagery communication psychotherapist cannot determine the symbolic meaning of an image, he/she can guide the

client to "stare at" that image and imagine that it can change. According to the generality or similarity of the original image and its changing images, the symbolic meaning of that image is judged.

(8) ICP can still continue even though it is impossible to judge the symbolic meanings of some images for a while. What should be done is based on the feeling of each image, respond accordingly. However, at the end of psychotherapy, the psychotherapist should analyze carefully and summarize.

3. The categories of imagery and their basic symbolic meanings

Note:

(1) The category of imagery is not strictly followed by the classification standards of natural sciences, such as zoology and botany, but by the symbolic meaning. The categories of each classification are larger than the corresponding categories of natural sciences.
(2) Every category has common symbolic meanings. At the same time, each specific image in the same category has its specific symbolic significance.
(3) The symbolic meaning of an individual animal shows a cultural difference between the east and the west.
(4) The symbolic meaning of all images is applied to the individual, subject to individual specificity.

3.1. *Animal imagery*

(1) Fishes: Wealth; sexuality; subconscious or intuitive (especially fishes that live deep in the oceans); soft; gentle; feminine beauty; auspicious nature; freedom; care; dedication; vulnerability; non-aggressive (except the shark).
(2) Birds: Freedom; nature; direct; concise; not hypocritical; sexuality; entry into the spiritual power.

(3) Animal symbols of inferiority: Insects; mice; ants; centipedes; frogs; toads; lizards; crocodiles and so on.
(4) Animal symbols of mysterious intuition: Snakes; bats; tortoises; cats; spiders; weasel; hedgehog; owl and so on.
(5) Felidae beasts of prey: Self-confident; powerful; kind-hearted; frank; brave; majestic; firm; glamorous; charming; being both very relaxed and very vigilant.
(6) Herbivores: Weak sense of security (except elephants); moderate; goodness; introverted; a little timid; internally sensitive and delicate; conforming tendency because of liking to live in groups.

    Note: Herbivorous animals have different personalities. They need to be treated differently and understood one by one.

(7) Cruel beasts: Aggression; destruction; conquest; loyal to their families and organizations (such as wolf and hyena); rich motherhood (such as wolf).
(8) Shellfishes: A strong sense of self-protection; internally soft, sensitive and vulnerable.
(9) Animal symbols of enactivism: Orangutan; monkey; swan; giraffe; peacock; fox; snake and so on.
(10) Combination of animals: A symbol of the combination of several animals. Need to be analyzed and comprehensively understood.
(11) Integration of animals: The auspicious animals are common, such as phoenix, dragon, unicorn and so on. They symbolize extraordinary mental health, self-realization and the transcendental self.

3.2. *Plant imagery*

(1) Trees: Male temperament
(2) Flowers: Femininity
(3) Fruits: Women often use a fruit as a token of their sexual self-evaluation.

(4) Special plants: Some special plants have special symbolic significance. For example, the cactus becomes somewhat aggressive due to lack of emotion. This knowledge needs to be accumulated over time.

3.3. *Natural objects imagery*

(1) Water: Vitality; emotional nourishment; reproduction; growth; creativity; female/ feminist/mother (reaction to water); deeper water or water in an underground cave symbolizes the subconscious; unclear and unclean water is often a symbol of psychosexual problems; also, notice if there are other sexual symbols.

   Note: Water images are quite rich. The water imagery not only has many variants (such as ice, snow, rain, fog, cloud, milk, wine, blood, sweat, urine, etc.) but also has other forms (such as sea, springs, streams, etc.). The symbolic meaning is related to the basic meaning of water and has unique symbolic significance.

(2) Fire: Life and vitality; creativity; wisdom; strong emotions; passion; fighting; danger.
(3) Light: Wisdom; knowledge; religiousness or transcendent wisdom.
(4) Sun: The divine wisdom; positive intelligence; source of vitality; the great love; strength; energy; masculinity.
(5) Moon: The divine wisdom; negative intelligence; mysterious intuition; unpredictability; femininity.
(6) Stars: Divine wisdom; inspiration.
(7) Stones: Stability; persistence; stubbornness; heaviness; oppression; difficulties or obstacles; lack of vitality. Also, fear is often associated with stone imagery.
(8) Jade and precious stones: The symbol of core personality — the real self.

Different jade and precious stones symbolize different states of personality integration, as well as of the real self-completion and purity. They represent the highest degree of one's mental health.

When a person's spiritual growth does not reach this level and when a person imagines a jade or precious stones, it represents the personality status he/she is looking forward to achieve.

3.4. *Artificial imagery*

(1) Metal: Solidified emotions; wealth. Different metals have different symbolic meanings.
(2) Means of transportation: The symbol of one's body or mind. Different means of transportation have unique symbolic significances. For instance, ships can symbolize intimacy. Planes can symbolize high rationalization and spiritualization.
(3) Clothes: Personality; appearance; identity; persona; characteristics.
(4) Weapons: Sexuality; masculinity; anger, hostility and aggression. Yuan Yuan made a detailed exposition in her book *Weapon Psychology* in 2018.
(5) Implements: Different implements have different symbolic meanings. For example, television symbolizes unconsciousness. Mobile phone symbolizes the connection between relationships and emotional communication. A video is a symbol of subconscious memory.

3.5. *Character imagery and ghosts and gods imagery*

The content that has been stated previously is not repeated here.

(1) Ghost imagery: A strong and negative psychological state; a serious mental illness; unresolved complex; evil; danger. The different kinds of ghost imagery have their own unique symbolic meanings.

    For example, the image of a female ghost with long hair and white and thin dress is often indicative of depression. Her long hair symbolizes the entanglement of emotions. Her white dress symbolizes sadness or innocence. She speaks and walks without a sound because her life energy is quite weak. Her pale face symbolizes severe mental anemia.

Note: When imagery communication psychotherapists do not have the experience and ability to face the ghost imagery and deal with it, they are not allowed to take risks with their clients! This is because the negative mental energy carried by the ghost imagery is very large and strong. The psychotherapist's mishandling could lead to new psychological hazards for the client.

(2) God imagery: Sages and men of virtue; Buddha; God and other images of gods. They are symbols of a very positive and healthy mental state or spiritual pursuit.
(3) Archetype: It is a symbol of collective unconsciousness. Archetype is human mental disposition. Archetype itself has no specific images, but it can be represented as concrete images, which were called primitive images by Jung. Jung divided the archetype into three categories — characters, natural objects and artificial archetype.

Character archetype: Birth Archetype, Rebirth Archetype, Resurrection Archetype, Death Archetype, Authority Archetype, Witchcraft Archetype, God Archetype, Devil Archetype, Great Mother, Wise man Archetype, Hero Archetype, Giant Archetype, Children Archetype, Prank Archetype and so on.

Natural objects archetype: Sun, Moon, Stars, Wind, Fire, Water, Animals, Trees and so on.

Artificial archetype: Rings and Weapons.

Chapter 10

The Topic, Principle and Application of Initial Imagery

1. The principle of initial imagery

Before elaborating on the principle of initial imagery, here again, Imagery Communication Psychotherapy (ICP) is not carried out according to a fixed, rigid, dogmatic and standardized formula or procedure; all the publicly published operational steps and clinical procedures can be flexible based on the principles of "client-centered" practice and ensuring optimal efficacy.

It is also worth emphasizing that the principles of operation and values of ICP are unshakable, whether strictly following procedures and steps, or being flexible. Besides, on the technical level, the psychotherapist must not omit the "end" part in every ICP.

In order to introduce ICP smoothly, the psychotherapist can apply the initial imagery in clinical practice. Which initial imagery to choose depends on the psychological problem of the client. The symbolic meaning of each initial imagery is relatively certain.

When we are training imagery communication psychotherapists, we will be devoted to explaining this part of the knowledge, and the process will be equipped with appropriate professional training.

Please make sure that each reader and ICP psychotherapist believes that if they do not treat a client sincerely and attentively, even though they have mastered this part of knowledge in theory, they will still be unable to accurately understand the client's inner feelings and subconscious demand, and they also cannot further interact with him/her in the depths of hearts, thereby making their help minimal. This is far from the original intention of ICP.

As an imagery communication psychotherapist, it is important to master the necessary knowledge and skills; nevertheless, personality and attitude are much more important.

2. The commonly used initial imagery

In the following sections, we will give an overview of the topic, principle and application of commonly used initial imagery.

2.1. *House imagery*

The house imagery symbolizes the basic internal state and emotional tone.

The house imagery is the most commonly used initial imagery in ICP. It can even be used as a psychological test to check the basic personality status and emotional tone of a client. Its related content has been discussed earlier. We will not go into too much detail here.

2.2. *Car imagery and ship imagery*

(1) Car imagery

Car imagery can represent a person's body or emotion. The direction of the car symbolizes the direction or pointing of the life path.

In a dream or an imagination, the concrete state of the car represents the specific status of one's own body or emotion. For example, a brake failure symbolizes out-of-control nature or being afraid of getting out of control. Being unable to control the steering wheel represents being incapable of controlling the direction of life or getting lost in it. A dysfunctional car light or windshield wiper symbolizes being unable to clearly see the direction of life. Lack of gasoline in the fuel tank symbolizes the lack of energy. Flat tires or punctures represent psychological frustration.

The driver in the car image represents the part of subconscious mechanism controlling one's life. If there is no driver in a dream or an imagination, or if one is not sitting in front of the steering wheel, but just a passenger, it means having no control over one's own life or some other part of it. A car is a relatively closed environment. Therefore, it is also a kind of house, which can be understood and interpreted as a house image.

The catch: The train is timed. In addition to symbolisms above the car image, the train often symbolizes time, times and opportunity. In our modern dreams and images, the train represents more opportunity. For instance, missing a train can be a sign of missing an opportunity or being afraid of missing an opportunity.

(2) Ship imagery

In the real world, ships are associated with water. Water can represent femininity. Thus, ships can symbolize femininity, such as a mother, maternity or the feminine part of the heart. A ship image is also a sex sign of females. The rocking of a boat can be explained as sex or sexual behavior. Ships can symbolize intimacy. There is well-known saying in Chinese known as "a thousand years in a ship".

In a dream or imagination where a ship leaving a country and sailing abroad, it symbolizes entry into an unfamiliar territory.

The crossing of a narrow waterway usually has three symbolic meanings. The first is the symbol of death. The second is the symbolic transition from one stage of life to another. The third symbol is a break from the past and beginning of a new life.

The car or ship imagery can be initial imagery when the psychotherapist wants to understand a client's basic state of body or emotion.

2.3. *Flower and insect*

The "flower and insect" is the most classic imagery in ICP. When the psychotherapist needs to understand a client's sexual relations, or a client has psychological problems in sexual relations, it can be used to enter the process of imagination and psychotherapy.

The "flower and insect" imagery has three symbolic significances: the attitude toward one's own gender and sexuality, the attitude toward isomerism and sexual relations.

In addition to sexual relations, through this imagery, the client's own ideas and attitude about sex can be presented. The client's gender identity can also be projected at the same time. The greatest advantage of this imagery exercise is that the psychotherapist and the client need not talk about sex on the conscious level. The two sides can deftly avoid some interference factors such as morality, evaluation and individual character and awkwardness of sexual discussion at the rational level, but instead direct the presentation, communication and resolution of the problems at the subconscious level. It can minimize the resistance in the psychotherapy process.

The common instructions:

In your imagination, you come to a beautiful big garden. There are many flowers in the garden. Please choose one of the flowers. Take a closer look at what it is. What color? Is it open? An insect is flying in the distance. What does it look like? When this insect is flying to this flower, what is the state of the two? Experience the feeling of the flower. And experience the feeling of the insect.

Flower imagery is the symbol of feminine temperament. Here, insect imagery symbolizes masculinity. This book cannot tell you all about the symbolisms of all the common flowers and insects. It is the knowledge that ICP therapists are constantly learning and accumulating. Even in the face of unfamiliarity, ignorance, and non-existence of certain flower images and insect images in real life, we can still help the clients because we are more concerned with the relationship between the two.

As a result, when using this initial imagery, we always ask how the flower feels about the insect and how the insect feels about the flower in one's images. It is worth mentioning that this inquiry itself has psychological therapeutic significance: guide the client (no matter male or female) to learn to respect the opposite sex, especially men to respect women, and learn to respect each other's feelings. This is one of the important foundations for building intimate relationships.

In this initial imagery, whether the flower is open and its degree of openness symbolize the client's attitude toward sex or whether he/she has experienced sex. An injured, damaged or dilapidated flower image often represents emotional trauma or sexual trauma, which requires the care, solicitude and healing from the imagery communication psychotherapist.

Sometimes, the flower image symbolizing emotional trauma is not only presented in image but also in color. For adult women, warm-toned flowers are more passionate or enthusiastic, and cool-toned flowers lack passion or enthusiasm.

For example, a healthy, married and middle-aged lady is imaging a flower that goes from red to white. The change in color is telling her innermost feelings. The white here symbolizes her desire to return to "girlish purity". She is expressing a wish. However, it is more likely that this white is a symbol of her emotional discoloration or "mental blood loss". This is because red may represent passion and exuberant vitality. When a lady feels that her emotion is hurt and she gradually gives up her confidence and enthusiasm for love, her feelings will lose blood, becoming "anemic". Thus, in her subconscious image, red turns white.

Therefore, in the experience and analysis of flower imagery, the psychotherapist also needs to consider the age factor of the client.

For a white flower, if it appears in the dream or image of a teenage girl, it is healthy and represents purity and unsophistication. This white isn't related to emotional damage.

I want to say more about flower imagery.

If the imagery communication psychotherapist is confronted by a young girl who encounters a severely injured flower in her imaging, for instance, an animal, a monster or an insect forcibly bites the flower or collects honey, these are likely to mean that the girl suffered from sexual trauma. Even if it is not in the "flower and insect" imagery, but in other images or dreams, such as house imagery, it still symbolizes sexual trauma.

In addition to providing care, solicitude, nourishment and supporting the work as well as helping the client heal in the process of ICP, when the client is young, where he/she lacks the necessary self-protection, awareness and self-protecting ability, we also need to teach the child client some essential knowledge and protective measures when the child is in a very sober and rational consciousness, after completing an imagery communication session.

2.4. *Seed and resurrection*

The "seed and resurrection" initial imagery is mainly used to activate the internal positive resources of the client to establish healthy beliefs after the dissolution of the more serious complex or mental trauma.

Usually, the instructions are as follows:

Please plant a seed in the area where you were injured. Then water it and see what grows out.

In order to identify complex or traumatic effects more clearly, the imagery communication psychotherapist can add a guide:

How would you feel if you left it now?

The principle behind it is that, in many cases, the complex is formed and extended because it could give the client some psychological benefits. In other words, thè psychological benefits promote the continuity of the complex. For this reason, when we help the client dissolve the complex, the client may not feel comfortable for a while. This guide can play a distinguishing role. Moreover, it can enhance the client's perception and awareness.

As we know, "water the seed" in this initial imagery is based on the purpose of emotional nourishment and awakening vitality. "What grows out" symbolizes some kind of mental transformation or rebirth of the client. The ideal and healthiest case is when the seed in the image grows into a new and better thing, representing good health symbolically.

In the client's imagination, if the seeds lead to the correct plant, such as planting corn and growing out corn, planting a bean and growing out a bean, it shows that the complex or trauma of the client has not undergone a substantial change, even has been fueled by trends.

In this case, it is necessary for the imagery communication psychotherapist to lead the client to resettle the complex or mental trauma, and to be as thorough as possible, without any subsequent problems.

If in the client's imagination, what grows out is different from the planted seed in form, but the symbolic meaning is not healthy, then it is probably because the mental problem of the client has transformed. It still requires the psychotherapist to direct the client to the point and then resettle the complex or mental trauma.

Citing an instance for example, a client plants corn and it grows out bank notes. It symbolizes that this client replaces his problem with the pursuit of wealth.

It is important to remember that only a new, better and healthier one is true "resurrection".

2.5. *Adopting animals*

This initial imagery is also called "the animal in the box". It is used to present the unconscious attachment of the client. We can analyze whether he/she has established a good attachment relationship with his/her caregivers, depending on the animal in the box that the client sees in the imagination.

The common instructions:

Please imagine you are in a strange boarding establishment for animals. There are a man and a woman standing on both sides of the door. What do they look like? What kind of clothes do they wear? When you walk in, you will find that the animals in this place are kept in the enclosed boxes.

You want to adopt an animal. But you can only choose one box at will. You do not know what animal is in the box, and you cannot guess it. This box is so magical that it can hold large or small animals.

Now, you choose a box. Please open it. What animal is inside?

It is important to note that no matter what animal is adopted by the client, this animal is not allowed to be abandoned or replaced. The symbolic meaning of such mental action is non-acceptance. Nevertheless, the initial imagery of adopting animals aims to increase the client's awareness of attachment and solve the corresponding problems. Thus, if a client makes such a mental action, it presents an attachment problem, which is a good topic for an imagery communication psychotherapist to work on.

If we want to understand the parent–child relation, we can turn it into "*God's gift box*" *imagery*. Its specific operation is as follows:

Guide the client to imagine that his or her father and mother received a gift box from God. Now, open these two boxes separately and see what animals are inside. What kind of food is used by the father and mother to feed their respective animal? Where do they arrange their respective animal to live?

Focus: Whether the love given by parents matches the nature of the child.

Therapeutic significance: To promote inner communication and build the parent–child relation.

In the process of applying this initial imagery, it is often necessary for an imagery communication psychotherapist to guide the imaginary parents to be proactive in paying attention to the animals' feelings. Its symbolism is to care about the child's soulful needs and respect the child's real feelings.

If the client is a parent and imagines the relationship with his/her child, the imagery communication psychotherapist can tell the client the following when necessary: good parents are not born, but learn it.

In clinical practice, we always encountered such parents who felt self-reproach and were even devoured by guilt for realizing the harm of their parenting style. After accompanying them to release the negative emotions with self-awareness, we must tell them that the best way to compensate the children is to take better care of them.

2.6. *Animals on the grass*

This initial imagery is dedicated to deconstructing personality by imagery, which aims to present the animal sub-personality.

Paragraph 1 instruction:

Please imagine you come to a grass field. You are going to have a special party here today. The party will be attended by all kinds of animals. Now, you just wait for them to appear...

In order to reduce resistance and encourage the presence of various animal sub-personalities, the psychotherapist can also add supportive guidance:

These animals may be what you know or you may not know. There are some you like, and some that you do not like or even feel afraid of... That is all right. It is just an imaginary party.

When the client reports all of the animal images, he/she can go to the next stage of imagination. Sometimes, given the timing, the psychotherapist needs to interrupt this imaginary process and enter the next stage of imagery communication. If time permits, it will be more coherent to deconstruct animal sub-personality by imagery at once. Its consistency will be higher. As to whether it is a one-off or occurs a few times, the psychotherapist decides on the basis of the situation.

Paragraph 1 instruction:

In your imagination, let these animals greet each other in their own way. Then, sit in a circle. They can sing and dance together if they want.

This stage aims to increase a client's self-knowledge. Hence, the psychotherapist can guide the client as far as possible to end the picture in a safe and peaceful atmosphere.

Some imagery communication psychotherapists are used to directing the clients to light bonfires in their imaginations and letting all the animals sit around and open a bonfire party. The clinical practice shows that not all clients are suitable for this imagination. Because for some clients, when some of their animals attending the grass party greet each other in the imagination, their basic feelings are safe and acceptable; however, when being guided to imagine "light a bonfire", they may be so nervous, or even scared. And the nervousness or fear at this moment is likely to be associated with the guidance of the psychotherapist.

As a result, in order to respect the client and avoid unnecessary tension, we suggest that imagery communication psychotherapists use "if you like..." or "if you want..." as they enter the second stage of imagination.

Furthermore, when the client appears in the following situations, the ICP therapist shall directly cut into imagery communication and carry out the targeted healing work:

(1) Sick or injured animals;
(2) An animal with obvious negative emotions;
(3) The relationship between two animals is unfriendly, such as contempt, anger, hostility, fear, etc.

In summary, it can be used to deconstruct sub-personality and move directly into the intervention of the personality level, using animal personality imagery for deep psychotherapy.

2.7. *Look in the mirror*

The purpose of this initial imagery is to understand the self-image of the subconscious mind. Because the exploration is deeper, and more to the negative images, thus, a novice is advised to carefully use it!

During operation, the client is guided to stand in front of a magical mirror in the imagination and observe what appears in the mirror. It is quite easy to see negative images. Many clients are too rational or intuitive to relax enough to influence the depth of their imagination. Consequently, in order to be able to have a more deep exploration well into the self-image, the imagery communication psychotherapist can lead the client into the cave or down the stairs in imagination, and then, encountering a mirror in this process, direct the client to stand in front of the mirror and see what image is in it.

For instance, the client is guided:

In your imagination, you are going down the stairs, a step down a step... walking to the corner, a mirror is hung on the wall. You stand in front of the mirror and see what is in it.

Here again, we emphasize that the beginners of ICP and people who just read the books about it rather than obtaining professional systematic training of ICP better not use the initial imagery of "look in the mirror".

The reason is that if they lack self-exploration experience, lack experience in dealing with a variety of negative imagery, and lack experience in coping with numerous strong negative emotions (such as fear, sadness, pricking of conscience, etc.), they will find it hard to handle this initial imagery.

As a guide, if they are unable to correctly deal with, it will cause the clients to have the following bad situations: the sense of reality abates or is even lost, mood indulgence or explosion, psychological trauma is expounded upon without corresponding healing and so on. It is dangerous not only to users, but also to the clients.

Please do not take risks with yourself or others!

2.8. *Look at the cave*

Like "look in the mirror", the initial imagery of "look at the cave" is also deeply involved in the imagery of negative images and negative emotions. For the beginners of ICP and people who just read the books about it rather than undergoing the accepted professional systematic training of ICP, it is best not to let yourself or others use this initial imagery.

The imagery of "look at the cave" has two purposes: the first is to explore one's own subconscious; the second is to understand one's own mechanism of regression. (Regression is a kind of psychological defense mechanism referring to a person who encountered some trouble in real life, whose psychological age and behavior unconsciously dates back to early childhood, in order to ease his/her inner anxiety.)

The common instructions:

Please imagine you come to a cave. You can walk in if you like. If you need, you can enter the cave with a torch in your imagination. After you walk in, look at it carefully. What is inside?

The cave symbolizes our subconscious and the mother's womb. This means that much of its exploration often reaches deeper psychological contents or early life, which is more likely to show and touch on the gruesome and grotesque images like skeletons and ghosts. The clients always need some mental support.

Therefore, in guiding this initial imagery, ICP therapists usually need to use sincere attitude and gentle intonation to support clients. For example:

No matter what you see in the cave, they are just images. Please believe that I will be with you all the time. You just have to describe what you see. If you have any uncomfortable feelings, speak up.

2.9. *Meditate yidam*

The initial imagery of "meditate yidam" aims to personify a certain positive and healthy mental quality to promote the client to deeply identify with it. In other words, "meditate yidam" is an imagery practice of connecting psychological qualities.

This term originated from tantra. To "meditate yidam" refers to the personal perusal of spiritual development in tantra. The refiner chooses a statue of Buddha, and imagines that the statue of Buddha enters into his chest. It grows bigger and bigger until it is as big as himself. It invades his entire body and integrates with himself. In doing so, the refiner believes that the Buddha's wisdom and compassion can be obtained and he will gradually approach the Buddha.

ICP just borrowed the phrase to express a similar psychological technique: to get someone's mental quality by imagining the integration with others.

The operational method is as follows:

First, choose your own "yidam" or role model. This person can be a celebrity or an ordinary man you know. For instance, if you want to improve your oral expression capability, you can choose someone with strong verbal ability to be your own "yidam".

The principle of selection: The gender, shape, temperament and personality are similar or same. Above all, this person must be positive and healthy.

Second, read the yidam's biography or relevant information, or contact him/her if possible. And you can find his/her photo and try to get to know him/her as much as possible.

Finally, choose an uninterrupted time each day and imagine that the yidam is integrated into your own body. Practice 10–20 minutes every day. Generally, it needs to be practiced for one month. You can imagine your chest being filled with images of him/her. The picture grows bigger and bigger, until it is as big as yourself, completely integrated.

Please note that in the practice of using this initial imagery, the imaginer only needs to be relaxed and imagine, there is no need to think and analyze and deliberately imitate or perform at a behavioral level.

2.10. *Pit or basin*

The initial imagery of "pit or basin" aims to understand the psychological problem that a client faces here and now.

The common instructions:

Please imagine there is a pit (or a basin) in front of you. Take a look. How big is it? How deep? Is there something inside? How far is it from you? If you are already in it, feel the mood at the moment.

The imagery is used to measure and learn about the psychological problems faced by the clients presently. Thus, not all people can see a pit or basin in their imagination. If a client has no mental trouble at the moment, or if a client wants to resolve a mental disturbance that is not present, chances are that he/she cannot see a pit or basin in his/her imagination. Therefore, we suggest that when the psychotherapist can determine the current psychological problem of the client, and it is necessary to further understand the specific circumstances, the psychotherapist can use this initial imagery to enter imagery communication.

Another thing to note is that ICP therapists should not force the clients to "jump into the pit or basin" in the imagination. We must respect the clients and their psychological rhythms.

Guiding principle: To seize the moment to get into psychotherapy, and to respect the psychological rhythms of the clients.

2.11. *Family photo*

The purpose of this initial imagery is to enhance a client's understanding of the inner family and promote self-exploration and spiritual harmony.

The common instructions:

A family photo is emerging in your mind. Please observe carefully. Who are in the picture? What are the location, appearance, dress and expression of each person? Looking at the family photo, what are you feeling now?

If the client has a special feeling for a certain person or persons in the photo, if there is something to say, or there is a desire to express it, the psychotherapist should guide the client to achieve it. When necessary, the psychotherapist can lead the client to imagine that everyone in the photograph is genuinely expressing themselves.

Or further guidance:

Please imagine you apply a magical liquid to the photo. The original image will slowly disappear and show a new image. Everyone in the picture has become something new, maybe a person, maybe an animal, a plant or something else. The situation in the photo also changes. Have a look. What is the picture of the moment?

The specific techniques involved in this section refer to "deconstructing personality by imagery" described in the previous sections.

At the end of this imagery communication, the psychotherapist can guide the client to keep the family photo in one part of his/her body. If the client has experienced the release of desire expression, gratitude and repression during the communication, the psychotherapist can reinforce these positive feelings and wishes at the end.

2.12. *Double imagery and consulting room imagery*

ICP stresses the importance of establishing consultative relations. Good consultative relationship is quite important for psychological counseling and psychotherapy, and can even yield twice the result with half the effort. Basically, an imagery communication psychotherapist's personality, mental state and empathic ability are the key to the clinical work.

To visually show the present consultative relationship, to give an insight into the current psychotherapist and client relationship, and to learn more about psychological counseling and psychotherapy from the eyes of the client, ICP specially designed two initial practices: double imagery and consulting room imagery.

Double imagery is used to evaluate consultative relation and promote the establishment of a good consultative relationship.

Double imagery is that in the whole process of imagery communication, the ICP therapist is always with the client and participates in the imagery experience of the client; at the same time, the therapist tells the client what he/she sees and how he/she responds to it in this process.

Double imagery can use all the initial imagery of ICP. The psychotherapist simply adds a sentence in the guidance:

Please imagine, in the process of seeing all this, I am with you.

The appearance of psychotherapist described by a client in the imagination represents the psychotherapist in his/her mind.

Consulting room imagery is used to understand the psychological counseling and psychotherapy in a client's mind. This initial imagery can stimulate the establishment of a good consultative relationship.

Its common instruction is similar to the house imagery:

Please imagine that you are in a different kind of consulting room. What texture is it? How about the light? What is in it? What are you feeling inside?

2.13. *Return from studying*

In general, "return from studying" has two uses. One is for psychological assessment during group training or group psychotherapy. The other is to make periodic summaries in case counseling or psychotherapy

The common instructions:

Please imagine you are a student. Now, you graduate. Take a look. What have you learnt?

Sometimes, the psychotherapist can facilitate a client's imagination by fortifying the singularity of imagination. For example, the guidance language can be changed:

In your imagination, you have been to a faraway place. Now, you come back in the plane. Beyond the mountains and across the sea, you return to where you started. Look, what are you bringing back?

Or:

Please imagine you are visiting a cave. What does the owner of the cave look like? When you leave the cave, the master brings you into a treasure house. There are a lot of things in it. You can choose one of them to bring home. In the meantime, you have to put aside something as a gift for someone else. What are you taking away?

The thing taken away by the client symbolizes his/her psychological harvest during the training or psychotherapy.

It is interesting to note that in individual counseling and group psychotherapy, with the solution of the mental distress, and as the spiritual growth deepens, many clients will have dreams spontaneously and express about "return from studying" in the dreams and the specific results.

2.14. *Authority imagery*

Each of us grows up with the influence of authority, and the authority image of each person is different. To this end, ICP designed an initial imagery: authority imagery.

In terms of symbolism, many images can represent authority, such as a crown, a dragon staff, a scepter, a high chair, a dazzling halo and so on.

The common instructions:

In your imagination, there is a tall chair in front of you. There is a person on the chair. What does this person look like?

Sometimes we can guide a client to imagine by using a chair in the counseling room. In order to deepen the self-exploration, in addition to lead the client to observe the authority image on the tall chair, let the client feel that part of himself/herself in the face of the authority, namely what the person looks like in the imagination, what the posture is, what the expression is and how the feeling is...

Immediately, the psychotherapist helps these two personality images truly express themselves and sincerely communicate, thus, promoting the client's self-awareness of the authority to coordinate interpersonal interaction and to improve the practical authority relationship.

2.15. *Drawer imagery*

Drawer imagery is used to organize psychological problems and to make them clearer. It can be conductive to calibrating the psychological problems of various layers and facilitating the targeted psychological counseling and psychotherapy, and can also benefit the personal growth of psychotherapists.

The drawer and the contents in it symbolize the psychological problems of various layers. They represent mental contents or some memories sometimes which are not necessarily "problems".

The common instructions:

Please imagine there are some drawers in front of you. Each drawer is labeled. Please see the contents of the labels clearly. If you want, you can open one of the drawers and see what is inside now.

In the process of applying this initial imagery, in addition to paying close attention to the symbolisms of the drawer and the specific things in it, an ICP therapist also needs to pay more attention to the psychological action of a client every time, especially those defensive actions, such as depression, isolation, withdrawal, etc.

Focus: To increase self-awareness and strengthen the sense of reality.

Those unprocessed or poorly handled "drawers" should be considered the main content of the next psychotherapy session. The psychotherapist can identify the work content by looking for the label on the drawer. In doing so, it is not easy to miss and ignore.

2.16. *Initiative selection and promise*

China has a traditional custom: There is an interesting party on the baby's first birthday. The highlight of the party is when the baby chooses and grasps an object that will symbolize his/her future. This custom is called as "Grasping a Week of Goodies" in China. For example, if a baby fetches a book, then it means that the baby will grow up to be a scholar or be intellectual.

This ritual is a choice. The initial imagery of "initiative selection and promise" is also a choice. The difference between them is that the ritual of the traditional custom is a random choice, because the one-year-old is the one who just casually fetches things, and as an initial imagery, "initiative selection and promise" has more autonomy and can be replaced.

When a client chooses what is not healthy in the symbolic sense in his/her imagination, the psychotherapist should guide him/her to select again. If a client chooses a healthy and positive symbol, the psychotherapist will encourage him/her to "save" directly in his/her subconscious mind.

Therefore. the selection is active and profound, and is a commitment.

2.17. *Haunted house on the desert island*

This initial imagery is used in the depth experience of ICP. Thus, it is not suitable for beginners.

The common instructions:

We are going to explore a desert island. You can prepare a toolbox or a first aid kit if necessary. Get ready to go. As if you leave the present environment, passing through a sea, into a separation zone, to a desert island. You walk around. You watch while walking. Do you find a haunted house? If you find a haunted house, please describe it. . .

To "prepare a toolbox or a first aid kit" in the instructions is designed to increase a client's self-support to reduce dependence on a psychotherapist.

The imagery of a haunted house on the desert island can not only find deep psychological problems, but also can focus on solving them. At the same time, it can exercise the mental ability of clients to survive on their own.

The image of the haunted house and its specific contents tend to be negative; even if the image is less negative, the time of psychological intervention will be long. Consequently, in general, only one haunted house is explored at a time.

Psychotherapy principle: Not much, but thorough-paced.

2.18. *Box hiding the terrible things*

This is one of the classic initial imagery in ICP. It explores what is truly feared in a client's subconscious.

An imagery communication psychotherapist can use this initial imagery when he/she can be sure that there is a fear in the client's heart, but is not very clear about the specific content or root of the fear.

The common instructions:

Please imagine there is a box in front of you. (Sometimes, in order to eliminate the resistance and fortify strangeness, this sentence can be modified: Please imagine there is a box under your bed.) There is something terrible hidden in this box. Only if you open it can you know what is inside. Do not worry. It is just an imagination, and I will always be with you. Ok, now open it, please. . .

This initial imagery is dedicated to presenting and resolving the problem of fear. Hence, for those psychological counselors and psychotherapists who have never dealt with their own feelings of fear, or who lack clinical experience in dealing with fear, please do not put the clients at risk!

In essence, taking clients' risks is taking our own risks.

2.19. *Danger and defense*

The purpose of this initial imagery is to learn about what a client considers as danger and the client's coping style at the bottom of his/her heart.

The common instructions:

Please imagine the most dangerous scene... In the imagination, at this moment, you are in it. What is the most terrible danger? How will you respond?

Focus: The psychological defense mechanism or means of the client.

If the defense mechanism a client uses lacks conduciveness and effectiveness (here, it refers to the positive and healthy validity), a psychotherapist should encourage the client to solve the problem by using the attitude and method of "confrontation".

There is an old saying in China: Hide for a while, cannot escape the world.

2.20. *Exploration of the jungle or desert island*

Unlike other initial imagery, generally, it is not used for psychological counseling and psychotherapy, but is more suitable for the early stage of learning ICP.

The purpose of this initial imagery is to understand the learners' desire, expectation and goal for ICP.

The common instructions:

In your imagination, you are going to explore the jungle (or a desert island). What do you want to put down before you go? What do you hope to get? What luggage do you take?

On the way, there is a river (or a sea). How do you get through it? What is the jungle (or the desert island) you see?...

Now, the adventure is over. You come back from the jungle (or the desert island). At this moment, once again, you are in front of that river (or the sea), please observe what it looks like. What is your vehicle this time? Go back to your departure and check your luggage to see if anything has been added. Or, what is missing from the luggage?

When sharing psychological feelings in the group, an ICP therapist should note that some words are for all of the learners in the scene and some of the words are for a certain learner. These differences must be clarified in public.

2.21. *Important relationships*

The initial imagery of "important relationship" was founded by Ms. Cao Yu.

The common instructions:

Please imagine you are in a room with someone important in your life. Look at each person's specific position, the orientation of eyes and expression, etc. Next, all of you become animals. Take a look at the relationship between these animals.

If a psychotherapist wants to explore the inner parent–child relationship of a client, after completing the above steps, the psychotherapist can continue to guide the client to imagine:

In your imagination, your father, your mother and you, one of the three persons quits, and the other two become animals. Please have a look. What are these two animals? What is their relationship like? What is the current state of affairs?

Either way, the focus of this initial imagery is to present "relationships". Therefore, the focus of psychotherapy is also on the interaction and communication between each other.

2.22. *Shop with wishes*

The initial imagery of "shop with wishes" was founded by Ms. Cao Yu.

The fulfillment of any wish requires a certain amount of effort in the real life. This is the exchange of value systems. The same is true in our inner world.

The common instructions:

Please imagine you are walking into a magical store called wish shop. There are many drawers and a wish in every drawer. But you do not know exactly what wish is in each drawer. You can only choose one of them and exchange it.

Now, please open one of the drawers and see what is inside. To take away this wish, you must leave a thing in this drawer for exchange. What have you left behind?

For instance, a client chooses to swap his watch for gold bars in a drawer. It symbolizes that he hopes to gain wealth by spending time in his subconscious.

This initial imagery can help us look back on our life choices, which is acceptance or rejection. It can help us clear our minds, make conscious choices, reinterpret life's past, and present the future we want.

Consequently, its clinical significance is to enhance the client's sense of reality and self-responsibility.

Chapter 11

The Matters Needing Attention

1. From heart to heart

Imagery Communication Psychotherapy (ICP) is "the words of the heart". Heart-to-heart communication is the most reliable. It is most important for an ICP therapist to be able to realize, understand and express the feelings conveyed by the client through the imagery.

In other words, the ICP therapist is just using imagery as a medium. The imagery communication therapist uses imagery and its symbolic meanings to guide the client to present the corresponding mental energy. The focus of psychotherapy is still on feelings, experiences and expressions.

2. Imagery communication psychotherapists must insist on self-growth

All psychodynamics schools of psychotherapy emphasize self-growth of the counseling psychologists and psychotherapists extensively. This is especially true for Imagery communication psychology.

3. Imagery communication psychotherapists must help and supervise each other in the team

For the qualification and evaluation criteria of Imagery communication psychologists, the Research Center of Imagery Communication

Psychology has established special rules and procedures. See the book *Guide to the Clinical Operation of Imagery Communication Psychotherapy*, published by the Beijing Normal University Press in 2012, for further details.

We encourage team members to help each other, promote each other, supervise each other and develop a healthy relationship.

4. Pay attention to the application of words

(1) In the process of imagery communication, the tone of the psychotherapist should be slightly gentle, smooth, steady and low, and the speed of speech should be slower than general conversation but not hypnotic in tone and speed. The principle of intonation and speed is to have a psychologically therapeutic effect, which can help adjust the emotional state of the client and guide the rhythm of the client's imagination and thinking.
(2) Use as little language as possible to trigger the rational logical thinking of the client. According to the needs of psychotherapy, if the ICP therapist must use language with a reasoning character in the process of imagery communication, please use a brief and clear sentence instead of a compound one.
(3) In the guiding language, the ICP therapist can remind clients to imagine strange scenes as much as possible, especially those which are very rational and defensive.
(4) ICP always emphasizes constructive expression.

5. Persistence and insistence

As a psychotherapist, when you are close to the core of psychological troubles, due to the resistance, a client will bypass it or confuse you and use various methods to guide you to leave the key.

Therefore, the psychotherapist needs to make a judgment as to whether the time is right for the client to address and solve the trouble and whether the client has the necessary mental preparation and psychological resources. If the time is not ripe, you will have to wait. If the time has come, you need to know how to be persistent and insistent.

- **Persistence**

It means that the Imagery communication psychotherapist clearly knows what the problem that the client needs to solve is and can recognize and grasp the opportunity rapidly and keenly.

Put another way, the so-called persistence refers to when the ICP therapist is not much countertransferential and can also clearly distinguish emotions between the client and his/her own, can feel the client's strong negative emotions, at the same time maintain the basic stability of his/her hearts and enable his/her own mental state to be kept within the ability scope of psychotherapy.

If the ICP therapist is able to do it, he/she can continue to carry out effective intervention. If not, there will be evasive, offensive or other inappropriate behavior unconsciously in him/her. That will affect the psychotherapy results.

- **Insistence**

The so-called insistence is when the ICP therapist understands quite clearly which issue the clients need to solve at that time and detects quickly and sharply which words and behavior are being avoided and which are actually related with the real problems. When the clients are evasive, the psychotherapist should be able to dispel briefly and expeditiously, and try to prevent the psychotherapy from taking too long and stop the attention of the both sides from straying from the core issue. The ICP therapist must insist that the direction of the focus of both sides be pulled back to the direction of the core psychological problems time and time again.

According to our clinical experiences, this is the best time to identify whether a psychotherapist has the professional workmanship and art. For the psychotherapists without professional workmanship and art, once a state of relaxation is set, the client will mentally escape. If they want to seize this problem, it will take a long time to wait for the next opportunity.

In order to avoid the core problem in their subconscious mind, the clients sometimes throw out a real psychological trouble that needs to be resolved indeed. Even for good psychotherapists with decent abilities, it is not easy to adhere to the core issue that was found originally and they might turn to solve the new problem. The psychotherapists may feel successful when they solve this new trouble. In fact, they do not know they have missed the boat.

There is even a possibility that the clients throw out further new troubles when the psychotherapists turn to deal with the so-called new trouble. If the psychotherapists follow them like this, the final result is likely to be nothing. But those excellent psychotherapists can ignore these so-called new troubles, or just very simply deal with them. They can always hold on to the core psychological problems.

Whether a psychotherapist can uphold or not, in addition to knowing how to do so in terms of strategy, another key is whether a psychotherapist can still stand strong when the client's mood (such as fear or anger) is very strong. This is of vital importance.

6. Demystify ICP and ICP therapists

Imagery communication psychotherapists shoulder a significant moral responsibility that makes the clients understand imagery deeply through psychological education. All images are but the visualization of psychological content, which is the visualization of human emotions, feelings, complexes, desires and demands, rather than entities. They are neither ghosts nor gods, nor psi ability.

After all, imagery is merely a symbol. Do not mystify it.

Chapter 12

Imagery Communication Psychotherapy Unites with Other Psychotherapies

1. Imagery Communication Psychotherapy and Psychoanalysis

At first, Professor Zhu Jianjun, the founder of Imagery Communication Psychotherapy (ICP), developed a strong interest and inspiration in imagery during the psychological interpretation of dreams.

For the strong identification of Jungian psychology, the founder introduced the analysis and interpretation of imagery symbolism to psychology, in particular to clinical psychology, which greatly enriched the understanding of the imagery, symbol and archetype theory, and thus expanded and deepened the "mental energy hypothesis" and the "deep theory of personality" in psychoanalysis, as well as the psychological dynamics theory.

In order to better help ourselves and others self-explore and self-grow, and in order to promote the clinical practice of psychological counseling and psychotherapy, imagery communication technology emerged. Later, it gradually matured and became ICP.

Therefore, ICP is the new branch and development of psychoanalysis. It goes deep into the subliminal world to explore and improve one's personality in a similar manner. However, compared with psychoanalysis, ICP has obvious differences and advantages.

(1) ICP deepens the understanding and application of the dreams

Psychoanalysis theory holds that dream is a disguise. ICP claims that all imagery, including dreams, is a manifestation of primitive cognition, an image of cognitive style, not the result of disguise. By using the symbolic meanings of the images in a dream, an ICP therapist can guide a client from a dream into imagery communication. It can not only deepen comprehending of the meanings of the dream itself, but also can moisten it silently by psychological counseling and psychotherapy.

(2) ICP expands the study of daydreams

In his book *Introduction to Psychoanalysis*, Freud says: day-dream is the product of fantasy... Not having a relationship with sleep, the second common trait, lacking experience and illusion, is just some imagination... Day-dream is called a dream, perhaps because it has the same psychological characteristics as the dream. As far as this feature is concerned, we know very little about it, but we are still studying it (Freud, 1997, 11, pp. 70–71).

ICP admits that daydream is a kind of imagination, but does not think it is just a product of fantasy. In a sense, ICP is a daydreaming mind communication. Nevertheless, daydreams also carry psychological experience, awareness, perception, motivation and mental energy, but may be weaker, lighter or less ambiguous. ICP can make daydreams magnify, deepen and dynamic, so that it has a psychological analysis meaning and clinical value.

(3) The object and method of interpretation are different

Psychoanalysis explains the meaning of dreams. It interprets a dream on the level of consciousness, making it concrete, so that a client can understand his/her subconscious mind to achieve the purpose of psychotherapy.

The interpretation object of ICP is imagery, which extends far beyond the dream, including all the mental objects expressed in the form of imagery, such as night dream, daydream, imagination, association and memory, etc.

The images appear in the client's mind when the psychotherapist is engaged in an imagery communication. The psychotherapist need not translate the symbolic meanings of the images, or even try to break through the defensive and interference of rational analysis. As a result, the two sides always maintain the state of deep unconscious communication.

At the end of an ICP session, the psychotherapist and the client have a cognitive interview, and the psychotherapist only informs the contents of some meaningful analysis when necessary. None of this will affect the clinical outcomes.

(4) The clinical techniques are very different

The clinical techniques of psychoanalysis include: Hypnosis, free association, transference, interpretation of dreams and so on. The clinical techniques of ICP are more abundant. Most of the ICP techniques, micro-technology and sub-technology are not available in psychoanalysis.

(5) The platform of psychotherapy is quite different

Freud's psychoanalysis transforms the original process into a secondary process and then psychotherapy is performed. But ICP directly carries out psychotherapy work in the original process.

This is not only the biggest difference between the two, but also the greatest innovation and advantage of ICP.

2. ICP and Jung's analytical psychology

Since the founder of Imagery Communication Psychology has a high degree of recognition of Jungian Psychology, the source of the two is deeper and closer.

ICP uses imagery as a medium and follows the primitive logic method for deep communication, which is quite similar to Jung's active imagination. I even read "image dialogue" in Jung's English literature.

This similarity, however, is precisely a great disagreement between the Jungian psychology and psychoanalysis psychology. Psychoanalysis uses rational logical thinking to understand the primitive logic, and Jung's analytical psychology uses primitive logic itself to understand the primitive logic.

The founder of ICP used to give a vivid metaphor: if the human unconscious can be compared to the sea, Freud and Jung are all great people studying the sea. The difference is that Freud stood on the shore of the sea, and Jung went into the sea.

To borrow this metaphor, I would like to say that, ICP not only goes into the sea, but also swims and interacts in the vast and profound ocean, and is dedicated to the treatment of sick "Marine lives".

Therefore, also studying the sea, Freud is like a scientific translator, Jung is like a brave adventurer, and ICP is like a wise doctor. In contrast, the active imagination technique in Jung's psychology is like an introverted warrior who imagines and communicates alone, and a psychotherapist gives instructions and explanations. ICP makes imagery "live" and "move", and emphasizes interaction more — the interaction between the psychotherapist and the client, which is between the client and his/her own images sometimes. For instance, a client is guided to "stare at" an image in the imagination, in which the client voluntarily or proactively changes this image.

Ultimately, when using ICP, the psychotherapist is with the client — imagining and experiencing together, confronting and solving together, the two of them explore images full of vitality together.

3. Imagery Communication Sandplay Therapy

Sandplay Therapy was named after Dora Maria Kalff, the student of Jung. Kalff once accepted to psychoanalyze Jung's wife and studied for six years at the Jungian psychoanalytic institute. Thus, Sandplay Therapy is basically a development of Jungian analytical psychology.

In the process of Sandplay Therapy, from the moment a client's hands touches the sand in the sand-tray, all the details are sketching out his/her inner feelings, such as the direction of the sand-tray picture, the movement traces of fingers on the sand, the action of sand-tools, the appearance transfer or disappearance of a certain sand-tool, the energy flow shown in the whole sand-tray and so on. Therefore, when faced with a picture of sand-tray, we need to feel the expression of the client from the bottom of the heart through external forms, and to feel the spontaneous presentation of his/her unconscious.

Whereupon, we can use the symbolism of imagery to make the sand-tray picture speak more. For example:

A child client put a tiger's head in the sand while setting up a sand-tray. The psychotherapist asked him: Why did you put the tiger's head in the sand?

He bit his lip and whispered: She is a tigress. That is awesome.

The psychotherapist: What does she do when she is awesome?

A handful of sand was added to the tiger's head.

He said: If I do not do well, she will hit me. She likes to hit my head.

The psychotherapist: Would you like to talk to the tiger about your feelings or desires?

In this Imagery Communication Sandplay Therapy, the tiger image represents not only the mother of this little client, but also the child's loneliness and fear. Here, psychological healing and growth can unfold.

ICP combined with Sandplay Therapy represents a kind of integration of "non-verbal psychotherapy" and "symbolic linguistic psychotherapy". It will impel the mental energy within the sand-tray itself to flow more vividly and evocatively, which can increase a client's self-awareness and help a client realize the important features of Sandplay Therapy more richly: getting to the heart, using of the hands, shape of the sand.

For the most resistant clients, we can use the fun of Sandplay Therapy to reduce their psychological defense and subtly introduce ICP.

4. Imagery Communication Sub-personality Constellations

Imagery communication is a work that explores the deep personality, so self-awareness, communication and integration of sub-personality are essential to the development of the mind. Our clinical cases show that the work is quite effective in combination with Family Constellations created by Bert Hellinger.

The psychotherapy power of Family Constellations is extremely shocking. It stresses that love should follow the hidden laws of "the great whole". The laws of love have a profound and long-term effect on each of us. When a stone sinks in the upper reaches of the river, the waves and ripples it causes are enlarged so that it affects the downstream parts as well.

ICP and Family Constellations can combine because they have many commonalities: Working in people's subconscious world; believing the love for wisdom and power; advocating minimal intervention in psychotherapy; emphasizing on the feelings of the mind and perception; adhering to the "confrontation", "acceptance" and "insight", and so on. At the same time, there are obvious differences. For instance, the language tools used in ICP are imagery, language rules are symbolic meanings of images, language logic is primitive cognition and so on.

However, the differences will not affect the combination of the two. During clinical operation, the psychotherapist can guide the client to constellate the sub-personality at the level of imagery, and can also bring the sub-personality into a certain form, such as writing on paper, or inviting other members of the group to play the family roles, etc. The key is that Imagery Communication Sub-personality Constellations put forward higher requirements for psychotherapists.

5. Imagery Communication Psychodrama

In 1921, J. L. Moreno, a psychopathologist, was the first to use Psychodrama Therapy at the Vienna psychiatric center. He went to America four years later and began to spread this psychotherapy.

Psychodrama Therapy makes the client discover and grow unexpectedly in the process of creativity and spontaneity by presenting the inner core of the client about the past, current or future. Moreno has always believed that action alone can help individuals awaken things that are not perceived. Psychodrama emphasizes on helping clients to "experience" and "taste" problems during the performance. Its common techniques include: Empty chair technique, role-playing, stand-in technique, mirror technique, magic shop, surreal fairy tales playing, etc.

The combination of ICP and Psychodrama mainly presents the imagery world of a client in dynamic and outward appearance. The plot of a psychodrama can be a client's dream or an image. In addition to focusing on the experience, emotions and interaction between the "roles", the psychotherapist still uses the symbolic meanings of imagery for psychological counseling and psychotherapy.

Before using the method of Imagery Communication Psychodrama, the psychotherapist needs to remind all of the participants that it is not a show for others to watch, but a psychotherapy method, and everyone just needs to be honest and spontaneous. As for expression, the participants also need to be reminded that even when they want to express negative feelings, they are not allowed to harm themselves and others. During the use of this method, the psychotherapist can flexibly combine the various techniques of ICP and all kinds of techniques in psychodrama therapy.

6. Imagery Communication Music Therapy

Music Therapy belongs to art psychotherapy. According to the authoritative definition of K. Bruscia, who was the former chairman of American Music Therapy Association and a professor at Temple University, Music Therapy is a system process of intervention; in this process, psychotherapists help clients become healthy by letting the client experience various forms of music as well as therapeutic relation, as a driving force, which is developed in the psychotherapy process.

Like all psychodynamic psychotherapy, Music Therapy also stresses on the experience and expression of inner emotions, as well as the flow and development of mental energy. To be sure, Music Therapy is not a simple and single psychotherapy, but a scientific and systematic process of psychotherapy, which includes applications of various methods and schools of theory.

In ICP, music itself is an image symbol. All the activities related to music, such as listening, singing, playing an instrument, lyric writing, song creation, improvisation, dance and fine arts, have a symbolic significance. As Gaston, the father of Music Therapy in the United States, points out — the music's strength and value are in its non-linguistic connotations. Therefore, the combination of ICP and Music Therapy is very natural.

You may have heard of the treatment of psychosomatic diseases by using music or dance, and traditional Chinese medicine for the treatment of visceral diseases, and so on. Here, take the inner environment as an example to illustrate Imagery Communication Music Therapy.

We can use music (or fragrance) to provide a new environment and even change the inner environment when a person is in a soft mud state. Nowadays, more and more people attach importance to fetal education. Music is one of the most common. For instance, pregnant women listen to soothing and gentle music every day. Well, what about after birth? What about adults? Do we still have the chance to "recreate the year" and even "rewrite history"?

The inner environment has always been a key point of focus for ICP. This is because a large number of clinical practices show that many clients have various mental disorders or more serious psychonosema, which are often related to the psychological experience in the womb.

ICP uses music expression to realize the other side — step in. As is known to all, all strong expressive mediums can be used as intervention tools, because the strong expressive medium is more easily accepted by others. This is a powerful and direct interpersonal influence. Music expression thoroughly through the individual's intrinsic connection pathways forms a semicircle of the most introverted outside, and we can, in turn, along the way back, with music freely involved in those parts that imagery is unable to get through and intervention, completes the semicircle of the outgoing, and achieves a complete circle.

The speed and intensity of a heartbeat reflects the state of the individual's vitality. Hence, music intervention with the core rhythm of a healthy heartbeat can be used to create a new and influential inner environment, especially in the soft mud state.

The specific operation is as follows:

(1) Preliminary assessment: The current life rhythm and state of a client.
(2) From the current rhythm to Music Therapy, while playing, the psychotherapist should guide the client to gradually change the tempo. If a standard deviation is fast, the client will be guided to stop playing at a slow standard deviation.
(3) After the client accepts a new rhythm that is the opposite of the original pattern, the psychotherapist should lead the client to perform the final standardized debugging and consolidation with a healthy heartbeat rhythm.

Chapter 13

The Self-Growth of Imagery Communication Psychotherapist

1. Self-exploration

1.1. *ICP psychotherapist's own in-depth exploration*

(1) Deconstruction and integration of personality by imagery

This section is detailed in Chapter 5.

(2) Color of character

Color by itself is also an image. People can use colors to express their character. For instance, people who like to wear black year around are either pursuing mystery or inner depression.

Method: Imagine what color or color system you are.

Key points to explore:

- The first is the color or color system of stability.
- The second is emotional color or color system. When affected by mood or the environment, the original stable color or color system will change. There should be some rules and characteristics.

(3) Emotional change

Method 1: Experience the basic emotions one by one, such as happiness, anger, sorrow, fear, shame, disgrace and guilt.

Method 2: Experience all the emotions you feel, such as happiness, superiority, achievability, emptiness, grievance, anxiety, etc.

Method 3: Experience the levels and the mutual transformation relationship of different emotions, which are as close to your primary emotion as possible.

Principles of exploration:

- First, it is necessary to express yourself constructively after the experience.
- Second, for negative emotions that cannot be expressed constructively and suppressed, you have to be aware and release them in a safe manner, such as by drawing pictures and tearing waste paper and so on. Hurting other people's property, personal safety or the mind is not allowed absolutely.
- Third, the general principle of exploring emotional changes is to increase awareness and encourage constructive expression. This safe release, that is also aware, is the bottom line.

(4) The reaction of the body

Method 1: Experience and detect the body's reaction which can evoke emotions, such as cold, heat, non-obstruction, oppression and so on.

Method 2: Experience and detect the emotional feelings carried by bodily feelings.

Method 3: Experience and detect the visceral images — heart, liver, lung, spleen, stomach, kidney, intestine. For example, the spleen image is usually a cow or bread.

Method 4: Detect your breath.

Method 5: Experience and detect the present body posture, find out the relevant potential language (subconscious language) and the emotions behind it.

Method 6: Detect the position of the body in space and the impact of the environment on the body, find out the relevant potential language and the emotions behind it.

Principles of exploration: Positive medical care and spiritual growth should be synchronized.

Instructions:

Consciously identify somatopsychic disturbance and psychosomatic disorder.

The viscus is both physiological and psychological. When your body is not feeling well, you should go to a regular hospital to seek medical attention and follow the doctor's advice. Remember: Psychotherapy and spiritual growth cannot replace physical medicine!

The earliest expression medium of human language is the body; thus, the deeper the mind grows, especially when it encounters an early psychological experience, the more likely it is to somatize, and more attention should be paid to positive medical treatment.

(5) Behavior patterns

Our behavior patterns can be understood by deconstructing animal imagery personality and the interaction between each other.

(6) External interpersonal relationships and internal relations

Apply all the methods and techniques of ICP to explore all the parts of the inner psychological conflicts and interpersonal relationships in reality, such as the parent–child relationship, intimate relationship, attachment relationship, authoritative relationship and so on.

Note: In the existing technology of ICP, there are some imagery practices that specialize in finding and adjusting specific relationships, such as "flowers and insects" — intimate relationship, "adopting small animals" — attachment relationship, "family photo" — family relationships, etc.

(7) Common ego defense mechanism

Method 1: Master the theoretical knowledge of ego defense mechanism.

Method 2: Discover and be aware of your own habitual ego defense mechanisms.

Method 3: Discover and guide your clients to be aware of their habitual ego defense mechanisms.

(8) Complex discovery and processing

There is an opportunity to touch our complexes in the above-mentioned process of self-exploration.

All the methods and techniques of ICP can be used to discover and understand our own complexes or the clients' and deal with it accordingly. More attention should be paid to discovery, understanding and psychotherapy of the core complex.

(9) Exploring countertransference in the course of ICP

An ICP psychotherapist must always be alert to countertransference. All ICP methods can give a psychotherapist a chance to find out, understand and deal with countertransference.

1.2. *Deep exploration of original family and the clan of ICP therapist*

Purpose: Understand your position in the original family and clan. Explore the interactive mode and interaction within the family.

Method: Classical psychoanalysis, Imagery Communication Psychotherapy, all the other methods of psychological counseling and psychotherapy.

Note: The goal of self-exploration is to improve self-awareness and self-perception of ICP therapists. All of the explorations contain the psychological resources that were originally available. Please note the findings and use them actively.

2. Quality training

Like other psychotherapists, ICP therapists have to keep widening their knowledge and strengthening their theoretical cultivation to constantly consolidate the professional foundation. ICP therapists must abide by the basic ethics, strictly comply with the law, social morality, moral rule and the basic professional ethics of psychotherapists, and should have a healthy and good lifestyle.

As an ICP psychotherapist, professional quality training needs to be strengthened constantly, and details are given in the following.

2.1. *The training of improving the ability of empathy*

(1) The training of "direct percipience" of psychological experience of others

This is a spontaneous process. You cannot train the process itself. However, you can make the process easier by some training.

- First, keep your body relaxed. You can do "relatively relaxed psychological counseling and psychotherapy".
- Second, you can imitate the client's posture spontaneously and naturally on the basis of physical relaxation. Do not do it deliberately or exaggeratedly in order to avoid the feeling of being offended.
- Third, pay full attention to the client during the process of psychological counseling and psychotherapy.
- Fourth, use all the processes as auxiliary, such as comprehension and imagination, to inspire direct feelings of the client to promote empathy. Keep in mind that these processes may or may not cause empathy. This is to say, empathy is not the guaranteed consequence of these processes.
- Fifth, it is used to focus on your own bodily feelings and inner feelings in daily life.
- Sixth, during the process of psychological counseling and psychotherapy, you need to train yourself to be able to empathize with your own internal countertransference by your psychotherapist sub-personality.

(2) The training of distinguishing between your own feelings and others

- First, do more psychoanalysis to figure out your own complex and main emotions and feelings that are easy to be generated in various situations.

- Second, as an ICP psychotherapist, if you are constantly experiencing the same psychological feelings on a number of clients, you need to remind yourself that you are likely to be projecting them.
- Third, group training: With the goal of enhancing the professional quality of the psychotherapists or ICP therapists, all group members or trainees have to feel the same object together and try to experience his/her feelings and emotions.
- Fourth, try to concentrate on the client during the process of psychological counseling and psychotherapy.
- Fifth, with the help of an excellent supervisor, work hard to learn to distinguish between empathy and your own feelings.
- Sixth, check the content of empathy with the client, and spin off your countertransference at any time. By focusing on the clients, check and correct the empathy section.

(3) The training of the ability to express feelings

- First, expand your vocabulary to describe emotions and feelings. It is necessary to pay attention to the subtle differences in the mental energy that are carried by different vocabularies.
- Second, practice how to express your physical and emotional feelings accurately and moderately.
- Third, at the right time, use the figurative metaphor (psychological imagery) effectively to express your feelings.

2.2. *The training of improving the ability of acceptance*

Acceptance means that the psychotherapist should allow the client to show his/her negative side, and not consciously or unconsciously deny, dislike, attack or repel clients. In a more positive way, acceptance means to get along with the clients in a caring and loving manner and attitude.

(1) Completely allow the client to be present in the current state.
(2) Make a difference between acceptance and agreement without giving serious thought.

(3) Separate "the client with a problem now" from "the problem" itself.
(4) Confront and endure discomfort with awareness, just keep "looking" or "staring".
(5) Do more personal mind growth to make your "container" more malleable and inclusive.
(6) Deeply understand the client's behavior, thoughts and emotions. Improve your acceptance by understanding.
(7) Do not defend or self-deceive the part that you can hardly accept. Do not express false acceptance to the client.
(8) When you cannot really accept it, please do your best to accept the client and your own "un-acceptance".

Note: ICP therapists cannot kill a person (including animals) or damage things in the imagination. ICP therapists must not act in disgust, dislike and avoidance. An ICP therapist should not reject, belittle and suppress the people or animals in the images, and only need to experience these images with uncomfortable feelings.

Here are some specific practices:

- First, use the "normalized" tone to respond to the clients' "unusual" statements. For example, you could calmly tell an abnormally frightened client "Yes, anyone would be afraid of such a thing."
- Second, you could express your concern and care to the client by asking some questions gently, after the client expresses fear of something that you would not accept.
- Third, express your empathy to the client, even if the empathy is merely a part of it.
- Fourth, when the client feels that he/she is not accepted and points it out to the psychotherapist, the psychotherapist should not be defensive, but be constructively expressive in a normal manner and should use a gentle tone to convey *that specific problems are unaccepted at the present moment.* More importantly, while sharing it, the psychotherapist should also express the real desire to accept.

- Fifth, when the client perceives your un-acceptance and asks if it is the case, you can use an image to faithfully express your "un-acceptance" or "difficult acceptance".
- Sixth, the psychotherapist should express the part of acceptance and love to the client duly and moderately.

Note: ICP therapists should avoid a mistake in expressing love and acceptance — love and acceptance is not just an expression. In other word, do not express it for the sake of expressing. Psychotherapists cannot confuse health with ill health, beauty with ugliness and the boundaries of what it is not. Psychotherapists should be tolerant, but not indulgent.

2.3. *The training of improving the ability to respect*

(1) Understand the differences between others and yourself

Example of group training:

Tell everyone to make a list of things on the paper:

- The things you like to do
- The things you do not like to do
- The things that make you feel the happiest
- The things that make you feel the most miserable.

Each kind of things can be written more than once. Take turns to read out and discuss the following aspects about the things written by others:

- Which things are similar to your own?
- Which things are different from your own? But you can understand it.
- Which things are hard to understand?

Group discussion:

* What is pathological?
* What needs to be changed for mental health purpose?
* What are the different preferences? It has nothing to do with mental health. For the latter, the trainees are suggested to express it in this way that "we are different people, so we have different preferences."

(2) Analyze the fundamental differences between people and their effects

Example of group training:

The trainees can be divided into different personality types with all kinds of personality scales. Then, discuss as a group. What are the characteristics of different personality types? How does this affect their feelings, thoughts and behavior patterns?

(3) Distinguish between your own needs and the needs of others

Example:

The trainees can talk about how they want to help the client and where to start, after reading his/her symptoms report or problem report. Next, they can ask about the hopes of the client. Then, compare both the similarities and the differences, and clarify the different needs of psychotherapists and the client.

To be sure, the client role here can be borne by one of the group members while adhering to the principle of confidentiality.

Note: To be an excellent psychotherapist, you should make more self-analyses to understand how much you need to control the clients.

(4) Use relevant methods of ICP to train

Sample:

Guide the trainees to imagine coming to someone else's yard and observe the barrier outside, such as fence, stockade or wall... then, tell them "if no one is inviting you into the yard in the imagination, but you want to go in. What that might be?"

Training focus:

What level of respect does an ICP therapist have for the boundaries of others? What boundaries does an ICP therapist provide more respect to?

Note: Excessive emphasis on respect should be avoided during the process of respect training so that the psychotherapist won't be afraid to break through the clients' mind boundaries when necessary.

(5) The basic point of showing respect is to focus on others. Pay attention to the basic etiquette at the same time.
(6) Another way to show respect is to ask more about the client's need.

2.4. *The training of improving the ability to be sincere*

In the context of psychological consultation and psychotherapy, sincerity means that consultants and psychotherapists don't provide false information to the clients and faithfully express their opinions, feelings and emotions.

Improving the ability to be sincere consists of two aspects. One is the ability to see reality. The other is the ability to express reality truthfully. These two aspects are always intertwined and cannot be separated.

(1) Psychotherapists should have the courage to face the problems brought by sincerity.
(2) By training in the ability to judge, psychotherapists can understand when to tell the truth, how much of the truth to tell and how to express the truth.

    The basic principle of sincerity is timely and moderate, which is beneficial for the spiritual growth of the clients.
(3) A practice can be used in group training "the part of me that you do not know".

Sample:

The suitable number for a group is 3–7. The group leader is the guide. Everyone takes turns to perform self-disclosure within 5 minutes. The initial sentence is "you may not know, I. . ."

Everyone needs to say one thing about themselves that is unknown to others. After someone has finished speaking, others take turns to give feedback. Each feedback is controlled within one minute. Finally, the self-disclosure person expresses his feelings in about 3 minutes.

Note: In this practice, due to personal threats, the content that is revealed is preferably mild or moderate. The disclosure is not appropriate for a very threatening privacy event.

(4) Role-playing methods can be used to practice how to express sincerely and constructively without hurting, and especially to not be offensive.

For example, practice saying "when you do this, I feel..." and not saying "you make me...". It is worth noting that when you say this, do not evaluate each other. The point is to say what you really feel inside.

(5) For ICP therapists, mere practice training is not enough. What is more important for psychoanalysis is to find the underlying causes that impede being out from within.

(6) Another way to express sincerity is self-disclosure, which means an ICP therapist can open up some of his/her own information to the client at an appropriate time during the process of psychological counseling and psychotherapy. The sole purpose of this is to help the client. It is true that the ICP therapist needs to be self-protective when he/she self-discloses.

2.5. *The training of improving the ability of insight*

There are some commonly used small exercises designed to improve the ability of insight of psychotherapists in ICP.

(1) Using the practice of "looking at the tree" of ICP to train the ability of insight into the clients' temperament.

Sample:

Let the simulated client stand in front of the trained psychotherapist. The trained psychotherapist just looks and feels with his heart. One minute later, he closes his eyes. After closing the eyes, he can use the memory to keep the client image in his mind. The trainer should tell the trainee that the image in his mind will turn into an appearance of a tree, which he should see clearly and carefully as far as possible. Then the trainee draws the tree or marks out the characteristics of the tree in the picture.

In the meantime, the simulated client can also see what kind of tree it is and write it down.

Finally, the image of the tree seen by the simulated client will be regarded as a reference answer to judge the accuracy of the trained psychotherapist.

Another way to do this is to compare the trees drawn by multiple trained psychotherapists and analyze their commonalities and differences. Generally speaking, the similarities of the trees can often reflect the temperament of the simulated client.

Instructions:

- As a cultural symbol or image, trees can symbolize a person's temperature, especially masculinity (the floral image highlights the femininity).
- This exercise is more difficult. Even the tree drawn by a psychotherapist with keen insight will not be exactly the same as the simulated client's. During the training, the trainer should demonstrate this to avoid unnecessary frustration with the trainees.

(2) Train the ability of perception of physical response to emotions

Training steps:

In the first step, the trainer identifies a certain emotion and then allows the trainees to recall or imagine a thing that triggers the emotion.

In the second step, the trainees try to visualize the thing as vividly as possible and experience the following carefully: which part of the body starts the feeling that emotions trigger? Then, which direction does the feeling flow? What happens when it is flowing? What is the final physical feeling?

In the third step, the trainees report the physical sensations they experienced. At the beginning, let the trainees freely choose how to express themselves. Later, they should use color, sound, weight, speed, temperature flow direction and so on to express the specific sensation states that they experienced.

Notes:

1. When a trainee's body sensation is found to be similar to other emotions rather than the preset, the trainer should determine whether the trainee experienced any other emotion by analyzing and interviewing the trainee.
2. The body's emotional response will be influenced by a complex if a psychotherapist has a complex. In this way, when a client shows a certain mood, the psychotherapist's body sensation will be affected by the client's feeling and his/her own complex. In other words, the physical response of the psychotherapist might be due to interaction of the client's feeling and his/her own complex. The psychotherapist should maintain a keen awareness of this.

Therefore, psychotherapists, especially ICP therapists, have to alleviate and eliminate their complexes as far as possible, or at least know what complex they have, to "minus" the feeling caused by the complex from their body sensations.

Instructions:

This exercise is very valuable, but needs to be improved.

2.6. *The training of ability to increase trust*

Psychotherapists should help clients increase trust in psychotherapists to strengthen and consolidate the effect of psychological counseling and psychotherapy. To this end, ICP offers some specific training methods.

(1) Trust yourself: Psychotherapists should boost their inner real self-confidence by solid mental and professional quality training.
(2) Trust intuition: A more and more clear sense of perception can lead to much more intuitive intelligence. The judgment by intuition that is not polluted by emotions and complexes is more trustworthy than any other thought.

(3) Trust the clients: Please believe that every life is naturally full of vitality and wisdom. This life knows better about his/her wants than the psychotherapists. Psychotherapists are just helping the clients wipe away the dust of the complex which covered the vitality and wisdom in order to make the inner power of this life show up more freely and fluently.
(4) Trust the Tao of nature and its causality: ICP therapists should open individual intellectual resources to connect with greater wisdom through constant mind growth and self-transcendence.

Special instructions:

ICP therapists should accept imagery training of "life and death" and "Belief, love, knowing, action" at the stage of a certain level of self-growth. However, such training must meet one of the following conditions:

(1) The psychotherapists should have participated in the first class and intermediate class of Imagery Communication Psychotherapy and passed the examination.
(2) The psychotherapists should have participated in the whole class of ICP.
(3) The psychotherapist should have received this deep training under the supervision of the ICP therapists.

3. Ability enhancement

3.1. *Be familiar with the experience of various image types and their symbolic meanings*

(See Chapter 8 for details)

3.2. *Master the use of basic initial images*

(See the relevant contents in Chapter 5 for details)

3.3. *Train basic skills: Interpret dreams, movies, myths, fairy tales and pictures*

This form of imagery is extremely rich. It is everywhere in our lives, such as dreams, films, myths, fairy, works of art, architecture, costumes, etc. If we are able to consciously experience, feel, analyze and share, we can not only master the basic skills, enhance the sensibility and acuity, and maintain learning interest but also add a lot of fun for this learning and application. (This is called "share" because ICP is opposed to closed doors and self-complacence.)

3.4. *Master the basic knowledge and methods of psychological crisis intervention*

An imagery communication psychotherapist is a qualified psychological consultant or a psychotherapist only when he/she masters the knowledge and methods of psychological crisis intervention. The generalized psychological crisis intervention refers to providing emotional support or psychological support during the acute phase of disaster (natural or man-made). Its primary purpose is to prevent the clients from hurting themselves or others and help them regain their balance.

Crisis intervention (CI) is generally of two levels. The first-order intervention is also called psychological first aid, which is for the clients to reestablish immediate coping to deal with the past in the present. It is often provided by people arriving at the site first, such as policemen, firefighters and first responders. The second-order intervention is also called crisis psychotherapy. The goal is to rebuild life, heal the crisis and integrate flexibility into life again. This work is usually done by counseling psychologists, psychiatric nurses and social workers.

CI needs to include the following factors:

"Two peace" — the peace of body and mind. Peace of body means a need for personal safety, medical needs, survival needs, information and communication. Peace of mind means to protect privacy, maintain secrecy, regain control, and not to be criticized by the physical and mental responses of the crisis.

"Two defusing" — solving and understanding. Solving is the ability to tell the psychological experience of trauma. Understanding means that the helper can express that he/she hears and understands what the client is saying.

"Two prediction" — forecasting and preparation. Forecasting is the ability to predict realistic problems and relevant emotional responses. Preparation means planning for possible problems in the coming days.

The important principles of CI are as follows:

(1) Teamwork: The helpers should respect and cooperate with the command system, and integrate with the basic material saving system to help the survivors and staff.
(2) Implement simple and unadorned contact and communication. The helpers ask the clients if they need help, for example, food, drink, clothing, sun protection articles, magazines, newspapers, communication tools, etc.
(3) Listen to the clients' stories. Listen to the clients without giving advice. Accompany them and adjust their negative emotions. Emphasize the security of the moment.
(4) Attitude is better than skills. Focus on the client's body language. Focus, respect, support, care and make comfortable physical contact (ask the client's wishes).
(5) Assess the need for referral. Carefully assess the symptoms and risk factors of the client. Give appropriate psychological intervention and necessary referral.

In the implementation of psychological crisis intervention, the helpers should have the consciousness of "self-help", in addition to mastering the common physical and mental responses of the disaster and coping with them as well as suicide.

Self-help essentials include the following:

- Setting up the concept of "who provide assistance are also victims". After crisis intervention, the providers also need to accept psychological intervention or counseling.
- Preventing vicarious trauma.
- Seeking team support.
- Maintaining a normal diet and resting.
- Being self-aware and asking for help.
- Managing stress effectively.

3.5. *Be able to perform differential diagnosis and psychological diagnosis*

ICP therapists should have the ability to identify neuroses, personality disorders, severe mental illnesses, suicidal tendencies and the temptation to hurt others, and all contraindications of ICP.

This requires that ICP therapists not only be proficient in ICP but also have mastery over the principal theories of psychology and fundamental ideas and methods of all schools of psychology and be familiar with the elementary knowledge of counseling psychology and abnormal psychology, as well as have basic skills of psychological diagnosis and psychological counseling.

3.6. *Insist on self-growth*

ICP psychotherapists should keep in mind that the improvement of professional quality cannot be stopped in a lifetime.

Chapter 14

Innovative Sub-technique in Imagery Communication Psychotherapy

Since Imagery Communication Psychotherapy (ICP) was founded by Professor Zhu Jianjun in the early 1990s, it has gradually matured during the span of more than 20 years with exploration and development. Under the framework of the essential theory and methods in ICP, some excellent researchers have been developing innovative and valuable sub-techniques.

Imagery communication innovation technology certification was launched from August 15, 2011 by the standing council of the Center for Imagery Communication Psychology, and a lifetime of authorship was granted to each of the new sub-techniques developers in order to encourage technical innovation to promote the academic development of imagery communication psychology and to give credit to the innovative contribution of developers.

All the innovative sub-techniques introduced in this chapter are certified by the Center for Imagery Communication Psychology. All experimenters and users are asked to fully respect the tenured authorship of each innovator.

The developers were sorted by their family names.

1. Cai Chenrui: Imagery painting

(The developer: Career psychological counselor in China)

After Cai Chenrui published a book titled *I Draw My Heart — Imagery Communication Understanding People* with Anhui People's

Publishing House in August 2008, he met many of his peers either at classes or at workshops asking him to explain and demonstrate his method. So, he started to teach "imagery painting" to the larger audience. At the same time, he applied this method to his ICP group activity and the cases he supervised or counseled.

The consulting technique of imagery painting is to guide a painter (client) to experience his/her painting on the basis of the essential principle of Imagery Communication Psychology. The process of exploring and making sense of the painting is the process of solving the client's mental problems and clearing up the mental distress.

One thing to notice is that the painting involved in the "imagery painting" technique is actual painting, not the imagination.

1.1. *Goal*

The fundamental purpose of imagery painting is to solve the psychological problems or eliminate the clients' symptoms. Although it uses the form of drawing, it does not have the function of projective tests, such as Tree–House–Person. Therefore, this technique is not used to evaluate the program and or to analyze the structure of the painting. For instance, it does not answer the popular question "can you (psychological consultant) see what is wrong with me?". The imagery painting does not do it.

Its main purpose is to help a client "experience the problems through painting itself", and to reflect and understand.

1.2. *Scope of application*

This technique can be applied to general psychological problems, serious mental problems and the early stage of neurosis.

In non-psychological consultation, imagery painting can be designed as a group activity.

Age range: 8–60 years.

The main criterion: The subject must have the basic ability of self-awareness and soul-searching.

Application form: Case consultation; group psychotherapy.

1.3. *Principle*

The fundamental principle of imagery painting is consistent with ICP. In imagery painting, painting works as the imagination. For example, when a client says "I cannot draw" or "I cannot draw it", it can be translated as "I cannot see any image" in imagery communication.

For imagery painting, we need to "experience".

When a client understands the images he/she sees, his/her psychological problems are resolved. Similarly, when a painter has a grasp of his/her painting, his/her psychological problems are dispelled.

The implication of imagery painting is still at the subconscious level, i.e. a subconscious adjustment to the subconscious. The subject of ICP is imagery, and the subject of imagery painting is the painting.

1.4. *The premise of observing the painting*

Both the psychological consultant and the client must follow two premises before observing the work finished by the painter:

(1) Not to explore the painter's motives and intentions,
(2) Not to explore the painter's drawing skills.

This is because the psychological consultant's direct purpose and task is to "see the picture", and neither the motives and intentions nor the drawing skill is relevant to the picture itself.

1.5. *The basic principles of observing the painting*

The unique aspect of mental consultation technique in imagery painting is the way it is used to "see the picture". The developer summed up a "20-word guideline" in Chinese to see the picture which can be translated as "Peculiarity; Seeing is believing; Self-justification; Fact Oriented; Back to the painting".

The psychological consultant only needs to follow this guideline to understand the painting and lead the painter to experience and discuss the painting. It is easy to remember, simple and practical.

The following is a detailed description of the "20-word guideline". It is extremely flexible to apply, just like the "16-word policy" of guerrilla warfare, which requires a process from skilled mastery to artistic creation.

(1) Peculiarity

When the painter puts the drawing in front of the consultant, it is the peculiarity that comes out. It should naturally appear before the consultant. It is the special, strange, fancy and unique parts that are worth emphasizing. Only in this way can the personal bias from the psychological consultants be avoided.

For example, it might be strange to see a house in the sky, a house without doors and windows, or some character images missing "parts" on them. When the consultant sees one or more qualities of "strangeness" in a picture, he/she can choose one to start from.

For instance, if the consultant sees a person in the picture with no ears, he/she can ask the painter how this person can live without ears.

This question leads to the painter's thinking and feeling.

The role of this principle is to create the starting point for discussion and exploration.

(2) Seeing is believing

Following the principle of "seeing is believing", the consultant should fully respect the original appearance of the painting and see it as real. Professor Zhu Jianjun once summed it up as "what you draw is what you see".

The purpose of this principle is to guide the painter from his/her own imagination to the actual picture.

For example, a painter draws a person who has three hairs and believes that three hairs represent a lot of hair.

The psychological consultant can state "I just see three. If you mean a lot of hair, please draw them out."

In fact, "a lot of hair" is in the painter's imagination, not in the person's actual painting.

The gist of this principle is to go "serious". It can help the painter return to the objective reality from the subjective imagination, and can also become a starting point for the communication between the consultant and the painter. For instance, with regard to that person with three hairs, the consultant can ask the painter "if this man really has three hairs, what's wrong with him? What happened to him?"

(3) Self-justification

Among the five principles, self-justification is the most difficult one to use. This is because after the consultant has asked about the "peculiarity" and "seeing is believing", the painter needs to provide a reason, and for that reason, it is more realistic and logical.

Again, taking the man with three hairs as an example, if the painter tells the consultant "he purposely left three hairs for the sake of fashion" then this is a logical "self-justification". If the painter says "his hair was blown off by the wind" then it isn't a logical reason.

The other difficulty is that, if the painter says "I cannot draw the hair, so I just draw three as representation. That is the reason!", then it will violate the two premises described earlier. In this way, psychological counseling seems unable to continue.

First, let's talk about the situation where we can continue the story of "three hairs".

Around "three hairs", the consultant can raise a series of questions:

It is not easy to keep only three hairs. How did he manage it?
What is the difference between this fashion and others?
Why not two or four hairs?
How to maintain three hairs?
How long has this image been maintained?
Why did he decide to keep this hairstyle? . . .

As long as the painter can self-justify, he/she will understand more and more about the character and become more and more aware of this person's state of mind, as if the person in the painting lives. In that case, the direct purpose of seeing the picture will be achieved.

Next, let's discuss the situation where we cannot continue. There are many reasons for this. Common ones include resistance, imagination, proficiency, etc. In this case, in order to ensure that psychological counseling can continue, the consultant can ask questions set out below:

If so, what tangible benefits will this person receive?
If so, what disadvantages will it bring to this person?

These two questions need to be thoroughly discussed so that the gains and losses can be compared. Then how you can avoid those drawbacks can be discussed.

This approach can also help the painter to further understand the emotions of a certain person or object in the picture.

(4) Fact-oriented

"Fact Oriented" refers to discussing only what is in the picture, or the way the painting is supposed to be.

For example, if a painter drew a pet dog and he always talked about the dog in his house when he discussed the painting with the counselor because he believed that what he had painted was the pet dog at home. But the consultant and the painter were talking about the dog in the picture. All the discussion centered on the dog in the picture.

Another purpose of this principle is to prevent the painter from moving his eyes from the painting, and to chat about things other than his painting. When "seeing the picture", stopping the painter from talking of what's outside the picture is to divert the painter's attention to self-awareness. At this moment, the "picture" becomes a "mirror". To this end, we need to make sure that the painter focuses his mental energy on the painting itself without leaving this "mirror".

(5) Back to the painting

It is impossible for the painter to not talk about reality at all in the process of "seeing the picture".

For instance, a female college student drew a child who was hiding in a corner (the sex of the figure was not obvious, the painter felt like a boy).

When the consultant used the principle of self-justification and asked her what good the boy in the picture would do for himself in the corner, she thought about it for a moment and said the boy could avoid making a fool of himself in public.

Right after saying that, she suddenly thought of one thing in primary school. When she was in fourth grade, she was a very good student in all aspects. She was often praised by her teachers. Once, however, she was late and was locked out of the classroom by her teacher. She stood outside the door and heard the teacher criticizing her in the classroom. All the students were listening. At that moment, she felt extremely embarrassed. Since then, she had felt humiliated in front of her classmates for a long time.

The painter was originally talking about the little boy in the picture, but suddenly reminded her of a traumatic event in elementary school. In this case, the consultant must allow the painter to finish what she suddenly remembered. The emotions involved also need to be released. After that, the painter will be directed "back to the painting". The consultant can continue "you were criticized by your teacher in public at that time, so you felt like you were making a fool of yourself. Then, what is the little boy in the picture afraid of?" In this way, the painter will continue to observe her painting and discover the real reason why the little boy is afraid of being ugly.

As long as the above five principles of "seeing the picture" can be applied flexibly, the consultant and the painter will be able to find out some "problems" in the painting, and then solve them successfully. This is the healing path of imagery painting.

To sum up, the principle is a kind of bottom line, and also a kind of measure. As a result, it leaves the consultant with a lot of room to create. As long as the principle is grasped, there will not be too much deviation in clinical treatment.

1.6. *Operating steps*

(1) State the problem

According to the convention of psychological counseling and psychotherapy, the clients need to state the problems they want to solve. In general, mental problems can be roughly divided into two categories. One is practical problems supported by external events, such as exam anxiety, marital relationship, insomnia, etc. The other is caused by some inner discomfort, which does not correspond to an actual external event.

Under the premise of following basic conventions, imagery communication psychotherapists generally encourage the clients to describe their inner feelings as much and as detailed as possible. Although the clients often talk about reality problems, imagery communication psychotherapists still pay attention to their mental feelings in reality. Every time a client's inner feelings are fully described, it means that the first step of imagery painting is completed.

After that, the focus will be on the client's painting.

(2) Expand the painting

The general instructions of "expand the painting" step are as follows:

Now, please draw your feelings. You can draw anything you want.

At the same time, tell the client three small requirements:

First, it must be painting, not abstract graphics or scribbling.

Second, no Chinese characters, English letters, numbers, symbols (such as arrows, +, −, etc.) can appear in the picture.

Third, as long as the client can understand the painting, he/she does not have to consider drawing skills.

The painting is usually set in 10 minutes. Of course, the consultant does not have to overemphasize the drawing time. Only if the client has been painting for more than 10 minutes due to long periods of hesitation or pursuit of perfection, the consultant needs to kindly remind the client by sentences like "two minutes! Please finish the painting in two minutes."

Our clinical practice shows that most of the clients can usually complete the painting within five minutes.

(3) Discuss

After finishing the painting, the consultant should have a discussion with the painter (client) according to the "20-word guideline" in Chinese. The following three discussion techniques are provided for reference only.

First, posture. If a certain person in the picture has a special posture, the consultant can let the painter imitate this figure in the same posture. The painter shall not move his/her body without the permission of the consultant. Give the painter encouragement when necessary. At this point, the consultant needs to ask three aspects of the feeling: physical sensation, mental feelings and emotions.

Generally speaking, the painter can experience the above feelings in two or three minutes. These feelings can be viewed as the feelings of the person in the painting. This method helps the painter learn more about the real feelings of the characters in the painting.

Please pay special attention so that no dangerous postures and poses that may cause harm are imitated.

Second, substitution. When a painter's subjective interpretation is too strong, it is recommended to use this technique. The consultant can guide the client by using the following sentences:

If this picture is not yours, what explanation will not fit any more? Or, if this picture is not yours, you may find something new, what might be it?

In this way, the "special" part will naturally emerge.

Finally, time and space. It is beneficial to help the painter find the contradictions or limitations in the picture. The contents of "time and space" include age, time, season, years, area, situation, etc.

(4) Outlook

After some discussions, the painter will find the problems in the picture. Next, the consultant and the painter can look into this painting from a distance. For example, the consultant can ask "if you want to redraw this picture, how do you want to change it?"

It is important to note that the new picture should be reasonable and not take on too much. If the painter insists on changing the new picture again, the consult must respect this. But even this new picture still needs to have an outlook. During the process, the consultant can put forward opinions about the new picture. To adopt it or not, however, must be decided by the painter.

(5) Set homework

The consultant can assign homework for the client to complete one or more new paintings at home (following continuous improvement).

It is necessary for the consultant to warn the painter not to draw many pictures at one time. There are two reasons for this: one is that the painter can make a concentrated effort to finish the psychological homework quickly; the other is that if the painter is not satisfied with each painting and keen to draw very well at a draught. Thus, it is recommended to only draw one picture per day.

(6) Save the painting

The client (painter) should take the pictures to the consulting room every time he/she receives psychological counseling.

Also, the pictures need to be kept in a strong folder or file cover in order to prevent stains and folding.

(7) Interview again

The painter should bring one or more new pictures (including drafts) and chooses one of them by himself/herself.

The consultant then asks specific drawing process details and discusses the new picture with the painter again. If the painter does not finish his/her homework or forgets to bring the new picture, the consultant can invite him/her to complete it at the scene of the consulting room, and then talk about it.

1.7. *Variants*

The above "imagery painting" shows the free way of painting. Clinically speaking, we can also use its variants according to the concrete situation.

Variant 1: Recall the painting.

Based on the different characteristics of painters, adopt the method of memory. It means encouraging a painter to recall a painting (especially personage), and then draw it.

Variant 2: Realistic painting.

The consultant puts a simple article in front of the painter, such as a household utensil, toy and so on, and lets him/her draw it.

The remaining procedures are the same. The variants have the same principles of "seeing the picture" and the operation steps are similar to that of the free painting.

1.8. *Taboos*

(1) No using this technique for non-psychological counseling, non-psychotherapy and non-psychology activities.
(2) No using this technique for the persons who lack self-awareness and self-reflection.
(3) No mixing the technique of imagery painting with the analysis technique of projective tests, such as Tree–House–Person.
(4) No damage or discard of the clients' paintings without authorization.

1.9. *Matters needing attention*

(1) For those objects (such as cars, buildings, shoes, hands, etc.) that the painter cannot draw, the psychological consultant should encourage him/her to learn. However, copying isn't permitted.
(2) The discussion about a painting is endless. When the symptoms of mental problems of the painter (client) are basically eliminated, imagery painting consultation can come to an end.

2. Cao Yu: Stratified empathy method

(The developer: Career psychological counselor in China)

2.1. *Goal*

When the content of a client's words is incongruous with the emotions in the heart, this method can allow the psychotherapist to communicate with the client by a type of mirroring without denying or endorsing the expression of the client.

2.2. *Principle*

People's rationality and emotions are often inconsistent. When we consciously express something, our emotions or mood are always inconsonant to it. This inconsistency is mostly unconscious.

When words are expressed, we often connect our inner feelings with speech. Therefore, when the verbal exposition is denied, we naturally feel that our emotions are also denied. It creates a dilemma for the psychotherapist: sometimes in order to be able to mirror the client's true feelings and emotions, we have to mirror his/her "distorted verbal exposition contents" together.

The stratified empathy method solved the dilemma very well. The psychotherapist can gently provide a stratified mirror and empathy to the verbal exposition and emotional expression of the client. This method does not let the client feel rejected and, at the same time, can effectively awaken his/her perception, thus separating the conscious and unconscious contents which infect each other without awareness, and then can more effectively return to the original mental truth.

2.3. *Scope of application*

It applies to the clients who are not aware that verbal exposition is inconsistent with emotional expression and the self-growth of psychotherapists.

Application form: Case consultation; group psychotherapy.

2.4. *Operation steps*

Step 1: First of all, the psychotherapist is in empathy with the content of the conscious level expressed by the client, which includes not only the content of direct expression but also the causal logic. In this way, the client can feel that what he/she expressed is heard and tolerated, and its rationality is understood.

This psychotherapy process also has a demonstration effect on the client.

Step 2: The psychotherapist is in empathy with the original emotion behind the client's surface mood.

Step 3: The psychotherapist checks with the client and connects with his/her emotion. If there is an error in deep empathy, the psychotherapist corrects the error in time and tries to keep up with the client's mental rhythm.

2.5. *Variants*

This technique can be finely adjusted in the face of highly performing clients. Its variant is to follow by empathy of the feeling of "director" and "audience" after empathy with a sentence of the "drama".

2.6. *Matters needing attention*

(1) When the psychotherapist is in empathy with the client's surface mood, the psychotherapist should not be in a hurry to clarify or confront, or even recklessly and forcibly break the resistance of the client, but mirror it with uncritical, non-defensive and uningratiating attitude.

In the process, the psychotherapist's "I" should not get involved as much as possible. The key to use the technique is that the function of the psychotherapist is only a "mirror" that clearly and truly presents the surface layer of feelings, emotions and the inner belief in order to increase awareness of the client.

(2) When in empathy with the deeper mental contents, the psychotherapist must first have enough sensitivity as a basic skill of using this technique. In addition, when expressing to the client, the psychotherapist must give himself/herself and the client room to stay.

Hence, in this step, it is better for the psychotherapist to use this sentence pattern:

But at the same time, I seem to feel something else that has not been expressed behind the emotion, for example. . .

It can give the client some space to feel inside, not stuck or focused on the surface and subsequent emotions. It also gives the psychotherapist a route of retreat in cases where the empathy is not accurate, or the client does not admit that there are deeper emotions at heart; the client will not feel compelled and be brutally analyzed, which leads to a tension or confrontation of the consultant–client relation.

(3) The first and second steps must be used in one expression, with no gaps in the middle. Otherwise, it is very easy for the client to focus on the superficial emotions because of empathy and then it becomes a discussion about surface emotions. In the "stratified empathy method", the main purpose of empathy with surface emotions is not being in empathy with the superficial emotions, but to loosen and breakthrough the client's resistance, and at that moment, the psychotherapist leads his/her perception to deeper and deeper mental contents.

2.7. *Case analysis*

Client: You did it all! I was not so miserable. Since you have started to give me psychotherapy, and when I see my father, I think of that! I could not face him! You have completely ruined my life!

Psychotherapist: I hear you are expressing anger at me. In your feelings, I reminded you of that terrible past. And you cannot face your father any more as if nothing had happened. But at the same time, I seem to feel something else that has not been expressed behind the anger like the sense of hurt that the past brought to you, and the sense of powerlessness and incompetence at this very moment.

Analysis:

The first sentence is the empathy within the client's consciousness. The psychotherapist is receptive to the anger that the client has projected onto her, and has an understanding and mirroring for it without subjective judgment. The psychotherapist has no defenses, no fights, no recognition and ingratiation, and simply subsumed this content into the current relationship between the psychotherapist and the client. It makes the psychotherapist not antagonistic to the client because of the need for self-preservation and clarification. On the contrary, the psychotherapist and the client remain in the alliance of friendly partners due to the mirroring reasonableness of the expression of the client and its causality. This virtually defuses the client's subliminal hostility and resistance.

The second sentence is a deeper push, mirroring the subconscious content and its emotion that the client has not been aware of. The understanding type of mirroring makes the client start to pay close attention to the deeper level of feelings and emotions. The client unknowingly removed defense of the surface, thereby turning to the present from falling into the past.

Client (eye sockets suddenly turned red): Yes, I am completely at a loss now! In any case, I have to face him. Whatever he did, he is my father after all. And he is old now, I cannot get rid of him.

Psychotherapist: Yeah! So you find yourself in a tight corner. On one hand, you are too hurt to forgive him, so you do not want to see him. But on the other hand, you cannot abandon him because he is your biological father and you are his own flesh and blood. You still love him.

Client: Um . . . (sheds tears) But what on earth should I do? I do not want to go on like this.

Psychotherapist: Now you want to solve this dilemma. That means we are starting to get a chance to focus on the solutions. If an engineer wants to fix an appliance, what should he do first?

Client: First, he needs to know what the problem is.

Psychotherapist: Yes, so, what is the problem you want to solve?

Client: My problem is that there are always two voices in my heart! One voice says "he died a punk! Never see him again!" Another voice says "how can you be so cruel! He is your father after all. And he was so good to you as a kid!"

Psychotherapist: Who are the two voices from respectively?

Client: The first voice comes from a girl of fifteen or sixteen. The second voice comes from a younger girl, about seven or eight years old.

Psychotherapist: Oh, I see. They must have their own stories. Let's listen to their stories.

Client: Ok. How to listen?

Psychotherapist: These two girls, who is closer to you?

Client: That seven or eight years old one.

Psychotherapist: What does she look like?

Client: She is fat and with doll hair. She is so happy. She is wearing a white and freckled skirt. She is very clean.

Psychotherapist: Is she willing to talk to you?

Client: She tells me . . . (enter the story)

Psychotherapist: No wonder she objects to that older girl about abandoning her father.

Client: Yeah.

Psychotherapist: But I believe that the older girl must have a reason for such a thought. Would you like to hear her story?

Client: She is wearing a large purple robe. Her face is unsightly and somewhat green. Now she is looking at me with hatred.

Psychotherapist: If this hate can be said, what does she want to say?

Client: I hate you! All of you don't even know me!

Psychotherapist: It sounded like she is expressing an anger emotion because we don't know her. At the same time, however, I feel a sense of loneliness and disappointment when I feel her heart carefully.

Analysis:

This sub-personality is formed in a traumatic event. Before touching that trauma, she naturally has a resistance. At this point, she began to use her anger and attack to protect her more internal sense of hurt. This happens to be the usual pattern of the client, which is just exactly the same as before.

The psychotherapist still used stratified empathy method. Her first sentence mirrored the client's superficial anger with understanding attitude. Her second sentence gently mirrored the deeper emotions behind the client's anger.

3. Cao Yu: Closed integral method

The "closed integral method" is the innovative sub-technique developed by Cao Yu, which is specially designed to improve sub-personality. This method can be used in conjunction with the relevant techniques of sub-personality described in the preceding text, and can be used independently.

3.1. *Goal*

This technique can integrate the over-divided sub-personalities that are disintegrated and refuse to "meet", solve the long-term irreconcilable internal conflicts, and as a result, improve the degree of self-acceptance.

3.2. *Principle*

Most of the time, the seemingly incongruous internal conflicts are caused by the excessive use of an ego defense mechanism — disassociation. The advantage of disassociation mechanism is that the individual can identify himself/herself with what he/she accepts, and the part that does not accept will be continuously depressed into the personality shadow or be abandoned outside the "self".

In this way, a person feels that he/she is what he/she accepts and meanwhile, continues to project the divided and unreceptive part to the outside world. Consequently, the internal conflict is externalized into external conflicts and will cause sharp external interpersonal conflicts.

The "closed integral method" provides an opportunity to connect the two divided parts of the self, to break the isolation, and to gradually mediate it in their interaction of relationship, to eventually make reconciliation of internal divisions that were incompatible like water and fire, and even to lead to integration. It allows the individual's inner original conflicts to be resolved and stops the individual from projecting an actual person as a "bad object", thus making the interpersonal relationship more harmonious.

In essence, this method is "should end it who tied the bell". The two split or isolated sub-personalities come from the forced division of super-ego. Hence, we need to take advantage of the obsessive integration of super-ego to restore things back to normal.

3.3. *Scope of application*

(1) The clients who want to deal with compulsive neurosis, phobia, homosexuality, sexual deviation and so on.

(2) The individuals who are used to the psychological defense mechanism of disassociation and isolation.
(3) The individuals who are committed to self-growth.

3.4. *Operation steps*

(1) If the two divided sub-personalities do not simultaneously reveal their true features, the psychotherapist needs to find the unaccepted and split "half".
(2) If the split sub-personalities are in isolation or refuse to meet, the psychotherapist guides the client to joint those sub-personalities who are willing to resolve the conflicts. The psychotherapist forces the split sub-personalities to be placed in a space and to observe the state of the two sides, and then leads them to release their negative emotions with self-awareness in a timely way.
(3) The psychotherapist gives both sides of split sub-personalities a mediator that connects and forces them to interact, so that the conflict between them can be presented. It allows the client's subconscious to realize that no matter how reluctant he/she is to let them meet, they will meet and clash in a certain situation. Therefore, isolation cannot solve the problem.
(4) In the process of ICP, the psychotherapist deals with the internal conflict by using the method of improving the relations of sub-personalities.
(5) The psychotherapist fully affirms the spontaneous reconciliation and integration and strengthens the effective internal adjustment mode in time.

3.5. *Variants*

The psychotherapist guides the client to convert the separate and isolated mental energy into two animals and keeps them in the same cage in the imagination. Inform the client that one of them might eat the other but it doesn't matter. Ask the client to keep track of the eaten animal (mental energy) until finally they reconcile in a healthier way.

For example:

A client imagined a sheep (weak) and a wolf (strong). In his imagination, the sheep was eaten by the wolf and turned into the dung of the wolf. The dung was broken down and became a part of Earth Mother. The wolf became a corpse after its natural death. The body was decomposed by microbes and turned into a part of Earth Mother like the sheep.

At this time, the division of two mental energies that seem extremely antagonistic finally was eliminated in the Earth Mother's embrace and reintegrated into a new one.

3.6. *Matters needing attention*

(1) In the principle of respecting and accepting the client, the psychotherapist does not need to force two over-divided sub-personalities to accept each other. The psychotherapist merely needs to constantly provide a mediating situation that prompts them to interact.

(2) The split sub-personalities are not required to be integrated every time. As long as the two sides reconcile, the goal of this clinical technique is achieved. Admittedly, it would be nice if the two split sub-personalities naturally integrated into a new sub-personality.

(3) Given the limitation of ICP, we should be careful when facing the clients who have a tendency of personality disintegration (for instance, there are many sub-personalities represented by alien images in the imagination) or have identity recognition disturbance. Do not use this technique alone. Please transfer psychotherapy when necessary.

Let's give a brief explanation by taking an alien as an example. Aliens in a dream often represent people who are not able to be understood by the dreamer and whose characters are distinctly different from the dreamer. As a kind of sub-personality, aliens mainly appear in schizotypal personality disorder, autistic personality disorder and in the early stage of schizophrenia.

The formation of an alien sub-personality is due to serious isolation in the client's inner self where some parts of his/her mind have been completely separated from the other parts, lost in combination with the other parts of the personality drastically, as a result of which he/she cannot understand them. This part has been peeled off from his/her overall personality in his/her mind, so this is the true "schizoid" of personality.

Therefore, the better way to deal with it is through the process of imagery communication where the psychotherapist guides the alien images to interact with other personalities to promote understanding until the alien images become human beings who can understand human emotions. For example, the psychotherapist can lead an alien image to make friends with children in his/her sub-personalities.

Such work can be extremely challenging for the psychotherapist because it requires the psychotherapist to highly accept the client. In addition, the psychotherapist has to face another reality that it is a difficult problem globally, that is, to solve personality disintegration thoroughly according to the development status of psychological science.

3.7. *Case analysis*

Client: I cannot stand shitty persons like them! I just do not want to see them!

Psychotherapist: If a human image can generalize these shitty persons, what image might it be?

Analysis:

The psychotherapist tried to make the bad sub-personality who had been projected to the outside apparent and to impel the client to draw his attention from the outside world into his inner world.

Client: This man is a beggar in his 40s. He is rustic, unkempt, shabby, dirty, smelly, self-contempt, and often picks his nostrils with his black finger nails. He is rubbing his own mud with his dirty hands in public. Others look down on him and spit onto his face. But he is laughing with a look of indifference. That is disgusting!

Psychotherapist: Who is disgusted?

Client: That lady I used to see. She is about 20 years old. She is wearing a snow white dress and a white jade necklace and bracelet. Her makeup is very delicate. She is spotless and so noble. As soon as she appeared, that beggar disappeared. That is always the case.

Psychotherapist: Oh, once she appeared, the beggar disappeared. But every time the beggar appeared, she was there and felt disgusted.

Client: No! Wherever there is the beggar, she will never show up!

Psychotherapist: I see. What if they meet on the narrow path?

Client: That is not going to happen! They are at daggers drawn because they belong to two different worlds!

Analysis:

The psychotherapist tried to put the opposite beggar and lady on the same awareness interface and let the client experience the lady's rejection of the beggar. However, the client denied the lady's response to the beggar. It was not that the client was lying intentionally or arguing irrationally, but that she was actually presenting her own subliminal content — disassociation and isolation.

Psychotherapist: I get it. No wonder you cannot bear to see the persons like that beggar in real life.

...

Psychotherapist: When I say that, I can feel a sense of sadness and despair.

Client slowly sheds tears.

Psychotherapist: If the tears of the moment can become a word, what is it expressing?

Client: I love you. But I really cannot accept the days I used to live with you! So we can only live apart.

Psychotherapist: Is this the lady's words to the beggar?

Client: No. This is what the lady says to the gentleman. The lady can never meet the beggar.

Analysis:

The refusal was so intense in the client's heart that she could not feel this psychological reality that the lady was always with the beggar. The psychological isolation has resulted in the couple's separation.

Psychotherapist: Please tell me the truth. Would you like to make some efforts to relieve the mental distress?

Client: Of course! That's why I came for psychotherapy!

Psychotherapist: What does this sub-personality who is willing to relieve the suffering look like?

Client: She is Meihui. But she could not do anything.

Psychotherapist: It doesn't matter. We can invite Meihui to find someone who is able to solve the problem. And this person isn't in this system. If there was a person, what would she or he look like?

Analysis:

When the client was stuck inside the contradiction that is unable to be resolved, the psychotherapist tried to drag her out of the system by looking for a third party who would be more neutral and was willing to adjust the contradiction, and then guided the third party sub-personality to build an alliance with the psychotherapist to implement mediation.

Another clinical technique is applied here: sub-personality third-party coordination.

Client: He is a rational, 40-year-old man. He is calm and has more autonomy.

Psychotherapist: I have a good idea but it might sounds like a bad one. Do you think he is willing to work with us to try to solve this problem?

Client: Ok. A dead horse is like a living horse. The problem cannot become worse.

Psychotherapist: Very good. Now ask him to lock the lady and the beggar in a closed room. There is nothing in this room. Please look at them carefully. Where are they in the room? What are their body positions and expressions?

Analysis:

The psychotherapist first fully evokes the client's willingness to solve the problem and then brings the method of closed integral into operation.

Client (with a long frown): They are in the diagonals in the room. The lady is standing with her back to the beggar, without even bothering to glance at him. The beggar is not afraid of getting dirty, and so sitting directly on the ground, smiling and looking at the lady's back.

Psychotherapist: What does his smile seem to say?

Client: Look at you, standing in high heels, not leaning against the wall, afraid of dirty white skirt. How tired you are!

Psychotherapist: The beggar seems to care about the lady. When the lady knows what the beggar thinks, how does she react?

Client: Nothing. She doesn't know it. Because she doesn't care about what he thinks at all.

Psychotherapist: Ok. Please imagine. One day passed. They did not eat or drink. There is nothing in the room. What will happen next?

Client: The lady is too tired to stand. She leaned against the wall. Her white skirt is dirty and her hairs are in a mess. But she still does not want to give a glance at the beggar.

Psychotherapist: What does the beggar feel when he sees the lady now?

Client: Why is this girl so single-mindedness? What a pity!

Psychotherapist: Does the beggar feel a little distressed?

Client: No use! The lady doesn't care.

Psychotherapist: Please continue to imagine. Another day passed. They still did not eat or drink. There is nothing in the room. What will happen next?

Client: The lady is so hungry that she has no energy. Her heels were taken off and thrown away. She is sitting on the floor with her back against the wall. Her skirt is dirty and messy. She has not brushed her teeth for two days and she has disheveled hair and a dirty face.

Psychotherapist: What does the beggar feel when he sees the lady now?

Client: The beggar sees that the lady has become down and out like him. He wants to comfort her. But she is still contemptuous of him. He doesn't go.

Psychotherapist: Are they sitting face to face?

Client: yes. But the lady doesn't take a look at the beggar.

Analysis:

In the arduous process, the psychotherapist patiently guided the client to be and experience the beggar and connect his emotions. In the imagination, although the lady was not willing to look at the beggar from the beginning to the end, and also did not know what a man he was, the client began to cross the image surface of the beggar so as to understand his inner mental quality and find out what was inside her heart, which means internal connections have begun to be established. Meanwhile, we can see that the lady's body position opens a door to further acceptance, from a scornful back against the beggar to sitting face to face.

Psychotherapist: Ok. Please continue to imagine. Another day has passed. There is nothing in the room. But someone finally brings a loaf of bread and a glass of water. What will happen?

Analysis:

The psychotherapist sets up a mediator to promote the sharing of food between the two divided sub-personalities.

The psychotherapist wanted them to interact and communicate passively.

Client: The beggar pounced on the food. When he is just about to eat, he suddenly feels sorry for the lady. He thought, as a man, he could not bully the weak woman. So he pushes the bread and water to the lady. The lady glances at the food and swallows. But at the thought of it having been touched by his dirty hands, she has no appetite at once. Finally, the beggar eats the food.

Psychotherapist: All right. Another day has passed. What do they look like?

Client: The lady is starved to death and lying curled up in a corner. She is ragged and dirty with untidy hair and black hands and feet. The beggar ate the food yesterday, and he becomes very energetic today. His clothes look a little cleaner. His face has a glow of health. His body is getting stronger.

Psychotherapist: At this time, someone brings a loaf of bread and a glass of water. What will happen?

Client: The lady no longer has dignity. She is so eager to pounce on the food. But she is so hungry that she has no strength. The beggar is very sympathetic to her and wants to hand her the food. But he is worried that the lady might think he is dirty. He is at a loss now.

Psychotherapist: So what should the lady do?

Client: She has to ask the beggar for help to give the food to her. The beggar lifts her up carefully and gives her water and bread. The lady rests for a while in his arms. Her face is better. Her dress also becomes less bad. At this moment, she suddenly feels that the beggar is actually quite good...

(In her imagination, the two sub-personalities finally started talking. They executed a compromise in the end. The lady was no longer harsh. The beggar became a sincere and honest young man.)

Analysis:

From isolation to negative relationships, and to positive relationships, that is where the technique of closed integral goes.

Usually, the goal of isolation is to avoid conflict. Thus, the negative energy of disassociation will be stuck and become unsolvable. However, with the setting of closed integral situation, the mental energy of isolation can be freed and resolved by confrontation and connection in the negative relationships, so as to eventually be able to realize natural reconciliation.

It is true that spontaneous reconciliation is just a common possibility in this case. Another common possibility is that one of the divided sub-personalities attacks and destroys the other one, since then, the attacker will gradually have compassion for the victim, even guilt and remorse, and eventually make the resurrection and reconciliation through the action of love.

4. Cao Yu: Resource introduction method

4.1. *Goal*

The goal of the resource introduction method is to break the endless loop of "resource scarcity — powerlessness — more scarcity — more powerlessness". It can change a client from lacking psychological support to gradually establishing a psychological support system, then to "independently and consciously using the psychological support system" in order to cope with various internal and external stresses, and eventually to restore vitality and mental health.

4.2. *Principle*

The object of resource introduction includes the internal and external psychological quality resources and relationship resources of the client. Among them, the method of discovering, cultivating and strengthening intangible psychological quality resources is called "quality resource introduction"; the method for the discovery, introduction and internalization of external emotional support in the object relationships is called "model internalization".

We often encounter some "difficult clients" in psychotherapy. Most of them were desperately short of support and mental resources in their early psychological experiences, which lead to a subjective feeling of "no resources" and "no support". When these negative emotions accumulated over a long period, they could form ingrained beliefs that were deeply rooted in their unconsciousness.

These beliefs are constantly being "verified" and validated later in life because of the "anticipation effect". Such clients will become more and more convinced, and accordingly form a series of psychological defense patterns and behavioral coping models.

While the client faces such a death cycle, the psychotherapists can find no way out. To wake up the clients to be sensible of external and internal psychological resources and support can make them consciously and actively internalize and understand these resources, which are simply ignored because their mental energy has been fixed at one time point.

It can make the clients gradually establish an internal support system of self-help and "repository" in the psychological world, so as to facilitate them to have more strength, more internal resources and more health to face the present and future life.

The method of "quality resource introduction" enables the client to discover some kind of a psychological quality resource and gradually apply it through internalization. The method of "model internalization" can make the client find an external object, which has the meaning of psychological support here and now, and gradually learn to call the mental resources of the sub-personality by internalizing this object image.

For example:

A dead baby appeared in the image of a female client. The imagery communication psychotherapist asked her about her attitude towards the dead baby.

Psychotherapist: Do you feel compassion, love or acceptance for this baby?

Client: Yes, I do.

Psychotherapist: Who says yes? Please give her a name.

Client:. . .

Psychotherapist: Good. From now on, she will act as the surrogate mother for the baby. She would lovingly nurture and care for him.

Analysis:

In the imagery communication above, the psychotherapist guided the client to discover the existence of so-called surrogate mother and then applied the mental quality resources of this healthy sub-personality to nourish that dead baby image. This method is quality resource introduction.

If no such nourishing sub-personality exists inside the client's heart, the psychotherapist can let the client internalize the psychotherapist's own image, and by removing contamination, make it become a new implanted sub-personality with positive mental resources. Indeed, the premise of this approach is that the client has established a good relationship with the psychotherapist.

In the above passage, the latter approach is called "model internalization". In essence, it is to awaken an adult helper with the most psychological resources who is best suited to repair or nurture a traumatized sub-personality currently present in the inner part of the client. Meanwhile, the psychotherapist needs to guide the client to connect with such an adult helper in his/her subconscious, and help the client break the old model of destructive object relationship, in order to build a new constructive object relationship.

Through repeated use of this method, the client will gradually build an internal self-supporting system in his/her mental world. Consequently, those new constructive sub-personalities can be proactive in helping those old traumatized sub-personalities. It will enable the promotion of the client's self-healing system and enable it to be activated and applied.

4.3. *Scope of application*

The resource introduction method is applicable to the following clients:

(1) Those who do not admit that there are positive psychological resources inside;
(2) Those who feel extreme inferiority;
(3) Those who seriously lack positive mental resources in the early growth experience;
(4) Those who have depressive neurosis;
(5) Those who have mild borderline personality disorder;
(6) Those who have mild narcissistic personality disorder, etc.

4.4. *Operation steps*

Step 1: Lead the client to discover some psychological qualities or a certain object image with positive mental resources.

Step 2: Through the elaboration of images, the client can create a complete positive image in his/her own inner self. The essence of this step is that, with the aid of external positive resources or an ideal companion and supporter, the similar mental energy in the client's subconscious can be aroused.

Step 3: Remove the contamination and make the positive image internalize the client's own sub-personality.

4.5. *Variants: The method of exporting an archetype image*

In a nutshell, the method of exporting an archetype image is to wake up a suitable archetype and internalize it into an image in the client's inner world. By gradual refinement, the image can eventually turn into a healer sub-personality within the client's heart.

Our most commonly used archetypes are Great Mother and Wisdom Old Man.

For instance, clients with borderline personality disorder are very suitable to internalize the archetype of Great Mother. For clients with borderline personality disorder, the psychological connections between them and their mothers are often exceedingly terrible. Thus, they always see the earth as a black hole or a vortex.

According to our clinical experience, clients with narcissistic personality disorder are quite able to internalize the archetype of Wisdom Old Man. It is so hard for them to connect with others, including psychotherapists. One of the key reasons is that they cannot trust an "incompetent" person. However, the trouble is that when the psychotherapist can be considered "competent" in the end by passing their heavy tests, which means they finally establish connections with the psychotherapist, this is often when they tend to be in a mental crisis. Because they suddenly realize that they are not the most powerful, they cannot bear the sense of vulnerability and powerlessness. So, they want to turn down the psychotherapist to regain a sense of strength. At the moment, they get into intense depression and sense of meaninglessness. The psychotherapist will face a severe test, as some narcissistic clients may choose to self-injure or commit suicide at this stage.

In this case, an effective way out is to let such clients become their own rescuer. The basic operation is that the psychotherapist directs the client into the collective unconscious to connect with the archetype of Wisdom Old Man, and to internalize it as his/her own sub-personality. In this way, the client can not only save himself/herself, but also feel powerful again. Even if he/she realizes that he/she has borrowed the power of Wisdom Old Man, for an individual's narcissism, he/she can accept it.

4.6. *Matters needing attention*

(1) The method of exporting an archetype image is to work at the level of the collective unconscious. It will pose a great risk if

not done properly. As a result, psychotherapists who are lacking sufficient self-growth, unfamiliar with archetypes, or not fully and systematically mastered in ICP are prohibited from using this method.

(2) When the client believes that he/she has no internal resources or they have been destroyed, the psychotherapist should not attempt to modify a so-called "bad object" to a "good object".

At that point, all inner companions and supporters in the mental reality of the client are "very bad". Thus, when the client has not set up other mental resources in the deep heart, focusing on those sub-personalities not only cannot provide any real help but might also hurt the client, due to them being exposed to the trauma without inner psychological support.

4.7. *Case analysis*

Let us share a case of "quality resource introduction".

Psychotherapist: Who is your favorite person in the world?

Client: Nobody! Other people have a little bit of something, but I have nothing! No friends. No one really cares and loves me. Who else in the world is like me who does not even know who my parents are?!

Psychotherapist: I am sorry to hear that. But seeing that you are still growing up makes me feel that you have enormous vitality in your inner.

Client: You are wrong! I am the walking dead. What vitality!

Psychotherapist: So what makes you grow up and find a place in society?

Client: Only because I am not afraid to die. Just live it! You do not have to kiss ass. I know who I am.

Psychotherapist: Please tell me who you are.

Client: I am an outcast. I have nothing at all.

Psychotherapist: How do you feel when you say that?

Client: No feeling. I am used to it.

Psychotherapist: In this way, you are so patient that you can persist in the absence of anything.

Client: As I have said, I am just not afraid to die. Do not compliment me. I know I do not have any advantages!

Psychotherapist: All right. I am not going to impose my views on you. I just want to know, what do you think is good in the world? Or what do you want to get?

Analysis:

At the beginning, the psychotherapist tried to help the client find mental resources in her relationships, but failed. The psychotherapist tried to find mental resources in her internal psychological qualities, but also failed. In this communication, we can see that the client was in a very bad mood. She said a lot of things that did not fit the facts. The psychotherapist understood she was expressing the irrational emotions, so did not confront her.

Instead, the psychotherapist inspired the client to focus her mental energy on a larger scale and to find some overlooked but positive psychological qualities. Obviously, this process was still full of tension. However, the psychotherapist's acceptance and persistence strongly contained her resistance.

In fact, the psychotherapist was a role model: she was repeatedly frustrated, but still did not give up. At the same time, the psychotherapist's consideration also conveyed human-oriented understanding to the client. These allowed the client to give the psychotherapist an opportunity to open a small window in the case of resistance.

Client: No good thing. I do not want to get anything.

Psychotherapist: You mean, love is not good for you. You do not want to be loved?

Analysis:

When the client habitually refused to see anything, the psychotherapist began to focus.

Client: Well... Actually, love is a good thing. It just does not matter to me.

Psychotherapist: Why is love good?

Analysis:

The psychotherapist selectively focused on love rather than the last sentence. Doing so is useful for the follow-up conversation. This is the focus of resource orientation.

Client: It makes people feel warm, dependent and not alone. Living in this world is not so meaningless.

Psychotherapist: If love has color, what color do you think it is?

Client: Red. It is like a drop of arterial blood.

Psychotherapist: Oh, what a living metaphor! If it could get into your heart, what would happen?

Client: Cannot get in! I have no heart.

Psychotherapist: When did you have no heart?

Client: Never had a heart. I am different from everyone else.

Psychotherapist: I see. If this drop of arterial blood could become a seed, what would it look like?

Client: It cannot be a seed, because it has no vitality. It can turn into a stone at best.

Psychotherapist: What kind of stone would it be?

Client: A very tiny chicken-blood stone, an impurity like a cataract.

Psychotherapist: Why?

Client: I do not know. Maybe that is what it was.

Psychotherapist: Do you really want to know?

Client: How can you not understand? I do not care!

Psychotherapist: How big is this chicken-blood stone?

Client: It is of the size of my little finger.

Psychotherapist: Smooth or rough?

Client: Smooth.

Psychotherapist: Cool or warm?

Client: Cool.

Psychotherapist: Please put it in your hands. Do not say anything. Just look at it for a while. How do you feel?

Client: I want to hold it tight.

Psychotherapist: Why?

Client: I am greedy! I want to keep it for my own. After all, it is a gem.

Psychotherapist: Good idea. Where do you keep it?

Client: In my stomach.

Psychotherapist: Aren't you afraid to lose it when you defecate?

Client: You are right. Where should I put it? What do you suggest?

Psychotherapist: If I were you, I would put it in the treasure box.

Client: Yeah! The jewels should be in the treasure box.

Psychotherapist: If there is a treasure box in your chest or abdomen, which one would you prefer?

Client: I would like to put one in every box. But I only have one. Put it in my abdomen.

Psychotherapist: Ok. What does the chicken-blood stone think? Will it stay there?

Client: It says it would prefer to go into the upper box. But if I want to put it below, it would also be acceptable.

Psychotherapist: It takes care of your feelings and desires.

Client (smiling): Of course, it is love!

Psychotherapist: Congratulations. You made it today.

Analysis:

The psychotherapist kept asking for details about the chicken-blood stone to help the client build the connection with her own quality of love deep inside her. After the hardships and a difficult push, the client finally put the image of chicken-blood stone in her abdomen.

The symbol of love was placed in the instinctive region. There was a little distance from the emotional region (chest). However, her love quality revived and began to communicate with her as a part of her life. It must have an impact on her beliefs.

In her imagination, the chicken-blood stone preferred to go to the upper chest area. It symbolized that the client was quite clear in her subconscious: in addition to being related to life's instinct, love should be more connected with emotion.

Client: Oh. But am I taking advantage of others?

Psychotherapist: You mean this chicken-blood stone belongs to someone else?

Client: No. It is in the ground. I find it.

Psychotherapist: So ah. It belongs to you.

Client: Um. I will be relieved.

Analysis:

The client began to focus on his inner feelings, which showed that his love had been activated with awareness.

Psychotherapist: You have a good conscience.

Client: Ha. It's nature!

Psychotherapist: Somehow, I am suddenly worried about its fate. Would you shut it in the treasure box and never take care of it again?

Client: You are worried. I will touch it a lot. Don't you know that jade needs to be nourished. The more you touch and nurture it, the more it will be lubricated and moist.

Psychotherapist: I cannot believe you know jade so well. Now I am relieved. You deserve to be its master.

Client: Of course. And I do not abandon it because I find it. It is my destiny.

Psychotherapist: Jade is the gem with the most integrity, it never despises the poor and curries favor with the rich, only finds the owner of the fate.

Client: I am going to make it a jade pendant to wear on my body, so that we are inseparable.

Psychotherapist: You put it in your stomach, isn't it inseparable?

Client: I cannot see it anytime! If you have a lover, would you like to keep him in your heart or see him every day?

Psychotherapist: Ha ha, you are right! I am convinced by you.

Client (suddenly opens her eyes): I am suddenly thinking, actually I can buy a real chicken-blood stone to wear on my body!

Psychotherapist: Good idea! But you are out of your images. How are you feeling now?

Client: I am fine! I feel refreshed. Because I have love! Today's psychotherapy is awesome!

Analysis:

After the client found the quality of love and allowed it to enter into her own inner self, she intuitively used the technique of borrowing the contamination. She wanted to buy a real jade similar to the jade image in her heart, which means reminding herself that she could be connecting with love all the time. As a result, she began to experience some joy. It is a good turn, but it is just a beginning. The psychotherapist has a lot of work to do.

In Imagery Communication Psychotherapy, one way to use this technique is to externalize a certain positive mental energy that is not easily perceived and put it into a concrete something that can be seen and touched at any time. This thing is like a good transitional object.

Cao Yu noticed that there is a special technique called "thumb stone" in Dialectical Behavior Therapy (DBT). It lets the client put some positive mental energy such as safety or comfort into a small stone that the client can hold when they feel uncomfortable. The difference between them is that ICP only borrows the contamination and must remove it after it is finished, so that the externalized mental energy can be recycled into the interior of the client. Otherwise, the client always puts mental energy into an external object. The client not only cannot be fully aware of the contamination, but can also be prone to a certain level of attachment. In this way, once this object is lost, the client will feel bereft of mental resources.

5. Cao Yu: Homeopathy of contamination

5.1. *Goal*

(1) Resolve the resistance in the process of ICP;
(2) Bypassing the resistance promotes the projection naturally to recycle into the interior of the client, and facilitates his/her understanding of this pattern.

In short, the ultimate goal of borrowing the contamination is to dispel it.

5.2. *Principle*

It is very difficult to perceive oneself in a strong emotional antagonism. Similarly, it is not easy to dispel contamination in a strong emotional state. Therefore, before dispelling contamination, do not confront it. Homeopathy of contamination is an effective method.

In the process of using this method, the client's negative emotions have enough space to be fully present and be expressed, which is like taking a drastic measure to deal with a situation, effectively reducing and defusing the drive of strong negative emotions. When emotional tension is reduced, it is much easier to remove the contamination. Here is a metaphor. The more muddy the water in a vortex, the more difficult it is to clarify by counterforce. If the muddy water can be kept still, we can clearly see the water and the sand.

Specifically, when the client shows a strong resistance, the psychotherapist had better not be in a hurry to distinguish and get rid of the contamination. Instead, he/she can first provide a safe and inclusive "screen" to make the rendering of the client's projected contents. Then the projected contents and projective target will separate naturally. And it will be easy for the psychotherapist to bypass the client's resistance, as well as recycle the projected contents into his/her heart.

5.3. *Scope of application*

(1) The clients who get used to outward projection or external attribution;
(2) The clients who lack the awareness of outward projection or external attribution;
(3) The clients with strong tendency of aggression and outward projection;
(4) The clients with strong resistance when projecting outward;
(5) The clients who have bad psychological boundary or poor sense of reality;
(6) The clients who have serious somatization in the process of psychotherapy and cannot be aware of it;

(7) Quite reasonable clients;
(8) Self-development of psychological consultants and psychotherapists.

5.4. *Operation steps*

(1) When the client projects psychological contents to the psychotherapist, the psychotherapist distinguishes and dispels the contamination in his/her own inner self to avoid projective identification to the client.
(2) The psychotherapist allows the client to regard him/her as a "blank screen" for his/her psychological contents.
(3) The psychotherapist asks about the details of the projected contents, makes them clearer, and guides the client to be aware of the catharsis to promote the mental energy of these projective contents to obtain a certain degree of "recycling".
(4) The difference between the projective contents and the psychotherapist will automatically present when these projective contents are showed safely and adequately. At the point when the difference is large enough, the psychotherapist gently asks the client to give up on the projected object in the real world, and thus makes self-perception.
(5) The psychotherapist directs the client to compare the object in the real world and the object image in the mental world and remove the contamination.

5.5. *Variants*

(1) Proactive borrowing contamination

When we somehow have a special feeling for someone, such as liking and loathing, imagine that the image of this person gradually melts away and becomes another image, which is usually a sub-personality within us.

If we want to explore ourselves further, we can experience another sub-personality with the special emotion for this sub-personality.

The pattern of interaction and emotion between these two subpersonalities is the pattern of interaction and emotion between us and a certain kind of person in reality.

(2) Independent involvement

When the somatic sensation is unable to be locked and perceived, the client's hand can "track" it on the outside of the body. And the connection between the hand and the somatic sensation is established in the imagination. At first, the client's hand passively tracks. Later, the tracking will become autonomous.

For example, a client reported a period of pain in his stomach. He was led to put his right hand on the stomach and move with the pain, and imagine that there was an invisible link between the hand and the pain. When this sense of connection got more and more clear, the psychotherapist guided his hand to move gradually, and then carefully adjusted the speed and direction, until the pain slowly stagnated in a particular location. Finally, his pain became a ball in the imagination. The psychotherapist directed his right hand outward and imagined that the ball was pulled out of his stomach through the link. Consequently, the pain stopped.

(3) Lucky article

This technique is especially applicable to the clients who deny that they have positive mental resources. It is often used in combination with the methods of resource introduction and dispelling contamination. The technique of "lucky article" is divided into 3 stages:

- Stage 1: The client is guided to seek a positive resource from the outside world, and feel its image in the imagination and the psychological connection with it.
- Stage 2: The client is guided to internalize the positive resource of the image and project it outward onto an article that is easy to find and carry. In real life, the client wears and contacts this article frequently, which can promote the positive mental resource to be aroused, connected and strengthened constantly.
- Stage 3: Dispel the contamination. The psychotherapist must show the client that the positive resource on the article is his/her own projection. In fact, it is always in his/her inner self. Even without

this lucky article, he/she can connect with the positive mental resource at any time.

5.6. *Matters needing attention*

(1) When the client projects psychological contents to the psychotherapist, the psychotherapist needs to pay careful attention to the natural resistance in his/her own heart and remind himself/herself not to make any comments or explanations, as well as not be eager to get rid of the contamination. Otherwise, the client will feel that the psychotherapist does not care and does not accept him/her, which will cause the client's resistance and confrontation to intensify.
(2) When the client regards the psychotherapist as a "blank screen" to show the mental contents, the psychotherapist should remember that this is only to help the client present the psychological contents without any comments or sharing of feelings. Otherwise, once the psychotherapist has his/her own attitude and forms an evaluation, the psychotherapist will lose the effect of the "blank screen" and will get involved in the client's "self-amusement", so as to echo the client's mental reality.
(3) In the process of pushing the client's projection back into his/her inner self, the psychotherapist should be careful to use the personal pronoun. Please refer to the following case.
(4) After imagery communication, the psychotherapist must remove the contamination from the client.

5.7. *Case analysis*

Client: Do not put on airs! You think I cannot see who-you-are? I just do not want to expose you!

Psychotherapist: Excuse me, what is my true face?

Analysis:

Here, the psychotherapist used "I" to imply acceptance to the client. It can defuse confrontation and give the client space to present the inner projective contents.

However, the premise of using this technique is that the psychotherapist knows very well that he/she is receptive and inclusive of the projection, but not to identify with it.

Client: On the surface, you are weak and innocent. In fact, your heart is very dark and dirty. You are good at controlling others for your own purpose!

Psychotherapist: What do I look like on the surface? What do I actually look like?

Analysis:

The psychotherapist has asked for two images. In essence, this gave the client a free choice — allowing him to choose one of the most sensual images at the moment, in order to enter a deeper presentation.

Client: On the surface, you look like a weak little girl who is bullied by others. In fact, you are pretending to be pitiful in order to take advantage of others to achieve your ulterior motives.

Psychotherapist: How old am I? Who bullied me?

Analysis:

The psychotherapist locked on an image to respond to and step in, so as not to confuse the two sub-personalities. Just from one of the sub-personalities, it is enough to push the projection back into his heart.

Client: A girl of 14 or 15. She was bullied by a boy.

Psychotherapist: What does the boy look like? Did he really bully this girl?

Analysis:

The personal pronoun used by the psychotherapist is no longer "I" but "this girl". It is "dispelling contamination".

Client: Of course not! He was wronged! (He is clenching his fists and blushing.)

Psychotherapist: You look like you are in a mood.

Client: Yes, I am so angry!

Psychotherapist: If this anger emotion can be expressed in words, what would you say?

Client: I was wronged!

Psychotherapist: Who are you saying this to?

Client: That old witch!

Analysis:

The projection of the client to the psychotherapist was fully presented — the two sub-personalities on the surface and their true faces.

Psychotherapist: What kind of old witch?

Client: Her hands are very sharp and long. There are black dirty things in the nails. She is wearing a black gown and a pointy hat.

Psychotherapist: Take a look at her face.

Client: Lined with wrinkles. Her yellow face is very ferocious with a sinister smile...

Psychotherapist: What did she take advantage of? What is her purpose?

Analysis:

The trauma in reality is presented. It means that the client has returned into his heart. The task of dispelling contamination was successful. The inner insight of the client has quietly taken place.

6. Cao Yu: The method of a connecting device

6.1. *Goal*

- Solve an individual's early complex.
- Resolve the profound influence of family complex on individuals.
- Actively reprint the original negative psychological print.

6.2. *Principle*

Psychological research has found that one's early imprint tends to come from the early stage of infancy or even in the womb. When regression is present at the stage, it is often difficult for an individual to clearly describe or express negative emotions. The individual is addicted to powerlessness, which will expose the individual to enormous trauma that cannot be healed. The experience of clinical practice and spiritual growth shows that the individual's problems at this stage are always the problems faced by his/her biological mother during symbiosis.

Therefore, tracing the source, we can go into the mother's mental world through the carrier of baby or fetus to split and save the trapped baby or fetus as well as let the mother confront her own problems by herself and use her adult psychological resources to solve them.

6.3. *Scope of application*

The method of a connecting device can be used for psychological counseling and psychotherapy, as well as mental development of psychological counselors and psychotherapists. In view of the depth of this technique, beginners are asked to accept the companionship and assistance of imagery communication psychotherapists.

The main scope of application: Clients with borderline personality disorder, individuals in the phase of symbiosis, individuals who automatically regress into symbiosis stage in the process of solving a complex, the treatment of individual early complex, the treatment of family complex, etc.

6.4. *Operation steps*

Step 1: When an individual regresses into the early stage of infancy or fetus, the imagery communication psychotherapist asks him/her about the details of his/her mother to lead the mental energy to this "mother" sub-personality.

Step 2: Guide the "mother" sub-personality to release the negative emotions with self-awareness.

Step 3: Promote the "mother" sub-personality to understand the cause and effect of her psychological trauma and heal it.

Step 4: Make the healed "mother" sub-personality reexperience the fetus in her womb, connect with him/her and reimprint it in order to transform the negative energy into positive.

Step 5: Complete psychological "gestation" and "birth" in the imagination.

6.5. *Variants*

(1) Separate containers

For some clients who are susceptible to others' emotional contagion, this technique can also be used to deal with their excessive emotional responses.

The operation is as follows:

Guide the client to imagine that he/she becomes a container that connects another container through a pipe. The contents in another container keep coming into his/hers container. In the imagination, the client blocks the pipe or separates the two containers and first focuses on and processes the contents in another container. After resolving those negative contents, the client returns to check and solve the issues in his/her own container.

(2) Loosen the mental energy pack

Its purpose is to loosen the two parts of mental energy that are half dead and entangled with each other. The imagery communication psychotherapist directs the client to allow the part that should be gone to get a rest and remain at peace, while encouraging the other part that should be alive to live well.

6.6. *Matters needing attention*

(1) When the client regresses to the early stage of infancy or even in the womb, lease note to not over-focus on the baby or the fetus. Do not allow the client to distinguish or express the emotions of the baby or the fetus because the client's identification with the early stage of life might lead to the inability to distinguish and express, as a baby or a fetus. Hence, we should direct the client's awareness to his/her mother in time, before he/she falls into negative emotions and feels powerless. In this way, by identifying with the mother, the adult psychological function of the client will start spontaneously.

(2) Use the technique of loosening the mental energy pack carefully when facing the subject of death. If used improperly, it will strengthen the death instinct in the individual's subconscious.

6.7. *Case analysis*

Client: I am drowning in black water and floating. I become a little fetus. Too painful! Cannot breathe! I am dying! I am dying! (She is suddenly huddled, trembling and grey.)

Psychotherapist: Please imagine this camera lens pulling out and getting out of the mother's belly. Feel your mother.

Analysis:

When dealing with a complex, the client regressed to the fetal stage automatically and showed a series of somatization reactions. This is because in the early days of life, human emotions are often presented and expressed in somatization. At the moment, it was difficult for her to describe her emotions clearly, and it was easy to indulge in them. Therefore, the imagery communication psychotherapist guided the client to focus on her unconscious mother and activated her adult psychological function naturally.

Client (gradually she calms down and frowns): Mom feels terrible!

Psychotherapist: What are the emotions in this "terrible"?

Client: Fear.

Psychotherapist: What will she say if her fear can be expressed?

Client: I am so young, what should I do later?

Psychotherapist: What is the mother worrying about?

Client: Mom is worried that her husband will not love her.

Psychotherapist: Why?

Client: There is another kid competing with me!

Psychotherapist: It sounds like you are angry.

Client: How could I not be angry? I am still a child! How can I take care of other kids? What's more, the kid I have to take care of is going to compete with me for dad!

Psychotherapist: How old is this mother now?

Client: Eight years old. She just lost her mother (the client's grandmother) who died in a car accident. So, she has got dad.

(The client bursts into tears. The psychotherapist deals with her grief and anger in her images. She is guided back to the images of her pregnant mother when she feels better.)

Psychotherapist: How are you feeling now that you are pregnant?

Client: I am delighted and feel that my life is continuing. But I also feel a sense of loss.

Psychotherapist: Speak it out.

Client: I have just been taken care of, and I am going to look after someone else.

Psychotherapist: You feel a little boy in your womb and he will take away your husband's love for you, right?

Client (nodding): Yes.

Psychotherapist: How old are you now?

Client: Twelve years old.

Psychotherapist: How old is that little boy fighting for love?

Client: He is just born. He is my brother.

Analysis:

By guiding the client to reexperience the mother in her psychological experience, the two mental traumas about the mother could be resolved, and the cause and effect of the trauma could be seen clearly, thus increasing her self-awareness. Consequently, the mother in her mind transformed into a healthier one — a healthier source of imprint.

Psychotherapist: How are you feeling now?

Client (smiling): I am fine. Very happy.

Psychotherapist: You are going to be a mother. You are beautiful when you smile.

Client: My child will be beautiful. I can feel that she is a lovely girl.

Psychotherapist: Do you love her?

Client: Yes! I love her so much!

Psychotherapist: How would she feel if this girl knew her mother loves her so much?

Client: I am in my mom's womb right now. I feel safe and warm. I want to sleep well.

Psychotherapist: All right. Sleep well in your mom's womb. This is your world.

(The client is smiling and seems to be asleep. A few minutes later, she suddenly says: I am going to be born!)

Psychotherapist: Welcome to the world!

Client: I am out! I see my mom! She is very young, with white skin and big eyes. What a beautiful mother!

Psychotherapist: What is her reaction of seeing you?

Client (smiling): She is also very happy and holding me in her arms. Her chest is warm and soft. I can hear her heartbeat.

Psychotherapist: Enjoy this quiet moment. Please keep this good feeling in your heart.

(A few minutes later, the psychotherapist gently awakens her and asks about her feelings. Her face is pink. She said: "This feeling is very good. It is the first time in my life that I feel safe.")

Analysis:

So far, the reimprinting has been done. The client's early sense of security was restored to some degree.

7. Cao Yu: Dreams come true

7.1. *Goal*

By "completing an unfinished wish", the fixed mental energy gets an opportunity to be released, defused or transformed into a new desire to be more realistic.

7.2. *Principle*

Everyone has many wishes and dreams in his/her life. Some dreams are put into action, while some are never paid for. Our psychological experience shows that some of the fulfilled dreams are not what we really want. For those dreams that we have never put effort into, we often take them to heart. As a famous saying goes "when one leaves this world, the most regret is not what he has done, but what he has not done."

As a matter of fact, many dreams and aspirations cannot stand up to facts. In essence, these mental energies are fixed because they were idealized and had no chance to be released or transformed. If we can use imagery to allow them to be realized and tested at the psychological level, these fixed energies will be reassessed, and thus loosened and deconstructed.

As time goes by, the wishes of the past are not actually the wishes of the present. But the persons still unconsciously cling to the past. Therefore, when "dreams come true" at the psychological level, it can promote those original "packaged" unmet emotions and unsanctioned desires to be disassembled, and get the opportunity to be resolved and reconstructed.

7.3. *Scope of application*

This technique is appropriate for all the clients and mental growers who are fixed with the "unfinished wishes".

7.4. *Operation steps*

(1) Guide the client to return to the time of the unfulfilled wish in the images, fully express regret and desire, and release the fixed mental energy with self-awareness.
(2) Direct the client to try to complete this wish in the images.
(3) This unfinished wish is spontaneously satisfied in the images. Or, in the process of implementing it, the client finds that it is no longer important. However, the fixed mental energy is still resolved or transformed.
(4) Guide the client to recycle the mental energy fixed in the past, truly stand in the present, and face the future freely.

7.5. *Variant: Fantasy photograph album*

This variant can be used in conjunction with the method of "dream come true" and ends with it. This technique applies to the client who is still attached to it after a certain dream has been realized in the images, and cannot solve or reconstruct it in real life.

For instance, a client was amputated due to misdiagnosis. For years he had been dreaming that his life would have been wonderful without that unfortunate misdiagnosis. The imagery communication psychotherapist guided him back into the unconscious to reconcile with the doctor whom he hated. Some of his fixed negative feelings were released. But he could not give up the illusion that his body was still intact.

The psychotherapist guided him to use the happiness script as a photograph album in his own mental treasure-house of resources or inspiration and to read it whenever he needed it to get life inspirations and positive experiences from it.

Later, this client turned his fantasy photograph album into a new life goal — he provided psychological assistance to those who had been amputated during the earthquake. Here, please share with us his famous saying: the moment you truly accept the loss, you truly open the gate to the harvest.

The principle of this technique is to acknowledge that there are some wonderful dreams that cannot be realized in life, to face the loss of reality, and to accept the regrets and imperfections of life, and at the same time, to keep a certain amount of space for an impossible dream. Most importantly, do not lose the feeling of reality, but with the feeling of reality and respect, allow a wonderful fantasy to become the precious experience and inspiration of life resources, and even allow it to become "a promising life script".

There should be a space for everything at the psychological level — the fixed mental energy has a chance to unclog and flow.

7.6. *Matters needing attention*

(1) After using the method of "dreams come true", the client should be guided back to the past or the current to promote the released mental energy to face the future. The system at this moment starts the positive circulation.

(2) When using the technique of "fantasy photograph album", the key point is to eliminate all kinds of negative energies one by one. A wonderful dream that cannot be achieved usually has both

positive and negative mental energies. We must break down the two parts.

7.7. *Case analysis*

Client: If only I had the courage to accept his love! Now, nothing can be done!

Psychotherapist: It sounds like you are remorseful. It seems that the choice is still bothering you.

Client: Yes. I regret it so much! I wish I had been brave in the first place!

Psychotherapist: If you could go back and face him at that time, what would you say?

Analysis:

The psychotherapist first gave him the empathy and then led him back to the complex fixation point of the past.

Client (tears): Dear, please forgive me! I know I have missed you forever. I can never be happy. It is my nemesis!

Psychotherapist: You must have difficulties at that time, so you have to make that choice. Maybe you can tell him the reasons to get his understanding.

Client: Dear, giving up our love is a necessity. Not that I did not want our love, but that I did not have the courage to face the public opinion. After all I am a third party!

Psychotherapist: What is his possible response?

Client: He understood my difficulties and did not hate me anymore. But he feels very sorry. Even so, he thinks, our love is worth the price.

Psychotherapist: What do you think of it?

Client: I agree with him.

Psychotherapist: What would you do if you were able to go back to your original choice?

Analysis:

There is an opportunity at the moment. The unfulfilled dream was tried to be completed. Regardless of the outcome, this intervention is a release of fixed mental energy.

Client (closes the eyes and returns to the images of the past): I must choose him without any hesitation and be with him! Actually, it does not matter what others say. The only thing that is important is happiness!

Psychotherapist: What if you were together?

Client: He would divorce and marry me.

Psychotherapist: And then what?

Client: His daughter would live with us. I will try to be a good stepmother.

Psychotherapist: And?

Client: There seems to be a problem. His ex-wife is angry that I have robbed her husband and daughter. She begins to put pressure on her daughter. The little girl struggles and feels miserable.

Psychotherapist: What do you feel?

Client (a rain of tears): I am feeling aggrieved and isolated. I want to leave them. But I still love him... Then I get pregnant. But my husband is not happy. My heart breaks again... It is not anybody's fault. I do not blame him. However, I am too tired. Truly happy love needs to be blessed. This time I really want to leave. I have a miscarriage and leave him alone.

Psychotherapist: You give up your love with pain, don't you?

Client: Yes, I do. I thought we would be happy. But now the pain is much more than happiness. I finally realize that the happy love was a fragile fantasy.

Psychotherapist: Now please return to the original.

Analysis:

The dream script was gradually presented through a series of refinements, and the client had a new insight about it. This communication is more effective and profound than intellectual discussion. Because the fixation occurred at the subconscious level, we cannot reach, transform and reconstruct it through reasoned discussions.

Client: Now I have a feeling of peace and quietness.

Psychotherapist: What would you tell him?

Client: Dear, I love you very, very much. I am dying to be with you. But life is not a fairy tale. Thus, I choose to bless you. I will bid farewell to our love.

I will thank you all my life for your love. As a woman, I want a more complete and happier life. Now I am on my way. Please also bless me.

Psychotherapist: What is his reaction?

Client: He is crying. But he knows I am right. It is hard to make the best of both worlds.

Psychotherapist: What would he want to tell you?

Client: My baby, you are the woman I love the most in my life. I must be responsible for my past. It is a pity that I have no way to fulfill our love. Please forgive me for not giving you a full love. Thank you for your love and understanding!

Psychotherapist: What do you feel when you hear these words?

Client: I am so moved. In fact, I just love him. It is enough that I love him.

Psychotherapist: Will he bless you?

Client: Yes. He will say "I sincerely hope that you will let go of the past and wait for a man who can truly love you and give you happiness. I hope he can give you what I cannot give you. As long as you are happy, I will be satisfied." Then, we are hugging and kissing goodbye affectionately.

Psychotherapist: Where are you now?

Analysis:

During the farewell ceremony, the client released the residual fixed mental energy and would spontaneously enter a new journey. The psychotherapist needs to verify whether her past mental experience has been reconstructed and whether her expectation for the future is positive.

Client: I am standing on a new path. Behind me is a fork in the road. I was lost. But now I know where I am going.

Psychotherapist: How is the road?

Client: This is a newly fixed road. It is very wide and smooth. The distance ahead of it is not yet fixed. But it does not matter. I can take a walk and take a break. Anyway, it is asphalt. The distant road is under construction and will soon be ready.

Psychotherapist: How are you feeling at this moment?

Client: I feel very fresh as if I suddenly put down something I have been carrying for a long time. I see the sun rising and the green grass on the sides of the road.

Psychotherapist: Good. Please take a deep breath three times and gradually get your attention to the real psychological consultation room.

8. Cao Yu: Emotional nomenclature

8.1. *Goal*

Calibrating emotion has a psychological therapeutic significance. The technique of emotional nomenclature names the emotions that lack awareness, and makes those original mix of psychological contents clearly identified and recognized. It helps dissolve the complex further.

8.2. *Principle*

Many times, our psychological troubles are difficult to solve because we cannot tell the different mental contents that are mixed together. When we are able to identify them with every detail, we will have an opportunity to understand each kind of mental energy carrying emotions, sensations, desires and cause and effect, thereby dismantling the fixed mental energy, and conquering each of them, in order to ultimately achieve the purpose of healing.

8.3. *Scope of application*

This technique is applicable to the following cases: Clients who are not able to clearly identify their negative emotions; several mixed emotions occurring at the same time; borderline personality disorder.

8.4. *Operation steps*

(1) When the client shows negative emotions, the psychotherapist first has empathy and discrimination in his/her own heart.

(2) According to the intensity of the various negative emotions, the psychotherapist communicates with the client about the most intense mood and invites the client to identify and check it together.

(3) The psychotherapist names this mood while guiding the client to release it with awareness.
(4) When the client calms down, the psychotherapist analyzes and discusses it in time to deepen his/her cognition.
(5) Follow these steps to deal with other negative emotions one by one.

8.5. *Variant*

Based on the depth of psychotherapy and the client's state of mind, the psychotherapist can name multilayer emotions seriatim in one psychotherapy session, and guide the client to understand their differences and conversion relationships, so as to promote a more profound insight and enhance the ability of managing emotions.

8.6. *Matters needing attention*

(1) In general, the psychotherapist guides the client to explore and name one mood during a single psychological therapy session. This prevents the client from being overwhelmed by the mixture of feelings. The above variant is used only for special cases, for example, after naming the first mood, the second emotion emerges automatically.
(2) In clinical practice, the psychotherapist should encourage the client to name his/her emotional experiences as delicately as possible, such as grievance, frustration, shame, etc. ICP believes that each person is unique. For different individuals, each emotion and feeling may have a unique meaning.

8.7. *Case analysis*

Client: Enough!

Psychotherapist: You are excited. What emotions are so strong?

Analysis:

The client bursts into a mood during the conversation. Based on the internal empathy, the psychotherapist felt that several emotions were mixed in the mind of the client. The top of the surface was anger. Behind the anger may be grief, or even fear or helplessness.

Client: I do not know. But as soon as I hear her name, I really want to slam the door!

Psychotherapist: I take your word for it. Because I can feel your anger at the moment, like a sudden burning fire.

Analysis:

The psychotherapist first mirrored the most obvious and superficial anger.

Client: It is not a fire, but a volcano erupting right away!

Analysis:

The client's sincere expression not only fixed the mirroring of the psychotherapist but also, more importantly, means that she began to pay close attention to perceive and express her anger.

Psychotherapist: Yes. Your fists are tight and your muscles are tense.

Analysis:

The psychotherapist followed the client's feelings and guided her to perceive her body in order to form a more complete experience and awareness.

Client: I feel feverish. My eyes are aching!

Psychotherapist: Yes. Your eyes are bloodshot. You are really angry.

Analysis:

While mirroring the body feeling, the psychotherapist calibrated her current anger.

Client: Yeah, I am really angry.

Analysis:

Because of the constant attention, expression of emotions and continually being mirrored, the client subconsciously accepted the calibration.

Psychotherapist: If you feel very angry, you can jump up and yell.

Client immediately jumps up and yells: Ha! Ha!

Psychotherapist: You can yell harder: ha! I am angry!

Analysis:

The psychotherapist encouraged the client to release her anger with awareness.

Client: Ha! I am angry! I am angry! I am so angry!

Psychotherapist: Do you feel better now?

Client: Much better. My anger is over.

Psychotherapist: What are the body reactions when you are angry?

Analysis:

The psychotherapist talked to her about anger after her mood had largely recovered.

Psychotherapist: Now, I notice that your voice is getting smaller and smaller, and your whole body paralyzes in the chair. Are you tired?

Client: Yes. I feel exhausted.

Psychotherapist: Helplessness or depletion?

Client: It is a sense of helplessness after exhaustion.

Psychotherapist: Would you please experience whether the two feelings are the same?

Client (silent for a moment): They are not the same. The helplessness is mainly physical. I have no desire in my heart. It is lazy, quiet and down. The exhaustion is mainly psychological. I have desires, but it far exceeds my ability. I desperately try to grab something, but I feel overdrawn. There is still a little bit of energy and resentment in my mind.

Psychotherapist: So that is it. You can tell very clearly! What are you feeling right now?

Client: I have both of them. The sense of helplessness is superficial. The exhaustion is more intense.

Analysis:

When the catharsis of the subsequent anger set in, the underlying mood started to show.

Psychotherapist: When did you get that feeling?

Client: Usually after the fury.

Analysis:

The psychotherapist inspired the client to perceive and reflect on her emotional pattern.

Client: At the moment, I do have a clear sense of exhaustion.

Psychotherapist: Is there an unfulfilled desire in your heart?

Client: Yes.

Psychotherapist: You can talk about it now or talk about it later or not. You decide.

Client: Let's talk about it next time. I am really tired now.

Analysis:

The client actively led the conversation to the current exhaustion, which indicated that she had the will and the motivation to solve the relevant complex. However, the client was feeling helpless and exhausted, which is not necessarily a good time to deal with the complex. Sure enough, the client found herself powerless. This sense of powerlessness happened to be one of the contents that she gave to her feeling of exhaustion.

9. Cao Yu: Follow the vine to get the melon

9.1. *Goal*

This is quite a practical way to deal with resistance. Especially when a client has difficulties facing certain images, the method of "follow the vine to get the melon" can effectively neutralize the resistance and promote the confrontation and presentation.

The other purpose is to help a client gestalt "psychological fragments" with a little bit of awareness, so as to understand the bigger picture, enhance self-awareness and further insight.

9.2. *Principle*

For individuals, the mental energy is often presented in the form of imagery. When individuals suffer from trauma, for the purpose of self-protection, some negative psychological contents are put unconsciously in their "shadow", which always shows up as local "fragments" in the images, such as a dead animal or a person's eyes.

The method of "follow the vine to get the melon" can make clients gradually enlarge the field of self-awareness to face those unaccepted mental contents, and promote acceptance and insight to occur inadvertently, so as to achieve a certain psychotherapy effect. For example, a female client cannot face the image of a character. The imagery communication psychotherapist guides her to observe from his shoes, trousers, clothes, face till the whole body.

In addition, in terms of the sub-personality system, we believe that there is no isolated sub-personality, but undetected object relationships. Therefore, this method can be also used for the gestalt of the sub-personality graph and to hunt for the "evil backstage manipulator" of "trapped complex" in the process of psychotherapy.

9.3. *Scope of application*

Deconstruction and regulation of personality imagery; the clients who can only see local mental "fragments"; post-traumatic stress disorder; borderline personality disorder; psychological adjuvant therapy for schizophrenia in rehabilitation period.

Note that psychological adjuvant therapy for schizophrenia in rehabilitation period requires a wide range of psychiatric knowledge and clinical experience. Please do not use it for beginners.

9.4. *Operation steps*

Step 1: Guide the client to fully see the local image that has been presented.

Step 2: Guide the client to release negative emotions with self-awareness.

Step 3: Guide the client to pay attention to and experience the image fragments and gradually expand the mental vision, until the client becomes aware of the whole image.

9.5. *Variants*

In the search for the "hidden sub-personality", the psychotherapist can find out "the man behind the scenes" who influences the client through certain partial clues, such as an evaluation or attitude, etc. For instance, there is often a "peeper" in the subconscious of people with phobia and obsessive–compulsive disorder. We can first guide the client to observe the eyes of the "peeper" and then gradually see the owner of the eyes to understand the true purpose of peeping.

In the images of clients with borderline personality disorder, an organ or a limb fragment of an animal or human is usually present. We can use the same method to help the clients experience the whole animal or person. It has a certain corrective function to their fragmented cognitive style, emotion and behavior.

9.6. *Matters needing attention*

The psychotherapist must keep an eye on the client's physical and mental feeling, especially in the face of some very negative images. Once the client resists, the psychotherapist should lead him/her to release the negative emotions with self-awareness in order to provide a safe psychological space as a mental resource to continue to face the problem.

9.7. *Case analysis*

Client: I can only see one hand.

Psychotherapist: Left or right?

Client: The left hand.

Psychotherapist: What does this hand look like? Is it like an adult or a child?

Client: An adult.

Psychotherapist: A man or a woman?

Client: It is like a man.

Analysis:

The client's report is not clear, and it is likely that the resistance is present. The psychotherapist will focus on the client's feelings and deal with them.

Psychotherapist: How do you feel when you see this hand?

Client: I am a little nervous.

Psychotherapist: How does this mental tension make your body feel?

Client: My back is cold. My neck and hands are tight.

Psychotherapist: Ok. We will be there for you. Feel it carefully.

Client (in a few minutes): I do not feel cold and tight. My hands are loose.

Psychotherapist: Good job! What are the characteristics of this hand?

Client: Its skin is rough. The veins are prominent. There is a lot of fine hair.

Psychotherapist: What is the appearance of the wrist?

Client: The wrist is sturdy and its skin is rough.

Psychotherapist: What is your body feeling now?

Client: I am all right. There is no discomfort.

Psychotherapist: What does the arm of this hand look like?

Client: The forearm is strong and seems powerful. The upper arm is very muscular.

Psychotherapist: The shoulder?

Client: The shoulder is also thick and strong.

Psychotherapist: And the neck?

Client: The neck is very hard and has prominent veins.

Psychotherapist: What is your feeling now?

Analysis:

When images were pushed forward, the psychotherapist guided the client to experience them. This would increase the security and support of the client, which would help face and transform the negative mental energy.

Client: The neck feels stiff.

Psychotherapist: Look at it.

Client: The neck feels relaxed now. I could vaguely see his face... He is my father!

Psychotherapist: Where is his right hand?

Client: He has no right hand. When I was so young, he lost his right hand in an industrial accident...

Analysis:

With this, the psychological content represented by one hand is presented in full. This hand image symbolizes the father of the client. Next, the psychotherapist can intervene with and resolve the correlative complex.

10. Cao Yu: Blind counseling

10.1. *Goal*

The method of "blind counseling" is mainly used to promote the establishment and construction of the consultative relationship.

This method can constructively break through the resistance, accompany the client with psychological defense, and make the psychotherapist and the client feel secure in deep communication when the consultation relationship is not good enough, the client's complex is too private, or when the psychotherapist needs to protect himself/herself (for example, the client is a criminal).

"Blind counseling" is quite effective in resolving "secrets or problems one does not want to reveal". It can promote the client to trust the psychotherapist, and can also avoid a real threat generated by mastering too much personal information, and then skillfully protect the psychotherapist's personal safety.

10.2. *Principle*

In a strict sense, almost all psychological counseling and psychotherapy are done under "covert monitoring" of some degree of psychological defense. Sometimes, a few clients unload their ego defense in the process of psychotherapy, but when psychotherapy is over, their subconscious insecurities may resurface, and the clients might even regret their "carelessness" and "impulsivity".

The developer encountered a male client with personality disorder. After his complex of "exchange of wife" was solved, this client was worried that his name would be made public, or that his secret would be known by his leaders in the company. Whereupon, he threatened the developer that he would destroy her career, or even take "more severe and thorough action" if she did not leave the city where he lived. It took a lot of effort for the developer to defuse his insecurities.

After reflection and exploration, the developer tries to use "blind counseling", which is to ease and adjust the mental energy of the clients without any privacy facts. The psychotherapist allows the client not to share internal mental activity and inner communication, but guides his/her processing method and lets him/her unclog the psychological problems in his/her own mental world.

For those clients who use "performance" to defend themselves, the psychotherapist does not respond to the hysteria images in order to prevent them from gaining psychological benefits. Their resistance will then be loosened and deeper psychological contents will be shown. At the subconscious level, the mental energy that has been wrapped up for a long time can be safely released. And the clients finally get the new insight.

As a consequence, the approach of "blind counseling" achieves "subconscious to subconscious" psychotherapy in a more tolerant manner.

10.3. *Scope of application*

The method of "blind counseling" is applicable to the following clients: Clients who need high confidentiality at the objective level, and for clients whose psychological trauma is open but insecure; placater or histrionic clients; clients with excessive use of projective mechanism and aggressiveness; there is an obvious or potential double relationship between the psychotherapist and the client; clients with narcissistic personality disorder.

10.4. *Operation steps*

(1) The psychotherapist had better use this method before the client overexposes his/her privacy. The psychotherapist can tell the

client that from now on, there is no need to answer the questions, but to present these psychological contents within him/her.

(2) In this process, the psychotherapist uses deep empathy to grasp the depth of work and ask questions.

(3) The psychotherapist will have empathy to the bodily feelings of the client at any time during the whole process.

(4) At the end of psychotherapy, the psychotherapist can tell the client "although I don't know what happened to you in your life, but I believe you do have the ability to adjust yourself by confrontation, acceptance and insight." The psychotherapist could still handle it in this way, if the client discovers a legacy problem later.

10.5. *Matters needing attention*

(1) The most important thing is that the psychotherapist should be well developed and have a high degree of empathy and strong mental endurance, and the courage to face all kinds of negative consequences as well.

(2) The key to successfully use "blind counseling" is timing. The psychotherapist needs to be quick and sensitive about when to introduce this approach to avoid the client's overexposure.

(3) This method is quite demanding for psychotherapists. Therefore, for those psychotherapists who lack clinical experience and self-growth, or who are afraid of clients, please do not use it!

10.6. *Case analysis*

Client: I see a dark red mouth. The lips are very thick and wet. It opens slowly and becomes a hole. It seems to suck the black snake in.

Psychotherapist: What does the black snake feel?

Client: It wants to get in, because it feels that the hole is very moist, warm and soft. But at the same time, it feels bad and tries to escape. Now, its body begins to swell and turns red and hot. It is rolling.

Psychotherapist: Why does it feel bad?

Client: Because that is not where it should go!

Psychotherapist: Who thinks that it is not where it should go?

Client: The owner of the hole.

Psychotherapist: What does the owner of the hole look like?

Client: He is a very big and tall middle-aged man. He is two meters tall. His face is square. His eyes are as sharp as a dagger, as if he could stab into the heart of the snake.

Psychotherapist: Why would he stab the snake?

Client: Because the snake invaded into his territory.

Psychotherapist: Is the snake male or female?

Client: Male.

Psychotherapist: How old is the snake?

Client: Fifteen or sixteen years old.

Psychotherapist: I am going to ask some questions, you do not have to answer them. You just need to look at these images carefully in your mind. Unless you want to share it with me, otherwise, you can say nothing. Ok?

Analysis:

When Imagery Communication Psychotherapy went on here, the psychotherapist was aware that this was a complex about incest. In this imagery communication, the lips and the hole symbolized the sexual attraction of his mother, the owner of the hole symbolized his father in the heart, while the adolescent male snake represented the client himself.

The complex about incest often leads to strong resistance. Not only is the client always unmentionable, but also the psychotherapist is usually implicated in the mind world of the client, especially when the psychotherapist is a maternal middle-aged woman. When the incest complex is exposed, the male client with incest fears would subconsciously project the psychotherapist into his own incest object — his mother. Hence, the psychotherapist used the method of blind counseling at once.

Client: Ok.

Psychotherapist: What does the snake feel about facing the hole?

His face is flushed and his neck is blue. Then he wants to throw up.

Psychotherapist: If you want to throw up, you can spit it out in the image and see what it is.

Client: Ok. (After a while, he calms down.)

Psychotherapist: You can ask the snake to speak to the hole what it wants to say.

Client: Um. It says.

Psychotherapist: What is the reaction of the hole?

The client frowns. His breath becomes short and his legs are clamped.

Psychotherapist: You are nervous, aren't you?

The client nods.

Psychotherapist: The hole can try to speak to the snake.

Client: Um. It feels better.

Psychotherapist: They can communicate sincerely with each other now.

Client: Well . . . they have done.

Psychotherapist: If the owner of the hole appears, what will happen?

Analysis:

Under the guidance of the psychotherapist, the client successfully confronted the incest fear, and in the images, the client communicated with his subconscious mother in a symbolic form, and released some repressed mental energy. However, this complex had not been completely resolved. It was an Oedipus triangle relationship. Thus, the psychotherapist began to introduce the essential element of father into the imagery communication.

The client turned his head to the left. He slightly raised his head and frowned. Then he regained his composure.

Psychotherapist: The owner of the hole does not harm the snake, does he?

The client nods. Soon, however, he frowns and swings his head.

Psychotherapist: What's wrong with your body?

Analysis:

The involvement of the father image must be causing anxiety in the client, as it also symbolized his superego. The psychotherapist carefully checked the body feeling with the client. On the one hand, it aims to ensure that the client can release the negative emotions with awareness, without being unable to bear it; on the other hand, it can verify empathy. In general, the accuracy of somatic empathy is often higher than that of imagery.

Client: I have a headache.

Psychotherapist: Where?

Client: I feel like there is a hoop on my forehead.

Psychotherapist: Please experience what it is and who put it.

Client: Um.

Psychotherapist: Do you see that man in your imagination?

Client: Yeah.

Psychotherapist: You two do not talk?

Client: No.

Psychotherapist: But both of you seem to want to say something to each other.

The client nods again.

Psychotherapist: If you want to, let them talk openly.

Client: Ok. (After a while, he takes a long breath.)

Psychotherapist: You feel more relaxed at the moment.

Client: Yeah.

Psychotherapist: Do you want the owner of the hole to talk to the hole? You decide.

Client: Next time. I want to get out of this hole now.

Analysis:

With respect, acceptance and companionship of the psychotherapist, the client successfully confronted the incest complex and bravely communicated and reconciled with his father in his subconscious. The owner of the hole no longer attacked the snake as an enemy in the images. This complex was largely resolved. However, it was far from reaching a real solution. The client's relationship with his mother is closely related to his parents' relationship.

From the client's attitude, the owner of the hole and the hole may not be ready for communication and reconciliation. In this place, the psychotherapist was very careful to throw out an intro. On the surface of it, she was asking for the will of the client, and the real goal is to make the client understand the unfinished parts of this complex. Otherwise, it is possible for the client to avoid subsequent processing.

11. Cao Yu: Regression to the overall

11.1. *Background and fundamentals*

In the process of psychological and clinical self-development, Cao Yu found that the existing technology of ICP needs to be supplemented. One of the most important parts is that, like classical psychoanalysis, ICP focuses on the complex of the past. Although the curative effects are always good, there are still limitations. This local psychotherapy is not perfect.

There are three main drawbacks.

(1) Once self-growth stagnates for a period of time, the curative effects may rebound. Because a person's life is a network system, only one line segment is modified or repaired, the influence of the whole system is still limited. For an individual, it is likely that there is a lack of clear insight and mastery of the overall life script.
(2) Traditional imagery communication technology focuses on the past, perceives the present and ignores the future.
(3) As a branch of psychodynamics, ICP takes the subconscious as the emphasis of the work. But as an inevitable limitation, we ignore "behavior" to a certain extent. It makes some clients and self-developers feel like the ability is not equal to their ambitions. For example, there is a car speeding toward the cliff. We check whether the steering wheel is broken. If so, we fix it. However, due to inertia, the car cannot stop or turn around immediately, but continues to glide for a distance in its original direction.

Based on the above thinking, Cao Yu tried to apply the method of "regression to the overall" to herself and clients. It is based on repairing the past now and the detection of the future, and takes a more complete view of one's life script to find the cause and effect, resulting in more essential exploration and insight.

It is as if we are intervening directly on the roots of a tree rather than in the healing of a leaf or a branch. The roots are restored and nourished, and will spontaneously produce positive transformation like "rebirth", thus achieving more profound awareness and autonomy.

11.2. *Operation steps*

(1) A dream fulfilled

This technique is to guide the client to realize his/her unfinished wish in the images. The client needs to be aware of every detail in the process, slowly and specifically. Do not swallow a date whole.

Theoretically, the end of "a dream fulfilled" is no more than two kinds. One is "false respect" (there is a famous Chinese idiom "Lord Ye Loves Dragons", which refers to an apparent love of something that one actually fears), namely when a dream comes true, you find in the specific details of life what you always want is actually the fixation of mental energy. Once you pursue this, your original fantasy is put down. The other is "wish fulfillment", in which a dream is realized in the images, so that the fixed psychological energy can be released and achieve a mental accomplishment.

However, the developer found that the danger remained in the second situation — the client may indulge in the perfect fantasy. Admittedly, this is not a big danger. In general, in our unsolved complex, we can more or less idealize the persistent object. Even if the client indulges in a certain perfect dream, we can continue to guide him/her to observe and detect this addiction. The most important thing is the clear boundary — a dream is only a dream, not the reality.

(2) Metempsychosis and reconstruction

The technique of metempsychosis and reconstruction is to guide the client to experience the past, the present and the afterlife, and then come back to reality to be aware of the cause and effect and talk about the insight. At last, the psychotherapist leads the client back to the past and "reincarnation". It is based on the past that has been spontaneously transformed through insight that reexperiencing the present and the future, reconstructing the life script, and realizing the goal in the deep heart occur.

The extension of this technique is to compare the themes of the old and new life script, explore the inner cause and effect, and achieve a deeper and more essential understanding.

Cao Yu would like to share her life script here. Her past is Qiu Jin (a heroine of the 1911 revolution in China) and the theme is freedom, resistance to failure and martyrdom. Her present is a sacrificial and the theme is to gain eternal life by giving up her life for a moral. Her afterlife is a yogi and the theme is to seek relief by transcending identity of physical life. Throughout the third, she found that the common theme was to achieve a more free life by transcending one life state. As a result, she understood that.

(3) System prediction + system returning

The former method is to guide the client to experience the three generations of his/her own afterlife in the images, draw the family tree diagram, discuss the family complex, and detect the influence of the present on the future. Then, based on the present, the next stage of psychotherapy and spiritual growth is carried out.

The latter approach is to guide the client back to his/her childhood with a new insight, to spontaneously modify the script of his/her three generations of ancestors, and to experience the growth in the new life script. After these psychological contents are completed, the client needs to save them in the deep heart. *It applies to family deep spiritual growth and the clients who are dealing with complexes. It is not suitable for beginners.*

(4) Back to inspection

This technique applies to every complex.

Its specific operation is to guide the client back to the original situation to reexamine after the imagery communication psychotherapist helps the client find and deal with a complex.

For example, a dirty trash can appeared in the images of a client. When the client experienced it, it became a beggar and then became a beautiful girl. At this point, the imagery communication psychotherapist led the client to look at the original trash can again in the imagination. When the trash can and the environment change in a positive way, the psychotherapy could be over.

Instructions:
All the above methods and techniques have been repeatedly tested in clinical cases.

11.3. *Primary variant — replacement manoeuvre*

(1) Fundamental principles and summary

The four methods described above are "regression to the overall" in psychological time. The method of "replacement manoeuvre" is in psychological space.

A large number of clinical experiences show that a person has three sets of systems — subconscious, conscious and behavior. One set of systems going wrong implicates the other two. In other words, for an individual, subconscious, conscious and behavior are indivisible, which like three intangible rings clasping together. Therefore, only psychological counseling or psychotherapy for one set of systems can achieve certain therapeutic effects.

The purpose of "replacement manoeuvre" is to solve the real problems directly and to change the original psychological, thinking and behavior patterns that are destructive in real life. The psychotherapist guides the client to understand the nature and cause of the problem on the conscious level, and then, through the spontaneous transformation of imagery, to complete the subliminal level correction; to complete the connection and reconstruction of the subconscious (life script) to consciousness (belief), through active awareness and insight, and to finally achieve the overall reconstruction of subconscious, conscious and behavior chains, by manoeuvres of the healthy life script in stages.

The method of "replacement manoeuvre" can avoid the disconnection between behavior, consciousness and subconscious and allow the client to change more autonomously and fully.

(2) Scope of application

It is suitable for people who are committed to long-term spiritual growth, personality reconstruction of mild personality disorder, and perfect family system relations. It is particularly applicable to the situation where clients are unable to adjust their behavior and to achieve reconciliation or positive transformation within the subconscious due to the long-term internalized conflict patterns or complicated family problems.

(3) Operating steps and technical essentials

- First, describe the imagery.
  The client is directed into imagery communication to describe a typical conflict scenario that is considered unmediated, including both sides in the conflict of body posture, manner, tone and dialogue, and to imagine it finally becoming a representative photo and to name it.

- Second, watch the imagery performance and gain insight.
  On the scene of psychotherapy, the client chooses two people to play the roles and present it as described by the client. The client watches and shares the feeling and insight. The psychotherapist can ask questions, but try to get the client to understand the answer in the next step.

- Third, play roles.
  The psychotherapist and the client play the roles again. The psychotherapist plays the client and the client plays the opponent. In the process of reconciling the conflict, the psychotherapist can give the client a sense of how different responses can make a constructive change. After that, the client shares the feeling and insight. If a new belief is believed and accepted by the client, the "enemy" can be changed.

- Fourth, internalize the conflicted sub-personality.
  The client plays himself/herself, and the psychotherapist or the other one plays his/her opponent. The new approach is used to resolve the conflict. At the end of the stage, the client shares the feeling and insight, and listens to the feedback from third party observers (who are often not involved in role-playing) and then summarizes.

- Fifth, cover the conflicted sub-personality.
  The final stage is the core and innovative point of this technique. The client is guided back to the past photo in the imagination and to redemonstrate the modified and constructive response process, to freeze the new photo and name it, and then to save it in the subconscious.

Instructions:

(1) The other variant of "replacement manoeuvre": reconciliation in imagery, discussion insight and changing unhealthy belief. Then experience role-playing in real life in order to establish a synchronous connection between behavior and subconscious.
(2) On the cases analysis: this method itself is a huge system of clinical application. This book briefly introduced it. We plan to discuss it in a more comprehensive and more detailed manner in future works.

12. Cao Yu: Conversion channel

12.1. *Goal*

The method of "conversion channel" has a more dimensional "stereo scan" for the whole picture of the client's mental world by calling different sensory and perceptual organs autonomously and flexibly. For instance, when the client experiences a powerful hindrance in the visual imagery, the psychotherapist can guide him/her to the auditory imagery in order to easily dissolve the resistance. Thus, the client can gain a deeper understanding and insight of himself/herself and the world.

12.2. *Principle*

What ICP stresses the most is the constant awareness. The method of "conversion channel" is to switch to the other when a path is blocked. In this case, the awareness of the client can be maintained, although the awareness path might be repeatedly converted. In addition, when it is used to a certain degree, the pathological persistence of the client to the psychological problems will be reduced.

At present, in ICP, the dominant working medium is visual imagery. But we are increasingly finding that the more primitive cognitive systems of hearing, smell, taste and touch play an important role in deeper subconscious. It's just that we have not done enough research on them. Therefore, we first introduce the more mature auditory imagery.

12.3. *Scope of application*

Psychological counseling; Psychotherapy; Deep psychological growth; Personality reconstruction.

12.4. *Operation steps*

This method is very flexible and unable to develop a fixed program. Please see the case below.

12.5. *Variants — finding sub-personality through five senses*

The method of "finding sub-personality through five senses" is to seek for different types of sub-personalities through the visual, auditory, taste, smell and tactile imageries. One's personality structure can be three dimensional. It contributes to deep psychotherapy and mental development. They look like different mirrors, presenting a different picture of the same thing.

There are two kinds of basic operations: initial imagery and timely guidance. For example, design a set of five initial imagery based on the subject you want to check. Each uses one sense. For the same memory scene, the client is guided to use different senses to recall and reproduce in imagery communication.

12.6. *Matters needing attention*

(1) The method of "conversion channel" can break the resistance quite effectively. Thus, the psychotherapist must grasp the rhythm and know how to stop it and where it should be stopped. Do not expect to solve a big problem at once.
(2) Carefully distinguish between escape and transformation. Sometimes, the client may use an auditory image to interfere with the presentation of a visual image. For this, the imagery communication psychotherapist needs to identify and "seize" an image to show it fully.
(3) The method of "conversion channel" has many variants. This tip is just a start. Please try your best to be creative. However, any clinical techniques that have not been repeatedly proven on your own are strictly prohibited from being tested on other people (especially clients)!

12.7. *Case analysis*

Client: No, I can see nothing!

Psychotherapist: That's ok. Maybe you are tired. Now, close your eyes in your imagination and take a break.

Analysis:

The client still maintained a connection to his mental world, albeit with a strong resistance.

Client (relaxed): Um.

Psychotherapist: How do you feel now?

Analysis:

When visual images cannot be easily presented, we first switch to feeling. The word of feeling is a pun in Chinese, which means bodily sensations and inner emotions.

Client: I feel better.

Psychotherapist: If you will, you can close your eyes to have a rest all the time. In fact, the feeling of our ears and body is interlinked.

Analysis:

The psychotherapist sets the stage for using conversion channel.

Client: When I close my eyes, I actually pick up my ears to hear.

Analysis:

It is clear that the auditory perception of the client has been called forth.

Psychotherapist: Yes. Ordinarily we are always used to relying on our eyes. In fact, there are many magic weapons in our body! You can try to listen to it. What is the difference that you feel from the sound of me and your usual impression?

Analysis:

The psychotherapist started with "what I look like" to test his auditory imagery. The key here is the gradual exposure. In this seemingly inadvertent process, the client was more aware of his own auditory imagery. It has a good paving effect on helping him face the previous mental trauma.

Client: Some places are the same, some are different. The difference is that you are very thin in my hearing, but much more tender and beautiful in my impression, laughing, without melancholy eyes, do not hate interpersonal communication, and will not always be ignored in the crowd.

Psychotherapist: You can hear so much information! What you feel with your hearing is like me when I was a child. It is interesting that your ears can feel what you cannot see in your eyes.

Client: I also found my ears strong!

Psychotherapist: So, what would you hear if you just heard it in your ears when you could not see anything?

Analysis:

The psychotherapist began to direct the client back to the scene that he just escaped from and asked about his auditory imagery, when he showed confidence.

Client (silent for a moment): I hear the voice of the night.

Psychotherapist: What is the sound of the night?

Client: It is death stillness, not even breathing, as if the air is completely sealed in an invisible balloon, and it could not flow at all.

Psychotherapist: Oh, so what?

Client: So what? It is still dead!

Psychotherapist: Please continue to listen to the dead voice. At the same time, pay attention to your physical feelings.

Client (after dozens of seconds): I suddenly hear a sound of cracking. Then, a sudden chill comes over my back. The outer skin of my two arms gets gooseflesh. You see, it has not subsided by now.

Psychotherapist (look at the skin of his arms): That is true. What kind of physical reaction does that sound bring to you?

Client: Look! When you say that, the goose bumps on my arms are back!

Psychotherapist: What does my voice let you hear?

Client: It sounds like an echo. I mean that the voice you spoke just now let me hear the split sound again.

Psychotherapist: What kind of sound it is?

Client: That sound is like an invisible black hole that can extinguish all things. It has no light and no temperature. No, it should be without warmth and cold. Specifically, it is gloomy. It will suddenly appear when you have no precaution. You do not know the existence of it. Or, you know it is there, but you do not know when it is coming. It is a kind of creepy sound, like... death.

Analysis:

We can see that when the psychotherapist asked about the details of the auditory image, the client could not help but describe the visual imagery and body's feelings. This is very meaningful. The client actually presented the same thing in different languages — death. It was no wonder that his previous resistance was so strong.

Psychotherapist: I notice that you get a shiver when you get here.

Analysis:

The psychotherapist constantly guided the client to experience his physical sensation. This is a very important skill. When the client is addicted to the mental world, or when a certain negative psychological energy is so large that it is "swallowing" the client, it can help the client continue to be aware and realistic. We suggest that, when dealing with the cases related to death, the psychotherapists use Imagery Communication Psychotherapy more for the body.

Client: You are right. When I spoke to you, I heard that voice again. And, this time it is particularly clear. It comes from my left molar tooth below the root.

Psychotherapist: Oh? What do you hear this time?

Client: I hear the cracked sound of the root of the tooth. It is like that a piece of black ice is suddenly poured by hot water and burst. At the moment, I see after molar tooth cracked. My tooth has been split into halves. There is a large black gap in the middle. All black inside and empty by worms. So disgusting!

Psychotherapist: You have just got two chills. There are goose bumps all over the body. Even on your face.

Client: I suddenly smell a very pungent taste, like a kind of potion used by the dentist.

Psychotherapist: Oh, and then?

Client: No, it seems to be the taste of preservatives. Formalin! I know, it is the smell of the corpse! My God! It is so disgusting! I suddenly see a corpse.

I saw it unintentionally on the site before. He is lying on the ground with the face down, whose seven apertures in the head have been eaten hollow by the small black worms. . . I am so miserable. I really cannot stand it!

Psychotherapist: You look awful all over. Which part of your body is the most painful?

Client: My arms and the skin. The goose pimples seem to be filled with small worms!

Psychotherapist: Besides your arms, is there any place that feels uncomfortable?

Client: My face, too, it is like a lot of bugs lying on goosebumps.

Psychotherapist: Are there any other places?

Client: My teeth feel uncomfortable, too.

Psychotherapist: How do you feel about your teeth?

Client: I cannot tell, but it seems to be a tall and strong tree on the surface, which is actually eaten out by worms.

Psychotherapist: I see. What would it be like to be eaten empty?

Client: Once someone touches it, it will collapse completely.

Analysis:

The psychotherapist carefully tested his recent region of psychological development. The tree image here symbolized the client itself, and being eaten empty represented his psychological status of being outwardly strong but inwardly weak. The so-called collapse in a touch means that it is not the best time to solve this problem at this moment. Otherwise, the client may face the danger of self collapsing.

Psychotherapist: What is the feeling of the tree, when it knows that it is facing this fate?

Analysis:

The psychotherapist understood the warning from the client and tried to awaken another detection of his heart, so that the client can be partially stripped of the identification to the negative life script of the tree.

Client: It has no feeling, because it is trying to make the outer bark thicker.

Analysis:

His answer showed that he needed more psychological defense and had no strength to face the complex. In this regard, the psychotherapist accepted.

Psychotherapist: It must be reasonable to do so.

Client: Yes, it has to do it. Otherwise, it will collapse right away. Only in this way it can survive.

Psychotherapist: It is right. Although the thickening of the bark cannot solve the problem of worms, it must ensure that it is alive after all. In this way it will leave the opportunity for the future.

Analysis:

The psychotherapist affirmed the positive significance and the necessity for temporary defense, but did not overly agree with it. At the same time, the psychotherapist pointed out the real problem in the attitude of acceptance and provided a positive guidance.

Client: Yes.

Psychotherapist: How do you feel at this time?

Client: Very calm.

Psychotherapist: How do you feel about your body?

Client: Nothing.

Psychotherapist: Do you want to be here today or continue to explore?

Client: It is here today.

Psychotherapist: So, we will end here, ok?

Client: Well.

13. Cao Yu: Active triangulation and dispel triangulation

13.1. *Goal*

The basic purpose of this method is to repair the double relationship that cannot be repaired by two persons. Meanwhile, the third party (usually the coordinator, the balance or the arbiter) is "rescued" to make the internal relationships of the individual live in harmony with each other.

13.2. *Principle*

In the sub-personality chart, the smallest sub-personality pattern is called a "unit". This unit can be a relationship between two people or three. In real life, we often see that when two people have problems and cannot solve them directly, one of them tends to turn to a third party to achieve a new balance. This often happens automatically in the unconscious, such as the triangular relationship of "the persecutor — the victim — the protector" in Transactional Analysis (TA).

The technique of "active triangulation" is to be active and aware of the introduction of constructive third party through the original destructive double relationship mode, so as to break the old vicious circle of relationship and form a new mode. Then, through the voluntary withdrawal of the third party, a good double relationship model is restored or built.

One good example of the techniques of "active triangulation" and "dispel triangulation" in real life is the third party coordination model in partner counseling. As a constructive third party, the psychological consultant joins the original destructive double relationship. Due to the intervention of a new constructive element, the dynamic mode of the original object relationship can be broken, and a constructive triangulation unit forms between the couple and the psychological consultant.

What is different is that in the specific application of ICP, "active triangulation" and "dispel triangulation" are carried out on the imagery level. This is to say, the third party of coordinator is not a psychotherapist in reality, but a certain constructive sub-personality in the imagery world of the client. In addition, "active triangulation" is not a purpose, but a chance for psychotherapy. Therefore, after changing the original destructive interaction mode, the third party should withdraw in time, remove the contamination, and leave the original conflicting sides to deal with and restore relations with the new healthy mode. In essence, the triangulated psychological resource is only a good object of transition.

The technique of "dispel triangulation" is that the third party of coordinator withdraws from the triangular relations unit with awareness, in order to restore or reform a constructive double relationship unit.

13.3. *Scope of application*

(1) Neurosis;
(2) A variety of psychological problems, especially marriage and family counseling, workplace interpersonal counseling, and other interpersonal problems.

13.4. *Operation steps*

(1) The psychotherapist guides the client to imagine three persons who have less than a perfect relationship living in the same room. They see each other's position in the image and show the basic relationship model of the moment.
(2) In the client's imagination, these three persons change into animals. The psychotherapist guides them to communicate with each other, and tries to understand the basic family dynamics, such as, who is the leader, who has a strong conflict with whom, what is their psychological relationship, what are the expectations of each other (self-expectation and recognition of others' expectations), what is the impossible expectation, and so on. The setting of concrete problems should be determined according to the specific theme of psychotherapy.
(3) Among these three animals, the animal that recognizes one's expectation and suppresses the other side first leaves the room. The other two animals remain in the room to express their expectations and communicate honestly.
(4) Or let the remaining two animals stay in the second room and the third room, respectively, then, the triangulated third party goes into the room of the two animals successively to communicate with each other. In this way, every animal image

(sub-personality) can face its own expectations and others' expectations more directly.

13.5. *Matters needing attention*

Sometimes we need to let the triangulated third party quickly withdraw and remove the contamination, and sometimes it is not the case.

For example, there was such a case: The client was a foundling. There were two disconnected sub-personality images in his mental world — "a discarded child" and "his mother". The psychotherapist helped the client find a good "alternative mother" internally and sent love into the original relationship unit, forming a new triangular unit. Under such circumstances, the psychotherapist did not have to let the "alternative mother" get out quickly. Instead, it was necessary for her to continue to undertake constructive psychological functions, so as to promote the final reconciliation of the traumatic mother–child relationship. Later, the client's "alternative mother" image was transformed into a "father" sub-personality and constructed a mutual love triangle unit with the former mother–child.

13.6. *Case analysis*

Client: I really do not know what to do. My son and his father are like enemies. They quarrelled as soon as they met! I have been driven crazy by them!

Analysis:

There are three tangled people in real life — the father, the mother and the son.

Psychotherapist: What happened to them? Please list a recent example.

Client: Last night, my son was not very happy to come home from school. His father had to tell him something about the pressure of employment. You tell me, isn't he pushing the child?

Psychotherapist: So?

Client: They were getting more and more angry, ended up fighting!

Psychotherapist: Wait, wait. We have to figure out how they started to get angry. His father told him something about the pressure of employment. Then, who said what?

Client: I walked up and said, why do you say this to your son? But his father did not look at me and continued to say it. My son said angrily "I don't want to listen to this right now." But he continued. How do I share this person! Earlier my sister said that he was a bad man, and I did not know what I thought at that time . . . Ah!

Psychotherapist: What were you doing in the process of saying this?

Client: I helped my son stop him. But he did not shut his mouth!

Psychotherapist: What did that mouth say that you dislike?

Client: Who knows? Anyway, it is possible to say anything.

Psychotherapist: For example?

Client: No. What he said did not matter. The important thing is that he is always talking and talking!

Psychotherapist: Are you annoyed? Are you angry?

Client: I am so annoyed! I didn't get angry, but I was especially anxious. They were really angry, anxious to take up arms in a fight!

Analysis:

Through embodiment technology, psychotherapist guided the client to reproduce a typical scene of a three-people conflict pattern in real life.

Psychotherapist: Well. Now please set the picture in your imagination and watch it carefully.

Client: I take a picture. The three of us are in a room. My son is in the center of the room and I sit behind him. His father stands near the door.

Psychotherapist: Which direction do the three of you see separately?

Client: My son is looking at his father. His father is looking at me. I am looking at them.

Analysis:

The position of space symbolizes the psychological position of each other. The eyes symbolize the point of concern.

Psychotherapist: Please imagine that three people in the photo become three animals.

Analysis:

Imagining animals can not only reduce the interference of real belief and resistance, but also present the unconscious contents of the client more clearly, and distinctly show the identification object of the son, as well as the psychological relationships among the three people.

Client: I become a tiger, my son becomes a little tiger, and my husband becomes . . . a donkey.

Analysis:

The son in the photograph looked at his father and his back to his mother, but became the same animal as his mother. This implied his duality — the superficial concern was his father, but the subconscious identity was his mother.

Psychotherapist: What would happen between them?

Client: The little tiger is going at the donkey and biting him again and again.

Psychotherapist: What about the donkey?

Client: He is jumping around the place and keeps calling. How hard to hear it!

Psychotherapist: Why does the little tiger do this?

Client: I do not know. He might be practicing hunting.

Psychotherapist: Why does he want to practice hunting?

Client: He can take care of his mother when he has good practice. Mom does not have to work hard.

Psychotherapist: Ha-ha, it turns out to be a very filial little tiger! How about the mother tiger?

Client: She is lazily lying on her stomach in the back and looking at the scene.

Psychotherapist: What is her feeling?

Client: She appreciates it so much.

Psychotherapist: Who does she appreciate?

Client: She admires her son to do well.

Psychotherapist: If the little tiger could feel this, what would he do?

Client: He would be more aggressive and bite the donkey again and again. At the moment, the ass's face is bleeding.

Analysis:

The internal interactions were fully exposed there and then: the son was attacking his father for his mother. The mother appreciated so much that his son attacked his father more fiercely.

It was not difficult to find that the mother had a feeling of collapse and admired his son in her deeper subconscious mind.

Psychotherapist: If only the little tiger and the donkey were left in the present picture, what would they do?

Analysis:

The psychotherapist started to dispel triangulation to check the relationship between father and son without the presence of the mother.

Client: They stop fighting. The little tiger begins to look around naughtily.

Psychotherapist: How about the donkey?

Client: The donkey heads down, smells everywhere, and finds grass to eat. Then, it turns out.

Psychotherapist: What about the little tiger?

Client: The little tiger follows the donkey, running a few steps on the grass outside. Then he suddenly feels too far away from his mother and returns to his nest.

Psychotherapist: How does the little tiger feel about the donkey going out?

Client: He is very curious and wants to go out and play with the donkey. But he is afraid of the danger outside, so he has to go back to his mother.

Analysis:

The mother was not present, and the son had no need to fight with his father. The father's attention might be outside. The son wanted to follow his father to explore the outside world, but he was too attached to his mother.

Psychotherapist: Will the mother protect the little tiger?

Client: Yes, she will. They protect each other. They love each other very much.

Psychotherapist: How does the little tiger protect his mother?

Client: For example, if someone bullies his mother, he will go up to bite him!

Psychotherapist: Who can bully his mother? Why bullying her?

Client: For example, that donkey. Mother wanted to treat the donkey as a prey, because she had been hungry for several days. But the donkey refused to give in and kicked her face with a hoof. So, I just jumped up and bit him!

Psychotherapist: Oh, so that is what it is. Therefore, the mother enjoyed him very much. Now please make another imagination. What will happen to the mother tiger and the donkey alone?

Analysis:

The psychotherapist used the technique of dispel triangulation again to check the relationship mode of husband and wife without the presence of son.

Client: The donkey is standing with his back toward the mother tiger, and does not see her.

Psychotherapist: How about her?

Client: She is very sad. She is too old to easily hunt as the young tiger. So now even the donkey looks down on her.

Psychotherapist: If the donkey knew the idea of the mother tiger, what would he do to deal with it?

Client: The donkey would say "You are wrong. Not because you are old, but because you do not have to be a wife and a mother at all!"

Psychotherapist: Why would he say that?

Client: I don't know either!

Psychotherapist: You can ask him.

Client: The donkey says "You always complain that I look down on you. But who really despises who?"

Psychotherapist: So who in the end disdains who?

Client: Of course, the tiger looks down on the donkey!

Psychotherapist: Why?

Client: The tiger should be with the tiger! But he is a stupid donkey!

Psychotherapist: It sounds like the mother tiger married the donkey?

Client: Well. So she is very bad. How can a donkey match up a tiger?

Psychotherapist: What will the donkey think?

Client: Even if I am a donkey, I have self-respect, too! Besides, it was you who pursued me. Otherwise, I would rather marry a donkey.

Psychotherapist: What is the response of the tiger at this time?

Client: She is roaring at the donkey and jumping on to him. The donkey is dodging, and she becomes more angry.

Analysis:

The problem was getting clearer. The wife looked down on her husband, and the husband showed disdain out of self-esteem. Apart from apathy, there is a conflict between them. They were trapped in an unconstructive death cycle. The psychotherapist decided to break the addiction, introducing the third party to execute the observer function.

Psychotherapist: What is your feeling when they are playing the game all the time?

Client: I feel bored. They simply disband. The tiger marries the tiger, and the donkey marries the donkey. So they will stop.

Psychotherapist: How does the little tiger think about this proposal?

Client: The little tiger is very anxious.

Psychotherapist: What should he do?

Client: He should keep his father for his mother.

Psychotherapist: How did he do it?

Client: He kept fighting with his father to stop his father from looking outside.

Psychotherapist: What does his mother think of it?

Client: I. . .

Analysis:

At this point, the basic dynamic model and its causes in this family are clear. Next, the psychotherapist can guide the client to explore and get a deeper insight.

14. Du Haiying: "Let's sign the contract"

(The developer: Beijing South Beach Primary School in China)

Du Haiying is an excellent Chinese teacher in a primary school and serves as a class adviser year around. During the process of learning and using ICP, she not only insists on self-growth, but also tries to explore how to combine ICP with daily teaching and student management. She has developed a new technique that specializes in the correction of children's bad behavior — "let's sign the contact".

14.1. *Goal*

We should guide children to communicate with their bad habits by imagery, to adjust their mental state, and to transform negative mental energy into positive ones, so as to achieve the purpose of mental health development.

14.2. *Scope of application*

Applicable population: Primary school children; children who can communicate in normal language.

Applicable forms: Case consultation; group psychological consultation.

14.3. *Principle*

In the process of growth, a variety of behavior habits are unavoidable. Some of them are not conducive to physical and mental health, social adaptation or interpersonal communication. In the past, the most common way we used was to get rid of bad habits. However, it is easy to see that it is difficult to remove them when our reason is clear and we emotionally cannot bear to give up, or due to the inertia of subconscious. Sometimes even the following happens, the more we want to get rid of a habit, the stronger it becomes.

If we can no longer treat them as enemies in some way, but in good faith to face and accept, even "shake hands and make it up", to be the same outside and inside, the effect must be different.

The technique of "let's sign the contact" emphasizes the attitude of confrontation and acceptance, encourages children to use their own positive power to help themselves, and turns bad habits into a positive driving force aiming at cultivating independence, self-esteem and self-confidence.

This technique also reminds parents and teachers that there are two ways to the education process: one is to use examples and the power of demonstration to guide the children to learn from better people and good things; the other is to cultivate dialectical thinking with dialectical perspective to explore the positive factors in everything and internalize them into positive resources.

14.4. *Operation steps*

(1) Let the body relax from head to toe.
(2) Let the client choose a bad habit that he/she dislikes and close his/her eyes to imagine its shape, size, appearance, and characteristics, etc. In order to arouse the interest of the child, we can increase the singularity and the richness of imagination. For example, guide the child as "this habit is something of a shape. It may be a man, an animal, a plant, or it may be a very strange thing..."
(3) Guide the client to chat with the visualized habit in the imagination, and talk about why it grows like this.
(4) Guide the client to communicate with it carefully in the imagination and try to find its advantages.
(5) Guide the client to contract with the habit in the imagination, and express the hope that this habit can help him/her.
(6) End the imagery communication. Bring the client back to reality by letting the body relax and adjusting the breathing routine.

Instruction:
According to the specific state of different clients, the guidance can be properly adjusted. The principle is unchanged — adhere to the face and acceptance.

14.5. *Matters needing attention*

Do not be eager to succeed. Do not ignore the details.

Pay attention to the rhythm of the client. Rather go slowly than quickly. And always follow his/her emotional changes. Moreover, in real life, pay continuous attention for a period of time. As long as the client is found to improve, he/she will be given approval and encouragement with time.

14.6. *Case demonstration*

The case is provided by the developer. She used the class meeting for three group consultations. Each interval is one week.

I often see some students throw garbage on the ground, some do not finish their homework on time, and when the children are angry, they use unparliamentary words on campus . . . As a teacher, I used to make sense to the children, or to solve some problems at a class meeting. Sometimes, the effect was not entirely satisfactory. After learning Imagery Communication Psychotherapy, I think about whether we can use imagery communication for these children, so that they can learn to deal with their bad habits in their hearts. I believe that the scientific nature of ICP will make me yield twice the results with half the effort.

First group intervention:

Guide the children to close their eyes and relax the whole body, the image guidance:

Each one of us has a lot of advantages and some shortcomings. Sometimes, it's not that we do not want to do our best, but there are some bad habits that stop us.

Please choose a bad habit of your own . . . OK, now let's deal with it. Look at it carefully. How much is it all? What shape is it? What is it made of? Please try to speak to it. Some bad habits may be very scary and strong. But we are just dealing with it in the imagination, so it is very safe. You just need to look at it quietly.

Look at it calmly. Make a good discussion with it in your own way. And try to reach an agreement with it and let it help you. Even if its attitude is tough, you have to work hard to find a way to do it. Believe in yourself! You can do it as long as you work hard. What are the advantages of it? These advantages can help you. Finally, please remember to sign a contract with it. When you finish, please slowly open your eyes when I count to three.

Next, the children reported their imaginations one by one.

At the end of the day, I told the children "the bad habit is in our body, we must treat it well, let it support and help us."

Second group intervention:

Guide the children to experience the bad habits again in the imagination. The focus of this time was its change.

The bad habits of many children became smaller. A few children asked me why their images did not change. I answered "Do not worry, as long as you do it with your heart."

After that, group discussion. What can your bad habits help you to do? Why have some changed, and some have not changed? What did you do for it this week? In the course of communicating with it, what actions have touched you?

Third group intervention:

I found that the children were changing slowly. When some children's bad habits disappeared, I guided them to say goodbye to bad habits in imagination, and told children to study and live well and remain happy.

There was a very lovely boy. He told me "my bad habit makes a girlfriend. It is especially interesting that its girlfriend is a good habit. Haha, I not only have made good friend with my bad habit, but also got to know a good friend."

15. Qiu Xiangjian: Looking for "explosive package"

(The developer: Career psychological counselor in China)

15.1. *Goal*

Its purpose is to discover the psychological defense and anger coping style of the client and the source of the related complex.

15.2. *Scope of application*

The technique of looking for "explosive package" can be used as an initial imagery and can be applied flexibly with other methods and techniques of ICP.

When a client is afraid to face anger directly, or lacks sufficient self-awareness (such as the root of a complex) which causes only partial release of anger, this technique can also be used to deepen psychological counseling and psychotherapy.

Applicable forms: case consultation; group psychological consultation.

15.3. *Guidance*

The main guiding words of looking for "explosive package":

Imagine yourself becoming a fairy flying into your body. You find that your body turns into a mountain, and you can fly freely in the mountain. Please observe carefully: where is the explosive package? When you find it, look at the environment where it is. How do you feel about the air and the temperature around you? Shape? Color? Size? Texture? Why is it here? What is the effect? If it is on you, where is it? Now, put on your protective clothing and put it in a safe place. Check what is inside and then handle it safely.

The explanation of the guidance is made here.

Imagine you become a fairy flying into your body. It is common in ICP to imagine oneself becoming an elf. Flying into the body symbolizes entering into the inner world.

Your body turns into a mountain. The mountain sometimes symbolizes repression. This is to promote the connection between the client and the depressed mood or complex in the subconscious mind.

You can fly freely in the mountain. Let the client have a free space of imagination. Open subconscious helps eliminate the resistance.

Where is the explosive package? Focus the attention of the client on the "explosive package" to strengthen the confrontation.

Look at the environment where it is. The environment symbolizes the atmosphere and the cause of anger. Air and temperature symbolize the psychological resources of the self. For instance, a client imagined a satchel charge on the bedroom's bedside cabinet. She experienced anger toward her husband and hoped that he could identify her dissatisfaction. But her husband never found it. After a long time, her disappointment turned to anger. In order to maintain the reality of the relationship between husband and wife, she suppressed negative emotions in her heart. As a result, a "satchel charge" was accumulated.

Observe its shape, color, size and texture. Its shape and texture are often related to the way of dealing with anger. For example, an explosive bag made of tarpaulin symbolizes that no tears are to be allowed. Its size and color often symbolize the degree and intensity of anger. It is worth noting that sometimes the client's anger is strong, but the explosive package in the imagination is small, even very small. This means a high degree of repression for the client. Once such clients have somatization symptoms, the situation is generally more serious.

Why is it here? This exploration is for a deeper understanding of the causes and sources of anger.

What is the effect? The aim is to enhance self-awareness and to understand the psychological significance of this process.

If it is on you, where is it? This is to explore the relationship between anger and the body. Pent up negative emotions may form somatic symptoms or psychogenic diseases. For example, a client felt that the location of the explosive package was in the heart, so it was clear that his anger repression caused the oppression feeling of the heart without organic lesion. Another client felt that a satchel charge was wrapped in his stomach. In real life, his stomach felt swollen for a long term, sometimes with searing pain. After a serious experience, he realized that the real reason was that he could not digest a kind of anger. The anger feeling couldn't be released and was stuck in his stomach.

Put on your protective clothing. It is out of necessary self-protection. Protective clothing represents self-protection consciousness and ability, and can reflect the psychological defense mechanism of the client. Whether or not to wear protective clothing itself is of clinical significance.

Put it in a safe place. This is to remind the client that he/she has the ability and resources to cope with the harmful effects of anger. In addition, in group counseling, this can protect the group as a whole.

Check what is inside. The interior of the explosive package is often related to the inner needs. For example, a female client saw cotton. It means she needed love and warmth in her heart. Another client saw ice in it and said to himself in his imagination "I was angry because no one loved me." In clinical practice, only a few clients see gunpowder or explosives in their imagination. In general, explosives are angrier than gunpowder. A few clients see wet gunpowder or explosives. In this case, it is necessary to explore the deep cause of wetness.

Handle it safely. Guide the client to understand how to deal with anger more healthily and more effectively. At the same time, ICP can also be used to guide the client to clear and release his/her anger with self-awareness.

15.4. *Principle*

The explosive package in the image symbolizes pent-up anger. Looking for is a process of discovery and exploration.

Looking for the "charge" in the unconscious is easier to find and understand the client's anger and its psychological factors. It contributes to the use of ICP for emotional cleansing and complex resolution.

There are many symbolic ways of representing anger, and the image of the powder is just one of them. When using this technique, it does not mean that there is no anger, even if there is no charge in the image.

15.5. *Variants*

This technique has a variant — removal of mines.

The starting guide of "removal of mines":

You come to a place. There may be some mines buried here. Please imagine that you are wearing protective clothing, taking others away from the mine area, and protecting everything that needs to be protected, such as seeds, food, etc. Then, you scan the ground with a special instrument. When you find a mine, you will see the hints on the instrument...

15.6. *Matters needing attention*

(1) Do not guide the client directly to detonate the "explosive package".
(2) For some clients, do not apply this technology, such as pregnant women, patients with cardiovascular disease or serious somatic diseases.
(3) If the client is not wearing protective clothing in the image (especially emphasize this point in group psychotherapy), the psychotherapist should pay special attention to and deal with it in accordance with the basic working principles of ICP, in order to protect the client.
(4) Please use this technique under the guidance of an imagery communication psychotherapist.

15.7. *Case demonstration*

In the following cases, "A" represents male clients and "U" represents female clients.

Group case:

A1: My body becomes a mountain. I see an explosive bag in a large warehouse. It is a black square and made of tarpaulin. It has a large size of a house. I am in a quiet mood.

(The warehouse has the symbolic meaning of isolation. The square symbolizes self- restraint and emphasizes on principles and norms. Black represents a deeper suppression. The tarpaulin symbolizes that the client does not allow himself to reveal such feelings of sadness.)

U1: I see an explosive package in the study. It was not found at the beginning, but it was later discovered under the desk. It is wrapped in cotton cloth. I feel it very soft and heavy when I take it up. When I drag it out, I am particularly afraid of exploding. I open it and see, the inside is cotton and needles. I am relieved.

(Cotton cloth is a symbol of soft emotion. "Dragging out" symbolizes the hardships of the face and repression. Fear of explosions means that the client is worried about losing control of her emotions. The cotton and needles in the explosive package symbolize the latent aggression — the client uses the self-thought good ways to subconsciously control her husband.)

A1: My explosive bag is very large, but it will not explode. The tarpaulin cannot be torn.

(He spoke in a hurry as if he was afraid of being asked. This sentence showed his psychological defense mechanism — avoidance and rationalization.)

The ICP therapist guided the clients to experience and analyze. If some experiences and analysis are spoken out loud by the group members, the effect will be better.

U2: I feel A1 is escaping his fears. U1 seems to be talking about the relationship with her husband. I found a bag of explosives in the kitchen cupboard. A small glass bottle is filled with explosives. Well, I often quarrel with my family when I cook at home. My husband once said that they should go home again after I have done a good meal. I often remind myself, but I cannot restrain myself. This bottle of explosives is like my mood, which is easy to break and easily dissipate. My understanding is that if the food is not well done, I will be picked on by my family. But I work and cook, my family should not criticize me. I always feel that they do not understand me, so it is easy to lose my temper. (She seems to be a little helpless.)

U3: My explosive bag is a biochemical weapon. I feel very surprised. (In this case, she swallows the saliva.) I am a little scared. (Her hands are clasped together.)

(Biological weapons symbolize deep psychological defense, which is often associated with resentment or fear of death.)

U3: I am afraid that the biological weapon will kill people.

(There was panic and unease in her eyes. Later, she realized that it was related to a traumatic experience in her childhood, so deep in her heart was resentment. In real life, she was lively and cheerful in interpersonal relationships, but she became lonely and depressed when she was alone.)

U4: My explosive is under the bed of my son, and there is also cotton in it. It is tightly tied outside with thick cotton threads. It takes me a long time to unlock it... I have been so dissatisfied with my son recently. He is going to high school this year, but he is playing every day... Whenever I accuse him, my husband criticizes me. I have to be silent. These days, I cook for my son as usual, but I do not want to talk to him.

Psychotherapist: So, you use the cold to "explode" your son?

U2 talked to U4: You take care of them, but you say nothing. You express your dissatisfaction in this way. That makes them guilty, right?

U4: Yes. This is the soft control.

At this point, we have noticed that every source of anger is different.

Individual case:

A2: 35 years old. He experienced the image of explosive package at home and exploded all the explosive bags in his imagination, causing the lake to be completely dry and gradually become a desert. He did not know how to deal with it and asked the ICP therapist for help.

Psychotherapist: Why did you think of detonating the charge bag at that time?

A2: I thought the water could be brought back again after the explosion. Who knows!

Psychotherapist: I remember in your images last time, there was a shallow lake with water in the middle, and the rest of it was mud. Many small explosive bags were scattered in the lake. There were some damaged wooden ships. The paddles were complete, but soon rotten. There was a red broken hat and a tattered book.

A2: That time we talked about the problem. It was an emotional trauma to me. Please analyze it.

Psychotherapist: Many small explosive bags were scattered in the lake, which was a symbol of frequent mood swings. I feel like your heart is flaking out in one piece. It is a heartbroken pain.

In this imagination, the shallow lake and mud represent lack of emotional nourishment and despair. The wooden ships here symbolize intimacy. The decaying paddle is a symbol of masculinity, which may be associated with sexual life.

The client was actually trying to relieve the depressed mood completely and desired to start a new life. He even wanted to grow lotus seeds in the lake to express his yearning for pure and beautiful feelings.

The choice of the case is to show that inappropriate detonating needs to be dealt with in time. The psychotherapist needs to guide the client to understand the environmental meaning and psychological needs or motives.

Inappropriate detonating includes active detonating, error guidance, accidental explosion, and so on.

16. Qiu Xiangjian: Mind "CT"

16.1. *Goal*

The technique of mind "CT" is to discover deep psychological problems and their sources. It is quite practical.

16.2. *Scope of application*

This technique can be used to respond to the client's resistance. It can also be used as an initial imagery to detect and interfere with somatization symptoms and psychosomatic diseases.

Applicable forms: case consultation; group psychotherapy.

16.3. *Principle and operation steps*

This technique is inspired by the imagery of light scanning in ICP. The so-called mind "CT" is to explore with the heart of the self.

Main instructions:

Please imagine a light on the top of your head. This lamp shines on one part of your body. There is a computer screen in front of you, showing some pictures. These pictures may be static or dynamic. The content of the picture is not a physiological structure. Look at the content of the picture and feel it.

Operation steps:

As an initial imagery or for group psychotherapy, please refer to the following steps:

(1) Provide guidance after relaxing from head to foot.
(2) For groups, share images and feelings; for individuals, explore in depth according to the specific circumstances.
(3) Share insight.
(4) End the imagery communication.

16.4. *Variants*

(1) As an initial imagery, the following variant can be used to explore the isolation of the psychological defense mechanism.

Guidance:

Please imagine that you find a box in a secret place in the room, such as a corner of a cabinet, under the floor, etc. What does this box look like? Can you find a way to open it and see what is in it? Maybe there is another box or interlayer inside it. There is a light on the roof. There is a table near the window. You put the box on the table. A display screen appears in front of you. What can you see when the light goes through the box? You look at everything in the box and watch the screen carefully.

(2) Explore the somatization symptoms and psychosomatic diseases.

Guidance:

Now imagine standing up and looking into this room. You see a secret door on a wall. You walk closer to it slowly. The words are written on the door: mind CT. You push the door and walk in. There is a light on the roof. At the bottom of the lamp is a movable bed. You can lie on the bed, or sit on it, or push the bed off and stand under the light. A display screen appears in front of you. The light gradually brightens and begins to scan your body, or directly scan the uncomfortable parts of the body. The display on the screen is not a physiological structure. Please see the picture clearly. At the same time, carefully experience your feelings of the body and the heart in this process.

16.5. *Matters needing attention*

(1) If the client reports mind "CT" is faulty, the psychotherapist leads him/her to clearly see the specific location, parts and cause of the failure, and then fix it in the imagination. The maintenance of the mind "CT" itself is of psychological significance.
(2) If resistance is encountered, the psychotherapist can increase the use of guiding language:

You find that there are some keys at the bottom of the screen, such as forward, backward, pause, signal amplification, picture magnification and so on. You can choose the keys according to the specific circumstances.

If the client cannot see the picture on the screen or cannot see it clearly in the imagination, the psychotherapist can guide him/her to press the key of signal amplification and add a sentence:

After amplifying the signal, the connection between the display screen and the light will strengthen and maintain stability.

16.6. *Case demonstration*

Case 1:

In the image of mind CT, there was a long, rusty knife in the chest of the client. She was in a very complicated mood. She felt regrettable, uneasy, angry, and scared. Her body felt a bit hard. Looking at the bleeding of the wound, she felt no pain. She seemed numb and was still smiling.

The client was guided to experience the feeling of the body in the present. She reported feeling little cold on her hands and feet. Then, she continued to experience that person with a knife in the chest in her images.

Case 2:

The mind "CT" is used in combination with the technique of looking for "explosive package".

In the imagination of the client, the bag of explosives was so delicate. It was made of cinnamomum camphorwood. But he did not know what was inside. Under the guidance of the imagery communication psychotherapist, the charge was brought into a laboratory. On an operating table, the client in a protective suit turned on the light, and then saw an ancient city on the display screen. The city had some big walls, like a fairyland on earth.

The cinnamomum camphorwood is a kind of tree that does not produce insects, symbolizing that it is not easily affected by the outside world, and making people feel good. Here, it also represents the psychological defense mechanism of the client — idealization and isolation. "Not knowing what was inside" means his heart was full of fear.

17. Qiu Xiangjian: Call and message

17.1. *Goal*

The purpose of this technique is to promote communication among the sub-personalities, and to establish a connection.

17.2. *Scope of application*

In the images, some sub-personalities are not willing or do not dare to meet or communicate, or they fear a certain sub-personality or animal image.

Applicable forms: case consultation; group psychological psychotherapy.

17.3. *Principle*

The telephone symbolizes the connection of relationship. Calls and text messages symbolize the connection and communication with the subconscious.

Guidance:

Please imagine that you take out your cell phone and experience it. You find that the mobile phone has changed and even turned into something else. There is a video window on the phone and you can see each other when you call. Feel the mood of the moment. Now you call a sub-personality who has not been able to communicate before. What is your feeling when you hear the phone ring? What is the first word you want to say? How does the other side respond? Both of you can talk for a while...

17.4. *Variants*

(1) Group chat. Multiple sub-personalities communicate on the image level.
(2) Leave a message. If nobody answers the phone, the other side can see the message.
(3) Send a message. The language must be healthy, concise and clear.
(4) The initial imagery of group psychotherapy. Main guidance:

Please call one of your sub-personalities. This sub-personality can be that you have not seen for a long time, can be that you want to see but not dare to see, or that you do not want to see very much. Just dial a phone, please try it bravely...

17.5. *Matters needing attention*

(1) The technique of "call and message" can quickly and effectively break the isolation mechanism. But do not just use it as a simple technique. Be sure to observe the specific circumstances of the client and respect his/her wish.
(2) Grasp the guidance flexibly according to the specific clinical situation. The key point is to give full play to the psychological function of the telephone.

17.6. *Case demonstration*

Case 1:

The client was reluctant to face his lion sub-personality. In the imagination, he could only look at it from very far, and he was extremely scared. He felt the lion was very thin and hungry. Any animal that it sees will be eaten. He was quite afraid of being eaten by the lion.

The psychotherapist guided the client to call the lion sub-personality in his imagination. After hard work, he finally said to the lion the first sentence "Hello, you look so hungry. I am afraid you will eat me." After hearing this, the lion sighed and did not speak. The client felt very sad. In his view, the lion was pitiful. After an attempt to communicate, he knew that the lion was not hungry to eat any animal, but had made a mistake, and it deliberately refused to eat to punish itself.

This technique helped the client to dissolve his deep fears, creating a safe and warm relationship with the lion sub-personality at the subconscious level.

Case 2:

The relationship between a client and his father was not good. After a period of psychotherapy, he could finally see the image of his father in the imagination, but refused to communicate with him.

The psychotherapist led him to call his father in the imagination. But as soon as the phone was dialed, he hung up. So he chose to leave a message to his father.

The message means that the client is still willing to connect with his father, which can pave the way for future communication.

18. Qiu Xiangjian: Interactive association and self-awareness

18.1. *Goal*

This is a technique of group imagery that guides the members into the image experience through interactive association and self-awareness.

18.2. *Scope of application*

This technique originated from an enterprise mentoring activity. The hope was that there will be some interesting group interaction, which could be combined with ICP. Therefore, after thought and practice, the developer created it.

It is suitable for imagery communication psychotherapists who have rich experience in group psychotherapy.

Applicable forms: family psychotherapy; group psychotherapy.

18.3. *Guidance*

The technique of interactive association and self-awareness has three ways of introducing and experiencing.

(1) When a member of a group enters the inner experience, the psychotherapist focuses on him/her. Other members can be self-aware, and can end the interactive association to experience him/her.
(2) Guide the group members to experience separately, and then interact and share with each other.
(3) Many people experience images at the same time. It requires a good sense of empathy and group psychotherapy experience.

Main guidance:

Let's get into the imagination game now. When I say "start", please tell me a kind of fruit or vegetable that you think of or can express your feeling. You can say what others have said. In this process, keep your feeling. We are together to imagine and experience. Whether or not you receive the influence of others, please try to focus on your own imagination and experience.

Start from my left hand and proceed in a clockwise direction. As long as I do not say "stop", it is going on. If I remind a member to withdraw from the interactive association to be selfaware, others do not stop until all of you get into your own inner experience. In this process, when you feel that you can enter the inner experience, please hold your right hand, and I will remind others that you are out of it. Now, start!

18.4. *Principle and operation steps*

This technology combines many psychological theories and clinical methods, such as Freud's free association, Carl Jung's active imagination, and the psychological energy theory of ICP.

The interactive association and self-awareness will create a group atmosphere. On one hand, it may increase the stress of the members, such as insecurity; on the other hand, it also makes the members feel supported and empathic. These atmospheres can promote an individual's deep experience.

Interactive association: the group members say their images one by one according to their first reaction. In this process, everyone is likely to be affected by others. The guide needs to call attention to them as the case may be. In order to avoid a few people talking at the same time, it is better to sit in a single circle and proceed in a certain direction.

Self-awareness: whether it is spontaneous perception or experience or influenced by group atmosphere or others, each member should concentrate on himself/herself and further discover his/her complex. In this process, it is easy to be infected and empathic. Therefore, each member has the opportunity to not only touch his own emotions and complex, but also improve self-awareness, resolution and ability to remove contamination.

Please refer to the following operation steps:

Step 1: Necessary paving.

The common guidance:

Let's play a game. Please respond to my guidance as soon as possible, and keep your feelings at the same time, which may come from your physical feelings or inner emotions, or from imagined pictures. In this process, I may be able to give some reminding. You decide whether to accept it according to your own situation. For example, when I observe that you are escaping or suppressing some kind of emotion, I will remind you.

For groups familiar with ICP, "play a game" can be replaced by "start interaction association and self-awareness".

Step 2: Guide imagination and experience.

Follow the previous guidance. Fruits and vegetables often symbolize the self-recognition of the subconscious mind, whose focus is to trigger the inner feelings and emotions of the clients. It has many variations. Different variations tend to lead to different psychological aspects. See the upcoming sections.

When any member shows a resistance state, the guide must take it seriously and cannot ignore it.

Step 3: According to the specific situation of a group, different ways of continuity are adopted.

(1) When group members have negative emotions, lead them to the self-awareness one by one, until all the members enter the inner experience and become self-aware. When the last member has an inner experience, the guide should leave some time for the experience to continue.
(2) When most members have feelings, guide the whole group to stop interacting associations and focus on their respective physical feelings, psychological emotions and image experiences.
(3) When a certain member has a strong mood, the interactive association can be suspended. Guide this member to experience internally and remind others to be self-aware, or to try to be empathic.
(4) Guide members to experience and communicate internally one by one. This is a serious challenge for the guider.

Step 4: Share their own experiences and insights.

If time allows, share it one by one.

For ordinary social groups, such as enterprise training, the guide should provide some analysis and explanation so that the members can understand the psychological meanings of their associations and experiences. For groups with the basis of mental growth, the guider should reduce the analysis and interpretation, and focus on enhancing their self-awareness.

Step 5: If necessary, the guider clarifies some problems further, aiming to make every participant gain and improve the ability of self-awareness, self-exploration and understanding others.

18.5. *Variants*

The other guide language is basically the same, mainly to make adjustments in the interactive association.

(1) Please say a word or a sentence that you think of or that can express your feelings.
(2) Please express your feelings in one or two sentences about the objects, characters or things that are related to your family.
(3) Please express your feelings in one or two sentences about the objects, characters or things that are related to your family when you were a child.
(4) Please say what you think of or feel as quickly as possible. Try to express it in a short sentence.
(5) According to the understanding of Imagery Communication Psychotherapy, other variants can be developed. The emphasis is on experiencing and understanding.

18.6. *Matters needing attention*

(1) The psychotherapist must carefully consider the specific circumstances of group members and individual clients.
(2) Please strictly observe the professional ethics and the work ethic of ICP. Without permission, it is advised to not enter the deep subconscious of the clients.
(3) In the third step, the guider should make decisions according to his/her own professional ability and the specific situation of

the group. Meanwhile, due to more pertinence and profundity of variants 2 and 3, the guider should use them carefully.

18.7. *Case demonstration*

In this group ICP, the members were asked to use a short sentence to speak about an object, character, or thing when they were young at home. Description: the number in front of the letter represents the ranking of members (from the left hand side); A represents male; U represents female.

1U: A little rabbit.

2U: I am playing alone.

3U: A desk lamp.

4A: My mother is cooking.

5A: A radio.

6U: A flute.

7A: I am playing with my sister.

1U: I am at home alone. (Her right hand twists her clothes.)

2U: I am drawing. (Her volume is a little higher than before, but she seems to be sighing.)

3U: A sewing machine.

4A: A kettle.

5A: A bicycle.

6U: An erhu. (A national musical instrument in China)

7A: A teapot.

1U: My brother and sister all go to school. (Her voice is a little trembling.)

2U: A bed.

3U: I dance at home alone. (Her tone is flat and the feet are moving.)

4A: There is a guest in the family, a comrade-in-arms of my father.

5A: My dad is repairing the wardrobe.

At this time, the psychotherapist noticed that 1U was biting her lips, then said: "1U, I feel that your body is tight, and your hands and feet are a bit cold." She nodded and her eyes were moist. The psychotherapist said: "Take it easy. Relax your chest and throat. Release your teeth. Do not bite the teeth together." Her mouth relaxed a little.

6U: Mom and dad are quarrelling. (Her voice reveals helplessness. The body leans back.)

7A: It is an old type of electric fan with color lights.

1U: I want to cry. (She is lowering her head. The voice is a bit hard. The other members look at her in the same way.)

Psychotherapist: IU can get out of the interactive imagination. The others go on. IU, I feel there is a sour feeling in your heart, and a slight sentiment in your chest is spreading around.

1U: Yeah. When I was a child, I used to be alone at home and felt lonely.

Psychotherapist: You were so afraid and very eager for company.

The tears flow down and 1U begins to cry in a whisper. The psychotherapist observes the other members, while guiding 1U: "Focus on how you feel. How old is the child crying at the moment? Do not speak in a hurry. Experience it carefully."

...

Psychotherapist: If someone wants to communicate with me alone, please hold your right hand and let me see it. I will communicate with you in sequence.

As you can see, as the leader of the group, an imagery communication psychotherapist must abide by the working principles, maintain continuous communication with an individual member, and pay attention to others in order to ensure the group atmosphere of "being together". Therefore, for beginners, please use it carefully.

19. Qiu Xiangjian: "Back garden"

19.1. *Goal*

In the technique of "back garden", it is easy to defuse defensive psychology, and the aim is to explore the self in depth.

19.2. *Scope of application*

It can be used as an initial imagery alone, and can also be combined with the classic imagery of the house or other techniques in ICP.

Applicable forms: case consultation; group psychological psychotherapy.

19.3. *Principle*

The so-called "back garden" is the garden of the inner world, which is often created by character and hobby. In the real world, the back garden is usually behind the house and its location is relatively secretive and private. For example, one was not allowed to enter the Imperial Garden of ancient Chinese emperors freely.

By understanding the construction characteristics of the backyard garden and its inner images, we can find the psychological defense mechanism of clients, thereby breaking through the resistance to further explore their subconscious world.

19.4. *Guidance*

The common guidance of the "back garden" is as follows:

Please imagine yourself walking into the garden behind the house. Does it have a wall around? What is the back garden like? What is inside? What is the weather like? Experience your mood. Somewhere in the back garden, you find one or some of the houses that are similar to the sundries. What is it or what they look like? Is there a door and a window? What is inside?

The utility room is used to store some unused items in real life, symbolizing what is isolated from the heart in the image. The psychotherapist can choose according to specific circumstances. For the symbolic meaning of the imagery of the house and its use, please refer to the relevant content of the initial imagery.

19.5. *Variants*

(1) Guidance: Please imagine yourself walking into a soul garden. What do you see? How do you feel?

(2) Before the imagery of the house is finished, the client can be guided to experience the "back garden".

19.6. *Matters needing attention*

(1) Because of breaking the resistance quickly, the psychotherapist needs to grasp the sense of propriety. In particular, the psychotherapist should decide whether to further guide the imagery of "sundries" according to specific circumstances.
(2) For the clients who are too weak in security or lack a stable relationship between them and the psychotherapists, please carefully use the technique of "back garden".

19.7. *Case demonstration*

A represents male; U represents female.

A: A little boy is playing with mud in the back garden. His mother is working. The little boy wants to get a hug from his mother, but he does not dare to say it. The mother has too much work to do and cannot take care of him. In fact, she cares very much about him. (At this point, he could not help choking with sobs.) In my memory, I was not held by my mama when I was a child. Now I see, because she was too busy. She was really worried about me, because no matter where I played, it seemed to be in her eyes.

A change in addressing means a change in the client's sense of parent–child distance in the heart. "Mama" is closer.

U: My back yard garden is an ancient aristocracy. This is a pretty big garden with a lot of flowers. There are sweet scented osmanthus trees and pear trees. The weather is not good. There is an embroidered building in the garden, with a lady and a servant girl in it. Without the permission of the adult, the lady is not allowed to go out of the embroidered building. There is a well in the blank area with a circle of flowers around it. The wellhead and the ground are flat.

The embroidered building and "the lady who is not allowed to go out without the permission of the adult" symbolize self-restraint and self-protection. The whole atmosphere of the images is cold and repressive, scattered with some sentimentality.

U was a rational and lively mind leader. In the group sharing session, she said she had no emotion before, and it would be strange to see someone cry. She did not think that she was shedding tears this time. Through this experience, she not only felt her other state, but also fully accepted this state, and increased her confidence and interest in self-growth.

20. Qiu Xiangjian: Imagery construction

20.1. *Goal*

"Imagery construction" aims to understand how the reality of feeling and behavior can be influenced by inner emotions and to help a client quickly find out the interactive relationship among "the real self", "the subconscious self" and "the self in complex", which is conducive to solve problems and enhance self-awareness.

Imagery construction is not the conversion of images, nor is it done at once. It is a more healthy connection between images, especially between sub-personalities, that facilitates an in-depth experience and understanding. It is especially important to emphasize that imagery construction is a technology, not the ultimate goal. It sorts out the early socialized level of emotion and complex, and resolves, transforms and works through the deeper complex, even before birth, so as to promote the reconstruction of personality and self-integration.

The technique of imagery construction can help ICP therapists integrate personality for clients more easily. The clinical effect is more significant for the sub-personality of the period and of the complex.

20.2. *Scope of application*

(1) In combination with other techniques of ICP, the inner relationship in a certain complex is quickly discovered.
(2) Present the internal sources of emotion and behavior, and carry on further with combination and dissolution.
(3) Explore and deal with a negative emotion, a bad behavior or a complex.

Applicable forms: case consultant and psychotherapy.

20.3. *Principle*

Environment is an indispensable factor for the survival and development of human beings. The same is true in the inner world. Our subconscious also needs to be constructed, and imagery can be the carrier of construction.

The technique of imagery construction focuses on two aspects: psychological and realistic. Psychologically, it is to attach much weight to the imagism and clarity of the internal psychological world of a client, including not only the mental content, but also the psychological process. In reality, it is to devote attention to respond to the emotion and behavior of a client in real life. In general, a client will be advised to consciously understand his/her most common emotion and behavior when encountering conflict situations. This kind of reflection may be consistent or periodic.

The object of imagery construction can be a character, an animal, a plant or a mineral. The basic principle is to promote internal communication, to build internal connections and to integrate personality.

Next, it gives a brief description of the important factors of this technology.

(1) **Phenomenon:** In the real world, every substance is formed through a connection. Different ways of connection make up an amazing world. Therefore, connection and relationship are a phenomenon in nature.

    One of the prerequisites for psychotherapy and psychological counseling is that there are all kinds of existence and relationships in the mental world. By holding hands and hugging, we feel closer. Standing far or near represents the alienation or closeness of interpersonal psychological distance. Through the sincere expression of care and by yearning, people can establish and maintain an emotional connection.

(2) **Energy:** Energy is the carrier of the existence of all things. Images, emotions, mood and the feelings of the body are different forms of psychological energy. The theory of mental energy is

one of the core theories of ICP. Refusing to feel or indulging in a certain emotion is not conducive to the growth of the mind.

(3) **Environment and scene:** The scene is smaller than the big environment, which refers to the background of the different sub-personalities. A certain connection to different scene images can promote the communication between the sub-personalities. This connection can be tangible, such as road repair, bridge erection, dredging the river course, sowing, mining mineral resources, etc. It can also be invisible, such as dialogue, expressing emotions and conveying wishes.

    Using the symbolic meanings and atmospheric feeling of environment and scene can effectively promote the flow of mind energy, which is a pretty important principle and one of the operation contents in imagery construction technology. Consequently, according to the need of psychotherapy, it can be combined with the methods of Music Psychotherapy.

(4) **Collective unconscious:** When the client enters a deep experience through a certain degree of spiritual growth, it is possible to touch the collective unconscious.

(5) **Vertical and horizontal:** When using the imagery construction technology, the psychotherapist must perceive and understand the vertical and lateral relations of construction contents, in addition to guiding the sub-personalities to communicate with each other.

20.4. *Operation ideas*

This technology has no strict operating steps, but ICP therapists should use it according to specific circumstances. Here are some ideas only for reference.

(1) Deconstruct the sub-personality. According to the topological graph, we explore different sub-personality's living environment, characteristics and relationships, and identify the sub-personality that needs to be dealt with at the moment and its relationship network.

(2) When the client feels afraid or timid, the psychotherapist can guide him/her to forwardly choose a powerful sub-personality (including an animal sub-personality) in the imagination and face psychological difficulties or spiritual exploration together through communication and consultation. When needed, remind the client to do some necessary protection in the imagery.
(3) Direct the client to understand his/her common emotions and behaviors, and to conduct targeted experiences, interactions and connections through imagery.
(4) For those sub-personalities with isolation mechanism, the psychotherapist can guide the client to release the isolation, to go in different directions in the imagination, to experience the mood, and to interact with the healthier sub-personalities.
(5) For a weak sub-personality, the psychotherapist can lead the client to find a personality image willing to accompany it, or direct it to exercise, such as planting trees and flowers, or opening up a road, and then to interact with the sub-personality in other scenes.
(6) Build a realistic environment. The client can be instructed to consciously choose or create an environment conducive to physical and mental health. For example, hanging a sword in the room to enhance sense of safety and confidence, posting landscape painting to create a relaxed and bold atmosphere, or putting the old clothes of the parent in the wardrobe, so as to maintain a sense of connection with the parent.
(7) Guide the client to find a tree in the original forest that can represent him/her, and to take care of it and communicate with it often. Moreover, before or after the formal psychotherapy session, guide the client to watch this tree in the imagination and share the joy of growth with it, and also let the tree of heart grow and nourish.
(8) If the client has formed a preliminary Mandala, the psychotherapist can guide him/her to implement the necessary imagery construction by combining the internal image of the Mandala.
(9) Through the construction and connection of the above aspects, the overall and preliminary imagery construction is completed,

which lays the foundation for the follow-up spiritual growth and insight. It is obvious that this is a more advanced imagery construction. Beginners do not have to use it in a hurry.

20.5. *Matters needing attention*

(1) Imagery construction often involves sub-personalities, therefore, the ICP therapist first needs to help the client to deconstruct personality by imagery.
(2) Imagery construction not only pays close attention to the imagery itself, but also focuses on emotion, mood, body's feelings, consciousness contents and the change process of subconscious. In addition to the use of ICP, it also includes the actual level of self-experience and self-examination.
(3) Imagery construction is really not a one-time thing that deals with everything at one stroke. With the exploration and resolution of the complex, as well as the deconstruction and growth of the personality, the times of use and interval are generally reduced.
(4) The construction and connection of images must be based on full experience and self-awareness, rather than just finding isolation or other psychological defense mechanisms. According to the needs of psychotherapy and the specific circumstances of the client, sometimes even a certain connection is disconnected. The interaction and influence of mental energy can best occur at the right time.

20.6. *Case demonstration*

Client: Female. 37 years old. The reason for the psychotherapy was that her husband became a vegetative due to an accident and had been in bed for nearly a year. She was suffering deeply, hoping to dissolve the pain in her heart, to adapt herself to life, and to keep the courage to live.

The deconstruction of personality by imagery is as follows:

a. A desperate woman, called "the woman looking for". 23 years old. Always vacant and helpless.
b. A 35-year-old woman who is very cold and does not care about others.

c. An extremely thin horse. (The client cried bitterly when she saw it.)
d. A stable little rabbit.

For the sake of protecting the client, this is only a part of the process of imagery construction.

In the sense of the client, the little rabbit is the only sub-personality with a little strength and a steady mood. Its good friend is a little monkey. The little monkey is so lively and can give the little rabbit some company and strength. The psychotherapist suggested that the client take a walk in the reality every day, even for ten minutes.

The client found a peach tree in the images that could represent herself. It was lonely, afraid of being squeezed out, and had to stay in the corner. (It symbolizes her desire to be valued and loved.) The psychotherapist guided the little rabbit and the little monkey to take care of the peach tree. The peach tree image became more and more powerful, and finally turned into a green willow tree. (A willow tree symbolizes being pliable and tough.)

In her imagination, there was a little match girl living in the woods, without name and homeless. She took the initiative to let the rabbit and the monkey take care of this girl and live together. (With companionship and emotional support, the original psychological resources of the client were aroused.)

The appearance of the dove image is a turning point. (A dove symbolizes serenity, gentleness, peace and hope.) From then on, the client felt more confident and powerful. Her family also felt that she had a great change. She is no longer so angry as she used to be, and more able to understand others.

When she was able to face the thin horse, an uncle named Mu Da appeared in the image. This is the first male character with great strength and wisdom.

So far, she has received 10 sessions of psychotherapy. The internal pain still needs to be resolved, but she has been able to face the real life bravely. She was responsible for decorating the house and buying furniture. Her original words were "it is the only major issue I did in my life."

21. Yuan Yuan: "Selection of weapons"

(The developer: Department of Psychology, Institute of Sociology and Psychology, Central University of Finance and Economics in China)

Since 2007, I began to teach the psychological defense mechanism systematically to the public. In order to guide the students to clearly experience how to subconsciously protect themselves in the stress situation, I added a link of image experience in the training — selection of weapons. In the process of clinical practice and professional training, I find more and more that it can always vividly and profoundly reflect an individual's way to deal with interpersonal conflict situations, especially anger.

21.1. *Goal*

(1) Survey the coping style in the context of interpersonal conflict.
(2) Show the unhealthy coping style in the situation of interpersonal conflict.
(3) Release negative emotions with self-awareness, solve interpersonal communication problems, and develop healthy coping styles.

21.2. *Scope of application*

This technology is suitable for the clients without serious personality disorders, and the counselors and psychotherapists who are willing to self-grow.

Applicable forms: case consultant; group psychotherapy.

21.3. *Group image guidance for "selection of weapons"*

As a kind of group course or group psychotherapy, it needs to be oriented to treat most of the members and most of the problems. Therefore, I hope the psychotherapist can highlight its experience and lead in the guidance of selecting a weapon image. When a case is encountered, the psychotherapist carries out one to one on-site psychotherapy. However, when it is over or at the end of the period, it is necessary to make a review so that all the members will get the best of it.

All the members sit in a single circle. After guiding them to close their eyes and relax their body, it can start.

Step 1: Guide to imagine.

Core guidelines:

In the imagination, there is an arsenal in front of you. What it looks like? If you want, you can go in and see it in a favorable way. Please choose one of the weapons and come out. (It is important to emphasize that, because it is in the imagination, it is not necessary to take into account the ability of reality. You can bring any weapon out of the arsenal.) Please put it in a place where you feel safe.

The interpretation of the core instructions is as follows:

This is a set guide. The purpose of using the word "arsenal" is to focus, and to increase the imagination and choice of the client.

"In front of you" is aimed at encouraging and strengthening the attitude of confrontation.

"What it looks like?" is a variant and concretion of "house" imagery. It mainly presents the following aspects: the characteristics of defending interpersonal conflicts, the basic state and style of protecting the inner self, the degree of anger's depression, and the specific ways to protect anger.

"If you want, you can go in and see it in a favorable way" expresses the psychotherapist's respect for the client. If the client is not willing to go inside, the psychotherapist will guide him/her to observe and experience the armory around in the imagination. Treating the arsenal as the house imagery can also explore the defense style of the client.

"Please choose one of the weapons". First, the limitations of group course and group psychotherapy are taken into account. Second, I want to go deep into the heart of the client through the first choice. (Whether by intuition or by rational analysis, the first choice is always particularly meaningful.) If it is a case of psychotherapy, the psychotherapist can carefully lead the client to choose more weapon images, in order to help him/her exquisitely experience self-defense in different interpersonal conflict situations, in different relationships and a subtle emotional state.

"Come out" is the action of a choice in the heart, and further determination and realization of the first choice. Some of the weapons brought out by some clients are completely different from the weapons chosen in the arsenal. This detail can help us understand their inner conflicts and changes. Moreover, "Come out" means that deep down the client is temporarily leaving the place, which is piled up by all kinds of negative emotions and the unconscious ego defense mechanism. It has three positive meanings: creating an opportunity for self-awareness, experiencing a moment's peace from being addicted to indulgence, and having a chance to comprehend how the weapon image is used in the real world, which is no longer suppressed and accumulated. The last meaning needs to be clarified in the third step — group discussion.

"Please put it in a place where you feel safe". The design of this sentence is mainly to take care of the groups that are not psychotherapeutic. For members without the training experience of psychology or ICP, we must guarantee the basic sense of security of the group. For individuals, there are two underlying meanings: one is not to use the weapons easily that might harm others; the other is to establish the basic sense of security so as to remain in the group.

Step 2: Describe one by one and communicate selectively.

In the process of group image guidance, we should not ignore any individual. A member has the right to not express, but we must give him/her the opportunity to express. At this stage, each member should be asked to describe his/her imagination without any analysis. In this process, the psychotherapist selectively communicates with members according to the clinical experience and their outpouring of emotions at the time. The psychotherapist need not do in-depth communication with each member. The specific contents of the communication are not the same.

For example, according to the different contents of their report, the psychotherapist can ask some details. "What does the man with this axe look like? Who does he want to cut? Why?" "If it is as old as a man, how old is the missile?" "Why do you put the gun in the office drawer and put the bullet at home?" "What is the mood when you are squatting behind the shield?" "What do you want to say if you do not thrust the dagger out, but use the language to express your anger?"

Step 3: Discuss in the group according to the category of weapon imagery.

(1) The training background of the group members is different so the way of interaction and the subject are different.

For groups that have learned ICP, every three members are divided into one group taking the "psychotherapist", "client" and "observer" roles, respectively. Use the way of ICP to explore. The focus is to understand the specific emotions that the "client" wants to defend and to carry out the corresponding mental intervention.

For groups that have not learned ICP, the subject of discussion is that "In real life, how do you deal with interpersonal conflicts? What is the bottom line of your anger? (Or, what's the bottom line of your tolerance?)" In the process of discussion, each group needs to sum up the commonalities and differences of the members. Its purpose is to increase self-awareness and strengthen the sense of social support.

(2) For those who are unable to enter a group according to weapon imagery category, who are quite imaginative and independent, make them as a separate group. In order to make this a little bit more interesting, the psychotherapist can give each group a name according to specific circumstances, such as the "magic group", "flying group", "singular group", "unreal group", "bare-handed group" and so on. They need to be reminded to focus on the "difference".

Step 4: Report by the representatives of each group. Commentate one by one.

The commented contents include explaining the symbolic meanings of the weapon images, the relationship between the weapon imagery and the ego defense mechanism, the advantages and disadvantages in the interpersonal conflict situation, the destruction and construction of the weapon imagery to the intimate relationship, and the healthy and effective interpersonal communication way.

Step 5: Summary guidance. Remind matters that need attention.

"Selection of weapons" is only a way to explore and understand the self-defense mechanism. No matter what kind of arsenal and weapons were chosen in the imagination, there is neither good nor bad. Every weapon contains power and wisdom. The key is our insight of the weapon and how we use it, so that the unconscious ego defense mechanism can be developed into a self-conscious and healthy coping style.

Before the end of every course group and group psychotherapy, please be sure to emphasize the precautions of the operation.

21.4. *Symbolic meanings of the common weapon imagery*

There are many dimensions to the classification of the weapon imagery. As an extension of ICP, it follows the principle of imagery classification, that is, on the basis of military common sense, more consideration is given to the similar shape, characteristics and functions of weapon images.

The simple examples are as follows. According to the historical order, the weapon imagery can be divided into ancient cold weapons and modern weapons. In use, they can be divided into direct use (such as knives, spears, swords, halberds, axes, tomahawks, hooks, forks) and indirect use (such as mines, missiles) weapons. There are many other dimensions to the division. For instance, the precision of aiming, distance of killing, whether it is filled with gunpowder and its quantity, whether it is lethal and its degree, whether it has the risk of self-injury and so on.

Each dimension itself is an image and has a symbolic meaning. For example, gunpowder and bullets symbolize the degree of repression of anger. It is obvious that the repression of the cannon is higher than the rifle. The killing distance represents the psychological interpersonal distance. People who are accustomed to using pistols and daggers in the subconscious mind, in other words, people with a pistol or a dagger as the dominant personality often have a strong endurance in long-distance social relations. Once the mood is erupted, those who are most likely to be hurt by them are usually people closest to them. There are two common cases: the closest people become the most innocent; the distant ones find it hard to hurt them, and only those in close relationships make them feel hurt.

Due to space limitations, this book only briefly describes the basic symbolic meanings of the cold weapons and modern weapons according to the rough chronological method. In clinical practice, I often encountered such weapon images that are not easy to be classified, with extremely specific characters and rich in imagination. For the sake of argument, I classified them individually and called it "personalized weapons".

(1) Cold weapons

The generalized cold weapons refer to all the combat equipment in the Cold War era. They are melee weapons without gunpowder, explosives, or other burning objects that can directly kill the enemy in the battle. In China, cold weapons can be divided into eighteen types, namely the eighteen weapons (the skills in wielding the 18 kinds of martial arts) that the Chinese say: knife, spear, sword, halberd, ax, tomahawk, hook, fork, whip, mace, hammer, catch, boring, stick, lance, club, crutch, meteor (Chinese weapon).

In Chinese martial arts novels, the role of weapons is always mythical, such as Xiao Li flying knife. The characters in the classical novels are often armed with uncommon weapons. It is also the same in ancient mythology and legends of the west, such as the mythological stories of ancient Greece. When the clients identify with the owners of such weapons in the subconscious mind, they tend to choose the images of such weapons. Thus, in addition to the symbolic meanings of such weapon images, they also permeate the personality characteristics of the original masters. During interpretation and imagery communication, these factors must be considered.

Usually, the clients who love the cold weapons in the imagery experience of "selection of weapons" are more honest, straightforward and direct. Among them, the clients who choose the images of wooden weapons are more simple and pure than those who choose metal ones. This is because wood is natural, and metal is the result of human civilization, symbolizing more reasons. In the context of interpersonal conflict, they dare to face it directly, even tit for tat. No explosives means that they use closer direct contact, and therefore, the degree of indignation is relatively low. The possibility of injuring the innocent will be lower. However, such clients need to enhance the awareness of self-protection and the flexibility to deal with problems.

Sword: A sharp knife cold weapon used for fighting in close quarters. The sword is divided into two parts — the blade and the hilt. It has sharp edges on both sides of the slender body and a sharp tip on the top. The hilt is generally relatively short, convenient for holding. A sword image with a scabbard means more concealment and protection. The tassel on the handle of a sword symbolizes the performance as a glamorous woman's skirt ribbon, just like wind and feather. The warm-toned tassel is more enthusiastic and the cold-toned tassel represents reasons.

The most prominent feature of the sword image is the pursuit of justice. In ancient times and modern times, and in the East and the West, we can find the cultural evidence that the sword symbolizes justice. Therefore, those who choose sword images or those who take the sword as the leading personality often have the chivalrous demeanor. They are likely to maintain justice and morality, and cannot endure injustice and lack of morality, so they will experience a special anger — righteous indignation.

A sword is double-edged, symbolizing injuring self and injuring others. Therefore, when using the sword as sharp and blunt, the "swordsman" should know how to protect himself and make it possible to reduce or avoid unnecessary cost. In real life, the sword's winning action is to prick into the vital parts of the opponent's body. This action symbolizes the pertinence of attack or anger, and can evolve into sharp language or articles.

Knife: A cold weapon with a close range for single combat. It consists of two parts — blade and handle. The blade is long and narrow. The cutter edge is thin and the back of a knife blade is thick. The handle of a knife is either long or short. There are plenty of types such as machete, saber, broadsword, falchion, and a sword with a long blade and a short hilt wielded with both hands. Compared with the sword, the knife is slightly blunt. "Knifeman" is pretty honest and forthright, but weak in flexibility.

Dagger: Short and small like the sword. From ancient times, the dagger has always been used, especially in the military. It is divided into single and double edges. Compared with the knife and sword, the dagger is more concealed. (Indeed, the strongest concealment cold weapon is the hidden weapon.) It is easy to carry and not easily found. Within the close range, the dagger's precision is high and the strength is fierce. Once thrust into the vital part of the other party, it is fatal. Hence, a person with a dagger as the dominant personality or a client who chooses a dagger image in "selection of weapons" needs to learn to deal with problems in intimacy and to raise awareness of projection mechanism. Otherwise, as soon as they are not careful, they will hurt their family or intimacy. The emotional and intimate relationships of the real world will be greatly destroyed.

(2) Modern weapons

Modern weapons refer to firearms that kill or launch with firepower or heat power, such as guns, cannons, grenades, rocket launchers, tanks, nuclear weapons (atomic bomb, hydrogen bomb) and so on.

Modern weapons use a large amount of metal materials. Gunpowder is not natural. It is made by human beings. As a result, modern weapons are more sensible and lethal than the ancient cold weapons, and have a wider range of destruction.

In imagery communication while picking a weapon, for modern weapons, especially the gun and the artillery, the psychotherapist should ask the client whether it is equipped with ammunition and quantity, the purpose of this is to understand his/her anger backlog, the realistic failure possibility of interpersonal relationships and risk coefficient.

Aircraft: Being able to leave the earth and soar at a high altitude, which corresponds to fantasy and avoidance in the ego defense mechanism. Here is a simple explanation. The earth can represent the reality, the sky can represent the spiritualization, and the underground symbolizes subconscious.

Pistol: A weapon for close range shooting. As mentioned earlier, it is easy to harm the relationships that are close to us and be easily hurt by them. In clinical work, I found that most of the clients and trainees who pursued perfection preferred to choose a pistol, and only one or two bullets were in it in their imagination. When asked how to use or distribute bullets, I always heard almost the same answer "this bullet is for myself." Or, "if he/she (the spouse) provokes me to get angry, I will kill him/her and then commit suicide."

Sniper rifle: A gun with high accuracy and strong fatality. The sniper must have super strong tolerance and toughness, be good at waiting in the hidden place, cool, rational, and have good mental quality. An excellent sniper is like a wolf. Therefore, the client who chooses the image of the sniper gun is quite good at patience and perseverance. In real life, once the anger breaks out, the feeling and relationship with each other will suffer irreparable damage.

Machine gun: Multiple bullets burst. It not only represents the relatively strong anger, but also means that it is easy to hurt the innocent if one is careless with his/her temper. For the client who selects a machine gun in the image, on the realistic level, their ability to control his/her own emotions is poor, that is easy to destroy the interpersonal relationships. However, the client often feels wronged and thinks that others do not understand him/her. Such clients often use projection and impulsive action defense mechanisms.

Tank: Offensive and defensive. Compared with the ordinary gun and cannon, the most prominent place of the tank is the metal shell and the moving track. The metal shell represents the isolation, avoidance and suppression in the defense mechanism, and has a strong sense of self-protection and protective function. The track is a symbol of action and flexibility. Tanks can cross a variety of complex and difficult terrain, which symbolizes strong adaptability.

Nuclear weapons: Modern weapons with great energy, devastating and destructive power and a wide range of impact. Excessive depression can avoid a sudden anger attack. But once it breaks out, it will appear similar to a volcanic eruption. Therefore, the image of nuclear weapon has a greater potential danger. The client who chooses the image of nuclear weapon in particular needs to learn to express his/her anger and dissatisfaction in a healthy way and communicate effectively in daily life, rather than to suppress them blindly. It is quite dangerous to accumulate the gunpowder in the deep inside day by day and month by month.

Interestingly, in the current clinical "nuclear weapons", I saw two rules: one is on plump and undemonstrative middle-aged women; the other is on a skinny young man. From the perspective of psychodynamics, these people choose nuclear weapons in their imagination, the former is over repression, and the latter is due to excessive compensation.

(3) Personalized weapons

The personalized weapons are always exceedingly strange and change constantly. For example, a poisonous lotus shaped brooch, the magical water that can become a sword, arms that can suddenly change into venomous snakes, bees that can be turned into laser, deadly Myron. Animals, plants, minerals, human bodies and artificial objects are available in all varieties.

As long as you know the conventional way of reading imagery, and pay attention to its use during a situation as a weapon and the specific effects, you can understand their symbolic meanings.

Take only the poisonous lotus shaped brooch as an example. Poison symbolizes strong negative emotions or serious mental illness. The lotus image is often associated with maternal individuals or females. The needle of the brooch has a stab wound with a small cut and no deep hole, but deadly poison. The brooch is worn on the chest, with both concealment and display. At the same time, it also symbolizes the importance of emotion (because the chest symbolizes the socialized emotion).

Compared with the ancient cold weapons and modern weapons, the more the client pursues the weird and changeable personalized weapons, the more they reflect the inner fear and sense of weakness.

21.5. *Matters needing attention*

(1) Give special attention to the projective language of the client in the description.

The projective language described here is only for the guidance. Whether in the individual psychological counseling, or group psychotherapy, the ability to capture the projective description of the client is an important aspect to quickly know and understand his/her ego defense mechanism in the process of listening to "selection of weapons", and also a valuable clue to explore his/her projection mechanism.

For instance, some clients speak "arsenal" in guiding language as "Zeughaus", "ammunition", "powder house", "explosive storage", "dynamite library" or "arm-shop"; "Please put it in a place where you feel safe" is said to be "when you let me hide the weapon".

(2) Respond constructively to the client.

From first to last, the feedback information of an ICP therapist should promote the client's spiritual growth, with no harm. Even when unfamiliar or incomprehensible weapon images are encountered, we should also express sincerity through listening, accepting and confronting. In other words, every word that the ICP therapist responds to, the client must be constructive.

(3) Remind the operating principles.

The principle of growth described above is at the core. In addition, the ICP therapists have the responsibility to remind clients or group trainees, when guiding those who have never contacted with psychology or ICP to experience "selection of weapons", not to be addicted to the specific category and characteristics and application at the realistic level, but to focus on the used situation, the function, lethality and destruction of a weapon image, as well as its impact on real human relationships (especially intimacy).

Facing any weapon image, we must adhere to the basic principle of operation of ICP: no killing, no destruction, not burial, no exaggeration, no extermination, no evasion, and no indulgence.

In principle, we do not encourage people who have not yet obtained ICP qualification to use it and its various clinical techniques. In real life, however, it is hard to control. It is inevitable that someone will take a risk. Therefore, in every workshop and training, we will repeatedly emphasize the use of norms and matters of attention.

(4) Ask teacher trainees not to use "selection of weapons" in the first class.

Unlike other occupational groups, because of a natural sense of responsibility and occupational sensitivity, teachers are very likely to think of giving their students an ICP experience. Even some teachers in primary or middle schools want to take "selection of weapons" as a psychology lesson in the classroom.

In the spirit of responsibility for the imaginer, I always suggest that such teachers do not use it in the classroom, especially for children with weak actual testing ability. The main reason is that the weapon imagery not only symbolizes anger, aggression or hostility, but also can represent "sex". The theory behind it is not only related to the ego defense mechanism, but also to classical psychoanalysis and even the whole psychodynamics. When other symbolic or more intense negative emotions are encountered, ordinary teachers who lack the experience of psychological counseling are hard to cope with or may even harm the imaginer.

To give enough emphasis, I will share a real case.

In 2008, a female teacher in a primary school took part in my training in Beijing. She felt a lot of benefit. Regardless of the reminding, she led the students to experience "selection of weapons" at a theme class meeting. A girl (11 years old) saw a red sword in the imagination and started crying on the spot. She cried and said, "I am afraid of that sword." This teacher did not know how to deal with it and told the girl "it was just an imagination. You do not have to be afraid."

From the second day, the girl did not go to school for three days. At home, she was very depressed, often crying, but not talking. Sometimes she sat alone in a daze. Her parents felt strange and anxious. No matter how her parents comforted her, she refused to go to school. And then, her mother called to ask the teacher what happened in the school.

At this time, she was quite worried. She sent me an email to tell the matter and to ask for help. After asking a lot of details, I made a preliminary judgment that the girl had been exposed to a sex addiction on her way home from school. In her imagination (or her subconscious), the red sword is the symbol of the man's penis. The age in the image was exactly the age she had encountered, that is, the age of sexual trauma.

I gave the teacher a detailed analysis and guidance. She went to the girl's home and helped her to dissolve the traumatic experience. The girl's mood quickly resumed and returned to school. At this point, a potential danger was transformed into an opportunity for psychotherapy.

If this teacher concealed the matter and did not seek any professional help, the girl would be the victim of selection of weapons. The teacher would personally create two degrees of trauma.

For me, this case has created a sense of vigilance. Consequently, I really want to tell all the readers and users:

Please do not let "selection of weapons" be a new weapon!

21.6. *Significance of the development of ICP*

(1) Add a new initial imagery.

Among the existing clinical techniques of ICP, there is nothing specific for interpersonal conflict. Interpersonal conflict is the external projection and concentration of inner contradictions, which can be used to assess a person's mental health. Therefore, the imagery interaction of "selection of weapons" can be added to explore interpersonal conflict and the self-protection model.

(2) Expand the application value of weapon imagery.

All those who have studied psychoanalysis can understand that weapons can symbolize "sex". But what is the relationship between the weapon imagery and anger, attack or hostility? Is there a theory to support? Can it be used in ICP? Ten years of clinical practice have proven that the weapon imagery is a combination point between the ego defense mechanism and ICP.

(3) Infiltrate the promotion of ICP.

In the past, most of the courses of ICP were independent, such as primary, intermediate, advanced and full courses. It must be a good thing if we can skillfully integrate the theories and methods of ICP into more social courses and group training to make it serve the society more widely. The image interaction of "selection of weapons" is an attempt.

Since the foundation of this technique, besides case psychotherapy, a great many people have studied and experienced it in group psychotherapy, workshops and group trainings, such as college students, graduate students, teachers, principals, bank staff, staff of the stock exchange, leaders of the tax system, staff of the community, and so on. They are generally able to accept this way of learning and highly recognize its enlightenment and application value.

Weapons in the real world will hurt people or defend them. I hope I can use my own strength to transform the weapons in the mind world into an effective scientific method of self-awareness, self-control, and for promoting communication and harmonious interpersonal relationship.

22. Zhao Yancheng: "Watermelon field"

(The developer: Career psychological counselor in China)

Zhao Yancheng is the most outstanding ICP therapist in China. Many years of clinical experience and keen intuition often inspired her. "Watermelon field" is one of her innovative techniques.

22.1. *Goal*

"Watermelon field" is used to check whether the psychological problems of a client have reached the extent to which they can be solved, so as to present the specific situation of current psychological problems, and to carry out targeted psychotherapy.

What needs to be explained is that as a fruit image (the universal symbolic meaning of fruit imagery is self-identification and self-evaluation regarding sex), watermelon itself does not represent mental problems. For the purpose of psychotherapy, the developer only borrows the image of watermelon, gives it the specific meaning, and then uses it to carry out psychotherapy. Thus, the psychological problem of watermelon is confined to this clinical technique.

When you understand and use the technique of "watermelon field", please do not confuse it with the universal symbolic meaning of watermelon.

The purpose of the "watermelon field" technique is to:

(1) Present the overall situation of the psychological problems that the client has been aware of;
(2) Examine the maturity of these psychological problems;
(3) Show whether the psychological problem(s) is/are suitable for the current solution;
(4) Understand the core issue(s).

22.2. *Scope of application*

This technique is suitable for clients without serious personality disorder, and the counselors and psychotherapists who are willing to self-grow.

Applicable forms: case consultant; group psychotherapy.

22.3. *Guidance*

Please imagine a watermelon field that belongs to you in front of you. You go in and see some watermelons with labels, which hint that this is a variety of problems that you need to solve. Look at it carefully. What are these problems? You can clap them with your hands or listen to them in your ears and feel the watermelons that are already ripe. Now, choose one of the questions you want to solve, and then feel the maturity of the watermelon. If this watermelon is ripe, open it; if not, do not open it, but put it back into the watermelon field and let it continue to grow.

22.4. *Matters needing attention*

(1) When guiding the clients to test the ripeness of watermelon, the psychotherapist does not have to worry that there will be no results. Clinical practice shows that almost all clients can feel the maturity of the watermelon through observation (for example, a cracked watermelon) and experience (such as flapping lightly, weighing in the hands and listening) in the imagination.
(2) The psychotherapist needs to understand the psychological significance of watermelons in different states. For example, a raw watermelon image symbolizes this mental problem is not suitable for solving at present; a rotten watermelon represents an overflowing mood; a half-raw watermelon means that the client lacks enough insight on this psychological problem and needs to wait for proper psychotherapy. For unfamiliar or unseen watermelons, the psychotherapist can use a specialization technique to help the client clarify the problem.
(3) In view of the psychotherapy principle of client-centered sessions and ICP's consistent working principles, do not guide the client to open a raw watermelon in imagination. Please do not take any of the clients into risk!
(4) If a client voluntarily opens a raw watermelon in the imagination (such as cutting it with a knife), once discovered, the psychotherapist should guide him/her to put it together in the imagination, and to put it back into the watermelon field and let it continue to grow. In general, such a watermelon will leave a scar, which symbolizes the client's self-injury or an overly exigent mood. The psychotherapist must keep an eye on it in future psychotherapy sessions.

23. Zhao Yancheng: Understanding intimacy through imagery

23.1. *Goal*

With regard to intimacy, Zhao Yancheng developed a series. Their purposes are the same: to present the true and profound intimacy of the client, increase the self-awareness of the client, and thus conduct targeted psychological therapy.

23.2. *Scope of application*

This technique is suitable for clients without serious personality disorders, and the counselors and psychotherapists who are willing to self-grow.

Applicable forms: case consultant; group psychotherapy.

23.3. *Guidance*

(1) Shopping in the shoe store

The image of a shoe can symbolize intimacy.

Guidance:

Please imagine yourself going to a shoe store. Choose a pair of shoes for yourself, and then choose another pair for your romantic partner. Next, imagine your romantic partner is right beside you. What kind of shoes does he/she choose for himself/herself? What kind of shoes will he/she choose for you? After selection, the shoe store owner comes out from the back room (or basement) with two pairs of shoes for you and your romantic partner. Now, observe the commonness and differences of these shoes. You can try them on your feet and feel them.

Choosing your own shoes symbolizes your understanding of intimacy. Selection of the other party represents his/her understanding of intimacy. The back room or basement is a symbol of your subconscious awareness of intimacy.

Clinical experience shows that the boss is an important image in this experience. In the process, the psychotherapist needs to pay special attention to the shoes chosen by the "boss" and the feeling of wearing them.

(2) The shoe cabinet in the doorway

Guidance:

Please imagine yourself going home. There is a shoe cabinet in the doorway. Whose shoes are there in it? What are they like?

It can present the current status of intimacy and the family relationships of the client.

(3) The bedside photo of the bedroom

The bedroom and bed are private spaces. For adults, they are often related with intimacy. A photo is a static or fixed memory. The bedside photo in the bedroom can be a symbol of intimacy.

Guidance:

Please imagine walking into the bedroom and seeing a picture on the wall of the head of the bed. You lift it and find another picture. What is the look of this picture? What is the specific content?

It can directly present the current status of intimacy of the client.

23.4. *Matters needing attention*

(1) In terms of symbolism, the "basement" is more symbolic of the deep subconscious than the "back room". Therefore, when using the technique of "understanding intimacy through imagery", we encourage psychotherapists to use "basement" in the instructions, especially for those clients who feel less secure.
(2) According to the psychotherapy relationship and the specific circumstances of the client, the above three sub-techniques can be combined with other ICP technique.

Bibliography

Freud, S. (1997). *Introduction to Psychoanalysis* (Gao, J. F., Trans.). Beijing: The Commercial Press.

Freud, S. (2005). *Freud's later writings* (Lin, C., Zhang, H. M., & Chen, W. Q., Trans.). Shanghai: Shanghai Translation Publishing House.

Hall, C. S., & Nordby, V. J. (1987). *Jung's Psychology Outline* (Zhang, Y., Trans.). Zhengzhou: Yellow River Art Publishing House.

Jung, C. G. (1991). *The Theory and Practice of Analytical Psychology* (Cheng, Q., & Wang, Z. H., Trans.). Beijing: SDX Joint Publishing Company.

Jung, C. G. (2003). *Jung's Character of Philosophy* (Li, D. R., Trans.). Beijing: Jiu Zhou Book.

Jung, C. G. (2012). *Archetype and Collective Unconscious* (Xu, D. L., Trans.). Beijing: Int'l Culture Publishing House.

Jung, C. G. (2012). *Symbol of Life* (Chu, S. H., & Wang, S. P., Trans.). Beijing: Int'l Culture Publishing House.

Lucien, L. B. (1987). *Archaic Thinking* (Ding, Y., Trans.). Beijing: The Commercial Press.

Piaget, J. (1986). *Child Psychology* (Wu, F. Y., Trans.). Beijing: The Commercial Press.

Rogers, C. R. (2004). *Client-centered Therapy: Practice, Application and Theory* (Li, Y. C., Trans.). Beijing: China Renmin University Press.

Shen, H. Y. (2004). *Analytical Psychology.* Beijing: SDX Joint Publishing Company.

Wu, Q. (2007). *Meet the Ghost Friend in Your Heart — Know Your Negative Emotions.* Anhui: Anhui People's Publishing House.

Xu, H. Y. (2003). *We All Have Psychological Scars.* Beijing: China Youth Publishing Group.

Xu, S. (2002). *New Version of the Origin of Chinese Characters.* Beijing: China Book Company.

Yuan, Y. (2006). *Self-acceptance and Imagery Communication Psychotherapy.* Hefei: Anhui People's Publishing House.

Yuan, Y. (2008). *Analyze Movies in the View of Imagery Communication Psychotherapy.* Hefei: Anhui People's Publishing House.

Yuan, Y. (2012). *The Clinical Operation Guidelines of Imagery Communication Psychotherapy.* Beijing: Beijing Normal University Publishing Group.

Yuan, Y., Cao, Y., & Zhu, J. J. (2013). *The Summary of Clinical Techniques Imagery Communication Psychotherapy.* Beijing: Beijing Normal University Publishing Group.

Yuan, Y. (2018). *Weapon Psychology.* Beijing: Beijing Normal University Publishing Group.

Zhu, J. J. (2001). *Psychological Analysis of Dreams.* Inner Mongolia: Inner Mongolia People's Publishing House.

Zhu, J. J. (2003). *How Many Souls Do You Have: Psychological Consultation and Deconstructing Personality by Imagery.* Beijing: China City Press.

Zhu, J. J. (2006). *Imagery Communication Psychotherapy.* Beijing: Peking University Medical Press.

Zhu, J. J. (2011). *Imagery Communication Psychotherapy and Traditional Chinese Medicine Science.* Hefei: Anhui People's Publishing House.

Zhu, J. J., & Yuan, Y. (2008). *The Psychotherapy from the Orient-Imagery Communication Psychotherapy* (In both Chinese and English). Hefei: Anhui People's Publishing House.

CPSIA information can be obtained
at www.ICGtesting.com
Printed in the USA
BVHW040824130919
558351BV00006B/20/P

9 789813 278936